D1146365

INVESTING
WITH THE
GRAND
MASTERS

"In a clear and readable way, *Investing with the Grand Masters* presents an invaluable interpretation of investment techniques that have proved their worth through the decades."
Robin Aspinall, Treasury Economist, National Australia Bank

"Lively insight into the philosophies of some of the UK's most successful investors, containing plenty of telling advice."
Alex Bance, SBC Warburg

"This authoritative review with a scintillating analysis comprises an immensely refreshing set of penetrative interviews with top flight practitioners of investment."
Dan Bunting, Investment Strategist, Matheson Securities

"As a stockbroker servicing investment institutions I used to work with most of the 'Masters' and found James Morton's book a fascinating reminder of their contrasting styles. Whether you are an active investor with your own ideas about how to maximise the returns on your portfolio or someone who relies on others to manage a portfolio for you, this volume will help you to improve the quality of the decisions which you take about your savings."
David Curling, Director, Williams de Broë

"Contains hard-headed, practical advice from top fund managers."
Chris Gilchrist, Editor of investment newsletter *The IRS Report*

"As the variety of investment opportunities continue to expand, the role of the money manager grows. This is illustrated with great clarity in James Morton's excellent new book *Investing with the Grand Masters*."
Mark Henderson, Director, Panmure Gordon and Company

"This book will be extremely helpful to both beginning and experienced investors. The conclusions are particularly valuable."
Julian Treger, Managing Director, Active Value Advisors

"At last, a book which will enable private investors to ask intelligent questions of (both their existing and potential) fund managers."
Justin Urquhart Stewart, Business Planning Director, Barclays Stockbrokers

THE FINANCIAL TIMES

INVESTING
WITH THE
GRAND
MASTERS

Insights from
Britain's Greatest
Investment Minds

JAMES MORTON

London · Hong Kong · Johannesburg
Melbourne · Singapore · Washington DC

PITMAN PUBLISHING
PITMAN PUBLISHING
128 Long Acre, London WC2E 9AN
Tel: +44 (0)171 447 2000
Fax: +44 (0)171 240 5771

A Division of Pearson Professional Limited

First published in Great Britain 1997

ISBN 0 273 62536 5

British Library Cataloguing in Publication Data
A CIP catalogue record for this book can be obtained from the British Library.

1 3 5 7 9 10 8 6 4 2

Typeset by Pantek Arts, Maidstone, Kent
Printed and bound in Great Britain by Biddles Ltd
Guildford and King's Lynn

*The Publishers' policy is to use paper manufactured
from sustainable forests.*

The Author

James Morton is Director of Investments at European American Securities and manager of the Chelverton Fund. The Chelverton Fund specialises in microcap stocks investing on behalf of high net worth individuals in equity markets around the world. Since inception the Chelverton Fund has outperformed the FT-SE by 100 per cent.

He is also non executive director of the Knox D'Arcy Trust plc, which is an active investor in UK small and medium cap listed stocks and Investment Adviser to the Tail Wind Fund Ltd. Tail Wind specialises in buying publicly traded equities at a discount to the market price. The Tail Wind Fund ranked in the top 5 per cent of all hedge funds worldwide, followed by the Republic National Bank of New York in the first half of 1996.

His twenty years in the financial services sector span commercial banking, corporate finance and investment management, and embrace some sixteen separate countries. Before CFA, James was a Director of Samuel Montagu Inc. and worked at Arthur Young, Bain and Citibank. He sits on the Board of Directors of several public and private companies in the UK, US and France. James has a BA in law from Cambridge, an MBA from Stanford Business School and an MA in Third World Economics from the Stanford Food Research Institute.

He was the Editor of *The Financial Times Global Guide to Investing* published in October 1995 and is a columnist for The IRS Report, a financial newsletter. When not managing money or writing books James likes to read investment newsletters from around the world.

Contents

Foreword

There are many different individual approaches to the challenge of performance in the stock markets. This book is an admirable and comprehensive introduction to over a dozen of the best British fund managers and how they achieved success. James Morton has taken an original approach in selecting his money masters and combined it with a fascinating insight into the history of British international investment beginning with the story of the Foreign & Colonial Investment Trust in 1868.

It is extraordinary to find that even at that early date, the first British investment trust had holdings not only in North America but also in the Far East, India and South America. The international prospective is still a dominant trend among British fund managers which puts them far ahead of their American and Continental European competitors. This book reflects that mentality well with some of the British managers working in Hong Kong as well as in London and New York.

The author also has the imagination to see that investment, in the broadest meaning of the word, can include innovative schemes such as The Prince of Wales Trust. 'Investing in People' is surely one of the key elements of successfully backing the right businesses.

It is difficult to draw many general lessons from these disparate individuals and their different approaches. Nevertheless it is clear that a good investment manager could be described as a man not only with imaginative flair and perception, but also a hard working detective or sleuth who is able to find an opportunity which the market has not yet identified. Good fund managers are also often cool and detached from their day to day activity and do not get emotionally involved, they are willing to be courageous and contrarian when occasion requires such as in the 1974 bear market. I believe that any private investor will benefit enormously from studying the fascinating characters in this book and learning how they have achieved success.

Robert Lloyd George
October 1996

Acknowledgements

It goes without saying that a book of this nature may be written by one individual, but only with the help of many others. I want to single out my wife, Ellen, who has been long suffering while I turned our kitchen into a research library and devoted many weekends and evenings to writing yet another book. Her tolerance and constant encouragement have been my greatest source of support.

A great deal of work has been done by a number of people at Pitman, most particularly by my publisher, Richard Stagg. He has been a font of improvements and ideas. Claire Powell and Sylvia Nash both laboured long and hard to salvage copy which went through many iterations. I want to acknowledge the help of Matthew Cartisser, Managing Director of Chelverton Properties, who made essential contributions to the completion of this book. Finally, I would also like to mention five other individuals who provided me with help in writing *Investing with the Grand Masters:*

William Eccles	Director	Foreign & Colonial
Christopher Fawcett	Finance Director	Fauchier Partners
Richard P. Pease	Director	Jupiter Tyndall
Michel Rolin	Director	Fauchier Partners
Christopher Stainforth	Managing Director	Corporate Finance, Guinness Mahon
Devina Watter	Director of Investment Management	Morgan Grenfell Asset Management

Note from the Publisher

Investing with the Grand Masters contains information, opinions and views on a range of investment topics. All information contained has been obtained from sources considered to be reliable and every effort has been made to present a balanced and fair assessment of the topics covered in this publication. Nonetheless, neither the accuracy nor the completeness of the information contained herein, nor any of the conclusions or recommendations can be guaranteed. There is no guarantee that future performance will in any way relate to the past, nor that any specific investments outlined in *Investing with the Grand Masters*, nor any of the strategies described herein, will be profitable.

Neither the publishers nor the author endorse the views of any of the individuals or organisations who have contributed to *Investing with the Grand Masters*. Opinions contained in the book are intended solely for information purposes and should not be viewed as any kind of recommendation by either the publishers, the author or the individual writers or their respective organisations and should not be relied upon by investors in making investment decisions. Investors should consult with their own professional advisors regarding investment decisions.

All investment markets are volatile and subject to fluctuations which cannot be reasonably foreseen. Any investment may result in losses as well as in gains. No responsibility for loss occasioned to any person acting, or refraining from acting as a result of the material contained in this publication will be accepted by the publishers, the author, the individuals featured or their respective organisations. The information presented in *Investing with the Grand Masters* is not and should not be construed as an offer to sell or a solicitation to promote any of the securities referred to anywhere in the publication.

Introduction

One in a thousand makes a fortune investing in financial markets. Most lose money. Why? The markets are not a zero sum game. Real wealth can be created, yet too many people plod along content to come close to the averages; while a few consistently do better. This is no statistical freak. It is the product of hard work, thoughtful analysis and superior execution. No-one has yet found a guaranteed way to make money in the markets; but there is one strategy which comes close. Find the top investors and follow their lead. These are the people the individual investor wants to watch. These are the people we profile in *Investing with the Grand Masters*. Their success has made their investors wealthy. Learning their secrets can make our readers wealthier too.

When editing *The Financial Times Global Guide to Investing*, I set myself one hard and fast rule, that the book would focus on practical insights and information from people who were in the markets every day making money for themselves and their clients. Lawyers, accountants and academics may all be brilliant in their own way, but they had no place in *The Global Guide to Investing*. Advice from advisors is like getting a tip on a horse from the trainer's GP. It sounds fine, in theory, but would you want to go and risk your savings on information once removed? We wanted to offer our readers practical advice direct from people who, year after year, have proved to be winners.

Without a doubt the most useful insights for improving the performance of my own investment fund came from conversations with the likes of Peter Cundill, Marc Faber, Michael Price, Christopher Mills and Sir John Templeton. They had been through the wars, seen markets rise 200 per cent and then fall 70 per cent and still managed to come out smiling. More importantly, their investors were smiling too. There can be no better source for guidance than the greatest names in the industry and, in the investment profession, as you look back 15, 20, or even 30 years, it is relatively easy to identify who these people are.

For one thing, most people do not last that long; and there are very few indeed who seem able to string together a series of successful years, one after another. While academics have found evidence of 'hot hands' among American mutual fund and British pension plan managers – at least in equities – the main body of individuals in the investment industry is confined to mediocrity. Few fund managers top the index. So few, in fact, that, in 1995, not one out of the 134 general unit trusts in the UK beat the stock market benchmark. 81 out of 82 classified as investing primarily for income failed to come up to that threshold. To do better on a consistent basis is a noteworthy achievement. A good year or two, perhaps, occurs with some frequency, but a sequence of unbroken successes is rarer than the white rhinoceros. When you look for outperformance by a wide margin over any length of time beyond ten years, you are down to a handful of names: the very best in one of the toughest and most competitive professions.

A large percentage of those select people are found in Britain. Investing must be in the blood, as here is an industry at which the British excel. Outside of the US, no nation has a greater share of the truly global investors, and even further down the rankings the average British manager is more at home investing in Nairobi and Sydney than his or her American counterpart. There is so much of interest which these professionals have to offer, and their experience is so wide ranging that every investor can benefit in some measure.

At Pitman/FT, we set out to identify the top British investors today. We believe we have succeeded and have persuaded them to share their investment insights and extraordinary expertise with our readers. The performance record of each and every person profiled in *Investing with the Grand Masters* is so superior it is not surprising that what they have to say is so powerful; and yet, these extraodinary minds manage to convey the most complex of subject matter in clear and concise terms. I have been privileged to spend a great deal of time with these people over the last year. Not only have they disclosed the secrets of their success but, comparing the various and varied approaches, it is possible to extract some common threads, indicators of superior investment performance. These are examined in Chapter 14 Keys to Successful Investing. I also attempt to answer the question: 'What makes a good fund manager?'

In the body of the book, a separate chapter is dedicated to each of the individuals highlighted as one of Britain's great investors. A chapter is too short to give a complete picture, but we have been able to pinpoint the most important reasons for their success and have highlighted accessible investment strategies of most relevance to the individual investor. There are lessons, too, for even the most experienced professionals looking for that elusive edge to extract the extra percentage point of improvement in their portfolio performance.

How was the choice made? There were three main criteria: first and foremost was performance. I was only interested in people whose track records put them at the very top of the investment industry. They not only had to be the best in their own particular patch of investment expertise, but they also had to be consistently in the top decile overall to qualify. They had to be British, though not necessarily living in Britain. They had to be responsible for investment decisions for at least ten consecutive years at some point between 1980 and 1996. There are many talented Brits in money management, but only the most exceptional, the very best of the best, made the cut for inclusion in *Investing with the Grand Masters*.

I need to put down a couple of caveats. The people chosen are not numbers 1–12 in any ranking of total returns for the most recent ten year period, nor are they the top 12 culled from a particular poll. One single dimension cannot capture the complexity of all the varied types of investing, nor provide a comprehensive range of investment insights of interest to all investors. There is no point covering only people who know how to make money in Egyptian equities if the average individual cannot follow suit. I went out of my way to ensure that those selected for coverage in *Investing with the Grand Masters* embrace a spectrum of different investment styles and approaches, most of which can be carried out by an individual investor.

It was also important that the people included were capable of articulating why they had been so successful. An idiot savant with computer capability might crank out good numbers, but where is the relevance of that? The team selected are well rounded, interesting individuals, widely respected, who have superior investment records and, on top of all that, can explain not only how they did it, but also have ideas as to how others can emulate their efforts.

Do such paragons of investment virtue exist? I believe you will find them profiled in the pages that follow. In my view, it is impossible for any investor to read this book and not learn of some new approach, or not come away with some new idea which will enable them to garner higher investment returns. That is the overriding objective of the book. I learnt a lot by writing it. I expect to manage my fund better, having had the benefit of the investment expertise and wisdom of these British gurus. I hope that all readers will end up better able to manage their investments and make more money than they would have before picking up their copy of *Investing with the Grand Masters*. If this book helps you achieve your investment goals, then I have achieved mine.

There is another message which matters. If *Investing with the Grand Masters* can persuade even 1,000 people who never saved before to start now, then it will have achieved something important. Reading the achievements of these great investment managers and realising how little a sum of money can be necessary, if invested intelligently, for someone to gain a comfortable cushion on retirement should cause every reader to make that decision; or if they already have an investment account then, hopefully, this book will encourage the reader to save more than they do today. The power of compounding is awesome.

Focus on the fact that as little as £50 a month invested with one of the better investment managers has, over the last 25 years, been able to produce in excess of £300,000. That sum should keep the wolf away. Past performance can never predict how the future will unfold; but one prediction is certain. The best way to ensure a reasonable standard of living for people as they get older is to begin to save while they are still young. You do not have to be a rocket scientist to realise that demographic trends throughout the developed world mean more people must save more money. 30 years from now, most countries which, today, take pride in providing state pensions will not have the resources to continue to make payments at their current level. It is hard to imagine a more important decision than how to invest one's savings. *Investing with the Grand Masters* should stimulate readers to start sooner, save more, and be smarter about investing.

It is essential to stress that the performance of investment managers has varied dramatically in the past, and that will inevitably continue to be true in the future. The same people will not necessarily provide consistently superior returns; but a few have done so in such a way as to suggest that the pattern is likely to repeat itself. *Investing with the Grand Masters* does not set out to provide investment advice as such but, clearly, I believe that these particular managers, selected after extensive analysis of their performance and after consultation with a large number of experienced and knowledgeable members of the financial community, represent the 'Best of British'. Ultimately, everyone has to take responsibility for their own investment decisions, and the outcome, good or bad. My point is that it is essential to invest. You cannot save and prosper if you are not in the game.

One other aspect should not be ignored. The multitude of problems that can crop up to plague investors attracts a full court press. Somehow the fun side of investing rarely gets the same sort of attention; and investing can, and should, be fun as well as rewarding. More and more people are realising that investment is an activity which can compare to gardening in providing the pleasure of watching things grow through one's own efforts.

Investing	*Gardening*
Research	Prepare the soil
Purchase the security	Plant the seed
Monitor with continual research	Fertilise and water
Sell losers/take profits	Prune and weed
Enjoy the capital appreciation (and a stream of dividend or interest income)	Enjoy the view (and a vase or two of fresh cut flowers)

Enough of analogies – stretched or otherwise. My point is that investing can bring both intellectual satisfaction and tangible benefits, and all without getting wet or dirty. Consenting adults can even do this together in the privacy of their own homes!

I welcome readers' comments and criticism. To the extent that this book helps, it is nice to hear. Where it falls down, it is essential to know, so the next edition can be better. Let me end by hoping that, after reading this book, you will be able to invest more wisely and more successfully in the future.

October 1996

CHAPTER
1

In a World Class

Who are the best British investment managers in 1996? How can a select few do so well when most managers fail even to meet the overall market averages? *Investing with the Grand Masters* should provide the answers to both these questions and more. Anyone who reads this book should come to the end with a much better understanding of how to improve their investment decisions and their portfolio performance. Let's not be shy. The aim of the game is to make more money, and the top strikers in this industry are those who achieve the goal of maximising the increase in net asset value.

Britain is still a world class player on the investment stage. Of course, the US is number one, but then comes Britain, and our ranking is very much a result of the efforts of a small number of people who are, themselves, among the best of the world in their business. Britain in the 1990s continues to produce leading investment managers who can more than hold their own with the top professionals from any other country. I hope *Investing with the Grand Masters* can contribute to a wider acceptance of this fact by telling the stories of British managers whose success deserves a wider audience.

What you, the reader, chose to do with this information has to be up to each individual. There is no one right road. Different people have different requirements. No two people will come to exactly the same investment conclusions, even when faced with identical facts.

The easy and, some would say, the safe solution, is to go out and put your money with the managers covered in *Investing with the Grand Masters*. Here I must stress that neither the publisher nor the author is in any way offering investment advice; and every investor should not forget that mantra, frequently recited but no less true for frequent repetition, that 'past performance does not, and cannot, predict future performance'. Equally, it should not be ignored. People who weathered the slump of 1992, the crash of 1987 or, even better, the chasm of 1974, and are still going strong are something special and, certainly, a cut above the crowd. Survival of the fittest is a dictum which applies in spades to the investment industry.

Alternatively, you can use these ideas to make direct investments. No-one has a monopoly on wisdom in the investment business. Even the best make mistakes. Knowledge is transient. The increasing pace in the rate of change almost guarantees that; and the computer model has yet to be devised that can predict security prices. Screening and analysis, yes; but no software package contains all the factors which can affect investment values, nor is any such alchemist's dream, neural networks notwithstanding, likely to emerge in our lifetime. The perverseness of market behaviour guarantees that, the moment someone succeeds in modelling a mantra which simulates how markets tick, and starts to invest in any size based on that model, the underlying assumptions would shift.

There is a middle course which may seem both prudent and practical. Entrust the majority of your portfolio to professional management and then keep a portion back to try out a few fliers on your own. *Investing with the Grand Masters* will give you several ideas on strategies, though results will inevitably vary, depending on the choice of individual investments. Such a split leaves the material part of your wealth in the care of people who devote their entire day to managing money, and who treat the business with the seriousness it deserves; yet you are still free to follow the odd tip, hunch or, better still, have fun using the insights in this book to measure your skill against the professionals.

But why a work devoted entirely to British investment managers? An American friend asked me this question during a recent visit to New York, when I was promoting *The Financial Times Global Guide to Investing*. It's a good question but, fortunately, there are some very good answers.

THERE'S ALWAYS BEEN A BRITISH INVESTOR

A little history may help here. Firstly, the British have been doing it longer than anyone else. Unlike the Dutch and Italians, the innovators in trading and banking, the British made the transition from merchant adventurers and closely held corporations to wide ownership of public stock companies and broad distribution of bonds earlier, and with more success than any other country. The antecedents of today's stock exchange can be traced back to 1553 when a group of merchants seeking finance for three ships trading in the Far East offered shares in the venture. The Royal Exchange, a more diverse commercial establishment, but the ancestor of institutions surviving into the 1990s, was up and running by 1570. Exceptions exist. The Dutch would claim, with some justice, that they pioneered the first forebear of today's flourishing investment trust industry. King William I of The Netherlands set up the earliest recognisable closed-end fund in 1822.

That was an isolated incident. There are a surprising number of investment trusts with a history of over a hundred years listed in London and still available to the general investing public in 1996, more of that ilk here than can be found in any other country. The oldest one of all still manages to sit at the top table today, and is a perfect example of the great tradition of investing after a thoroughly successful and remarkable run of 125 years. The Foreign & Colonial Investment Trust and its masterful manager, Michael Hart, are covered in Chapter 6.

> *The British made the transition from closely held corporations to wide ownership of public stock companies and broad distribution of bonds earlier than any other country.*

Markets of all sorts were proliferating in Britain in the seventeenth century, though they were, for the most part, restricted, private and informal. By the end of the eighteenth century, wealthy investors could chose from a range of investment alternatives and a span of asset classes that would be recognisable to today's portfolio manager. A widely held public securities market, primarily in Government stocks, was a well established feature of the British investment scene by the turn of the nineteenth century.

Along with evolving markets names emerged whose success was to set the tone for generations to come. More often merchants first, often investors by default, they dealt in letters of credit, bullion, insurance, commodities and lowly loans. They might dabble in annuities, government securities, distressed bonds, as well as the shares of joint stock companies. They were, inevitably, the main force in foreign exchange, with some merchants, the precursors of George Soros, able to shift rates by significant percentages intra day. British they were, but barely. Nearly all were first or second generation immigrants. Still, if they came from elsewhere, they found something special in the air in London which stimulated them to start financial institutions and allowed them the freedom and flexibility to develop with diversity, and on a scale not feasible anywhere else in that era. Names that still bestride the British investment stage in 1996 have their roots in that period 200 years ago, like:

- The Cazenove family
- Nathan Rothschild (from Frankfurt)
- Francis Baring (his father was from Bremen)
- J Henry Schröder (from Hamburg)

Banks were also booming or, at least, proliferating. Their role in pure investment was more tangential; but many of the household names that populate the financial landscape of Britain in the 1990s are the corporate offspring of personal partnerships whose names were familiar to depositors and borrowers of the late 1700s and early 1800s:

- Hanbury, Taylor, Lloyd & Bowman (Lloyds)
- Vere, Glyn & Hallifax (Glyn Mills)
- Barclay, Tritton, Bevan & Co (Barclays)

Jobbing, banking, providing indemnity, sub indemnity and dealing in other financial specie were well established as separate, if, at times, somewhat seamless activities. Conflict of interest issues were clearer then. There were none! The message was that investors could exercise their ingenuity with plenty of scope to make and lose a fortune.

Cross border investment was well understood. Barings was busy making money in Portugal. The Rothschilds had a network spanning most of the 'developed' world – a term which included several countries now categorised as 'emerging'. Others found fertile territory in South America. India and the Indies were more popular destinations for investment capital. The only significant absentee, from the investment point of view, was the USA, which was not especially united and hardly American, at the time.

Our financial forebears were a more 'global' group than popular folk-lore would allow. The business in third world debt was booming in the late nineteenth century. Values, in real terms, probably dwarfed the comparable market since the turn of the century up until this decade. So investors in Britain, as far back as 200 years ago, had the best part of the range of investment alternatives both geographically and in choice of instruments which survive to today; but they had one advantage – a tolerance for risk and a freedom of action which would leave most modern managers either feeling faint or extremely envious.

These firms and individuals have left a legacy which is still kept alive in the merchant banking community. For a detailed examination of this great investment journey, you may enjoy *The City of London* by David Kynaston, probably the definitive work in the field and packed full of interesting anecdotes. Do not let the title put you off. It is a rollicking good read.

Today's integrated investment house has a way to go to claim the mantle. And most investment managers in the 1990s are increasingly confined into narrow niches and hardly able to see the 30 year Treasury from the five year, let alone a Swedish warrant from a Korean convertible. Yet there is still hope that, once the specialists have had their say and the computer programs have told us all precisely how to allocate our portfolios over the next 12 months, the outstanding investor will shine through wearing the garb of a generalist who grasps the great trends that shape society.

While many of the larger and better known financial houses are now controlled by foreign firms, London continues to be the centre of operation, at least in Europe, for activity in bonds, stocks, currencies and, indeed, most major categories of financial asset. No other market is more innovative or more inclusive. Ownership is almost academic. The employees and the expertise remain in Britain and are, to a large extent, British.

A long history of trading and investing in public markets has brought other benefits. Britain has arguably the best body of securities law, both common and statute, to protect investors. Many safeguards for minorities exist which are absent elsewhere in the world, with the notable exception of the United States and a few other markets, mostly those with a strong British pedigree, including Australia and Canada. A legal framework that not only exists, but is also actually applied, promises fair play for all and attracts external capital. The regulatory regime has also evolved in a way which, while far from perfect, inspires added confidence among investors.

It is, perhaps, no surprise that Britain, with this wealth of tradition, has such a high percentage of its corporate sector in the hands of the investing public. At year end 1994, the ratio of market capitalisation to gross domestic product at 112 per cent was markedly higher than the comparable statistic for mature markets elsewhere. In Germany, the ratio was 27 per cent and France clocked in at 34 per cent. In Japan where all the valuation multiples are much higher that in the UK the ratio ran to 78 per cent. Even the USA only weighed in at 80 per cent. The UK stock market is still an important component in the FT/S&P Actuaries World Indices, with a weighting of 9.25 per cent as of the end of March 1996, which is a good deal higher than the current relative importance of the British economy put in a global context.

London's history as an investment centre is an important reason why the financial services sector remains one of the few areas that is flourishing in Britain in 1996. There are estimated to be 600,000 people working in financial and related services in greater London, a number approximately equal to the entire population of Frankfurt, which is billed as Germany's financial capital. London's role as one of a triumvirate, carefully sandwiched between the capital and currency giants in Tokyo and New York, gives it the perfect position to fit within a revolving 24 hour trading book. The centre of gravity may have shifted, but the participation of London is secure within a more open global system which, in turn, brings up another reason why British investment expertise continues to prosper and remains at the cutting edge of one of the world's most demanding professions.

> *There are estimated to be 600,000 people working in financial and related services in greater London, a number approximately equal to the entire population of Frankfurt.*

Evidence of London's pre-eminence is abundant but this book is not an academic text – far from it. *Investing with the Grand Masters* is about the experience of the best practitioners offering examples based on their own success of how the individual investor can make money. So I shall not bore you with a whole host of supporting data but will advance one slightly offbeat example to reinforce the proposition.

In the late 1980s the London Stock Exchange grabbed the lion's share of the cross-border equities trading business in Europe. During 1995 London traded no less than £54.3 billion of Swiss shares, that is about 30 per cent of the total trading in Swiss listed stocks which took place that year anywhere in the world, Switzerland included. The case for London as a leading global financial centre is so easy to make. The most bumbling articled clerk could take on the most eminent QC and win this argument.

GO GLOBAL, YOUNG MAN

Even more important than its prestigious past is that investment management in the UK has always been global in nature from its inception. It's
obvious that Britain's wealth, in large part, stems from its pioneering role
in setting up overseas trading companies employing the joint stock structure to support that expansion. The history of the Empire is one of a
mercantilist economic policy driving military decisions. Britain employed
its armed forces to achieve maximum profit for its corporate sector in the
nineteenth century. In due course, many of these great trading houses
evolved and became publicly trading companies offering investors an
internationally diverse group of businesses in which to invest.

The composition of the Foreign and Colonial Investment Trust
(FCIT), as of 19 March 1868, is instructive. It was highly diversified,
with a geographic spread which embraced 15 countries and states.
Twentieth century credit pariahs, such as Egypt, Peru and Russia, fea-

Table 1.1 Geographic Split of FCIT Holdings
(as of 19th March 1868)

Country	% Total Capital
Peru	10
Italy	10
Egypt	10
Spain	10
Turkey	10
Chile	10
Brazil	8.5
Russia	8
Austria	6
Danube	6
Portugal	5
Argentina	4
Canada/Nova Scotia	3.5
US	2.5
Australia/New South Wales	1.5

ture prominently. Italy, not known for fiscal rectitude of late is the highest ranking European entry. France in contrast does not appear at all, the Franc not being so *fort* back then. The US appears second bottom on the list with a meagre 2.5 per cent allocation. The breakdown then is tabled on page 9.

Not only did Britain export a mercantile culture, but colonists also introduced the British concepts of financial markets in each trading centre where they emerged as the dominant expatriate community. Stock exchanges sprang up around the world in countries which, voluntarily or otherwise, became part of the Commonwealth. In Asia, reputably the oldest formalised organisation was in India, where a stock exchange was set up in Bombay in 1875. Hong Kong established an organised exchange as early as 1891, though records of stock trading exist which date back to 1866. Other examples can be found in far flung fields of empire. Canada was operating a recognised stock exchange by the end of the 1870s. Johannesburg was in business by 1887. In each and every case, British investors were actively involved.

Contrast this picture with countries which remained outside the orbit of British influence. Bond markets may flourish, but stock markets have received scant respect until recently. You do not find the same tradition in Indonesia as in Malaysia or in Algeria compared to Kenya.

Why does India have the largest number of limited companies outside the US? How come a country like South Africa has the tenth largest Stock Exchange in the world measured by market capitalisation? It is because of the British influence.

The prevailing mentality has been attuned to investing overseas for the past 400 years, with public stock exchanges picking up the investment baton in other English speaking nations for well over a century. Given the access available to British institutions through the Empire, what seemed alien to a German banker was second nature to a British broker. This attitude is pervasive, and is reflected in the current composition of portfolios which varies across countries to such a degree that no directive from Brussels is likely to rectify the difference in our lifetime. The gateway to emerging markets for many continental investors runs through London.

BRITANNIA RULES THE INTERNATIONAL MARKETS

In 1995, the average British investor had the highest percentage of assets invested outside their home market of any of the mature economies. Look at holdings by pension funds in overseas equities for example as a percentage of *total* net assets. It came in at 24 per cent in 1995. The USA which, in many ways, is the most advanced market, is much less adventurous. The nearest comparable number for 1995 was roughly 9 per cent. The French, Germans, Japanese – name any developed country with large amounts of capital – individuals in all these countries are much happier investing at home. Germany managed a measly 5 per cent.

> *'Go with the growth' translates to 'let's go global'. British investors have always understood that relationship.*

Truth to tell, forays overseas have been a mixed bag. The history of the 1880s includes all too many losses for British investors in that pre-eminent emerging market, the USA; and a rash of bad news from Latin America punctuated the following 30 years. That said there is no substitute for direct, hands on experience. The British have been there, done that and, hopefully, learned some of the lessons to become better global investors today.

It is now a matter of necessity not preference, since the opportunities in one domestic market cannot encompass more than a few of the best investment options, particularly when that market is mature. 'Go with the growth' translates to 'let's go global'. British investors have always understood that relationship. They have had no choice. Individuals may buy foreign securities, but British companies have also been voracious purchasers of overseas businesses.

What holds true for investors, both individuals and institutions, is even more true for corporations. Look at almost any British company of size. You will find some portion, and often a considerable proportion, of their earnings is derived from operations in foreign countries. America has proved to be the most popular destination for outward investment from the UK in the last 20 years. There have been spectacu-

11

lar errors of judgement repeated *ad nauseam* in the press, of which Midland's purchase of Crocker probably ranks at the top, or bottom, of the heap, depending on your point of view. There have been many, many more successes, and these do not get nearly the same level of coverage. Hanson, in the 1970s and early 1980s, stands out. Siebe has confounded its critics. Wolsely has pursued its strategy quietly, but with superb execution.

Europe has proved to be less fertile, with failures far more common. Elsewhere in the world, British companies have been disproportionately active; not just in places with close ties, such as Australia and Hong Kong, but in emerging markets where British companies often have some historic affinity. Glaxo in India, Standard Chartered in East Africa and BAT in Brazil all illustrate the point. Figures are not always precise, but the earnings for the FT-SE top 100 companies increasingly come from outside the UK.

The pattern can be pronounced. Take Grand Metropolitan, a prestigious UK name, but most of its profits arise in the US, while the UK has contributed less than 30 per cent of late; or RMC, a leader in aggregates, an industry which is not an obvious selection as an international business. Yet RMC makes most of its money in Germany. Go further down in size to less well known names. Emess, the lighting group, is another company where Germany looms large. Filofax has a market capitalisation of only £44 million but it is a well known British brand with products available in over 40 countries. In 1995 more than 50 per cent of Filofax's operating profit was generated overseas.

This means that UK investors not only need to understand their domestic market, but also require an understanding of international business and overseas markets to assess whether to buy, hold or sell even domestic securities. So much of the earnings of UK companies comes from overseas, directly or through exports. Given the effort involved to evaluate those foreign sourced earnings, investing directly overseas becomes a relatively easy, and even natural, next step. British fund managers have to be global thinkers to succeed, even in circumstances where their remit restricts their holdings to UK listed securities. They must be able to consider a much broader array of factors to arrive at any worthwhile assessment of value, which leads into the last, and most important, point of all.

British investment managers are among the best in the world. Investing is one industry where the British still are pre-eminent and where the top tier can hold their own with any peer group in any other country. Performance proves the point. If we fall down, it is, perhaps, in the area of publicity. There is an innate personal reticence among many of the great investment managers in Britain. It's considered slightly un-British to sing your own praise or even allow someone else to script the song. There is merit in a collective corporate consciousness which preserves what is best about the history and tradition of the institution and plays down the accomplishments of the individual manager. This is so far removed from prevailing practice in the US, which is to recognise, and even glorify, superior achievements of individuals – stars in the investment firmament. A better balance is needed between these two extreme positions. *Investing with the Grand Masters* intends to provide that balance.

THE INVESTMENT INDUSTRY IN BRITAIN – THE HISTORY OF JOHN BULL

There is no better example of how well the British investment industry can work in practice than the story of Foreign and Colonial, but others, like Bankers Investment Trust, confirm the argument, and M&G has popularised British investment prowess.

Perhaps we need a bit more positive press. The successful investment manager is far more deserving of accolades than a top soccer player or chart topping pop musician. Their accomplishments are not transitory and, when investment managers do a good job, they improve the lives of all their shareholders, large and small alike. It is time to take the light out from under the bushel and name the Grand Masters of the investment industry of Britain in 1996.

The successful investment manager is far more deserving of accolades than a top soccer player or chart topping pop musician.

Britain may have no George Soros, but Peregrine Moncreiffe, of Buchanan Partners, can give him a run for his money. Anthony Bolton, at Fidelity Special Situations in London, shares many of the same characteristics

13

with that eminent US investor at the same firm, Peter Lynch. Sir John Templeton probably qualifies as an honorary citizen of Britain and certainly deserves such recognition. In Colin McLean, of Scottish Value, formerly Managing Director of Templeton in Europe, he has found a worthy disciple. Perhaps no British money manager can emulate the travel record of Jim Rogers of *Investment Biker* fame, but Nils Taube has a portfolio every bit as global and on his performance record he can go toe to toe with Rogers. The British venture capital industry has no founding father who could compare with Bill Hambrecht, but consider the accomplishments of the Prince of Wales, who has created more entrepreneurs and successfully backed more start-ups than anyone else around today.

No other country can boast an institution with an unbroken 130 year record of investment success of the calibre of Foreign and Colonial. That story stands alone. Michael Hart, who manages the leading investment trust at Foreign & Colonial, deserves a reputation every bit as large as that other great Michael across the Atlantic, Michael Price. The Swiss superstar, Dr Marc Faber, a guru in emerging markets, stands tall in Hong Kong, but so does Peter Everington, with a record to match any investment manager active in Asia.

There can be no better reason than this. *Investing with the Grand Masters, Insights from Britain's Greatest Investment Minds*, has been written because the best investment managers in Britain have a lot to teach every investor – not only about successful investing in the British market, but also, more importantly, about successful global investing in markets around the world. No other group of managers can make this claim with such conviction. International investing is a glorious British tradition, one in which the country can take pride, and which shows as much of the vibrancy and spirit of adventure going into the twenty-first century as it did when the sixteenth drew to a close.

> *No-one should make the mistake of thinking of this book as parochial and of relevance only to British investors.*
> *These grand masters have developed insights into markets all around the world.*

That said, no-one should make the mistake of thinking of this book as parochial and of relevance only to British investors. Far from it. By the very nature of their brief, these Grand Masters of the investment spectrum have developed insights into markets all around the world. They cover North America, Europe, Asia and, indeed, all emerging markets. Value is close to being one of the few universal truths, and many of these managers have made much of their money out of exploiting the inability of investors in, say, Finland to see how a stock or bond there could be compared with one in Taiwan.

Every investor in every country should be able to find a multitude of ways to better their current performance by blending domestic expertise and knowledge with insights from overseas. As the world economy becomes more international, and individual economies start to be submerged into a global whole, so investment markets have to cease to be insular and reflect relative global valuations. This is one area in which British investment managers excel, and many of the strategies described in this book have application from Australia to Zambia. Making money does not recognise nationality, but Britain has contributed more than its share to the top tier. If there were investment Oscars, any impartial jury would give Britain a high proportion.

Crammed into some 374 pages is the accumulated wisdom of over 250 years of exceptional investment achievement. The secrets of Britain's star investors are worth discovering. Since investors increasingly must employ global asset allocation as one essential element in protecting and building wealth, the experience and record of investors of this calibre have a lot to recommend to investors the world over. Read and reap.

＊ Top European Fund out of 85 over six years

＊ One of London's leading hedge fund managers outperforming
the European market benchmark by a factor of 5×

＊ Described by *International Asset Management* as
'The best European stock-picker around'

JOHN ARMITAGE

Tactical about Markets, Strategic about Stocks

True hedge funds, à la Soros, are still something of a rarity in Britain, and do not settle comfortably into the traditional investment landscape. Well publicised stories of complex trades which have unravelled, have not helped the reputation of this sub segment of the market. The reality, as always, is rather different. The press has picked up on a few misfires and chosen to publicise the failures rather than report on the  stream of successes in the sector. While still a small group, British hedge fund managers are prospering and producing performance which ranks up there with the best around the world.

One of the newest, but also one who has quickly acquired a reputation as one of the strongest fund managers is John Armitage. Egerton Capital, a joint concern with his partner William Bollinger, was only started in May 1994; but already the firm's main European Fund has racked up returns *net* of all fees of 39 per cent, as of December 1995, as against the FT European benchmark which managed a mere 8 per cent gain during the comparable period. There's another feather in Armitage's cap: in 1995, the Egerton European Equity Fund achieved returns which exceeded the performance of the King of hedge funds, George Soros' Quantum, by a full 8 per cent.

That is impressive, but Armitage – at 36, the youngest of our top twelve British investment managers – earns this rating because of his truly outstanding performance during his time at Morgan Grenfell. Armitage spent 13 years there, the last six as manager of Morgan Grenfell European Growth Trust. That fund was ranked number one on a cumulative basis since inception for the period under Armitage's direction, by Micropal, beating 85 other comparable funds run by many very strong teams at other blue chip institu-

> *Unlike most hedge fund managers Armitage makes money the old fashioned way.*

tions. Armitage came top with a stellar 27.1 per cent annualised rate of return, in one of the trickiest sectors of the investment spectrum.

Unlike most hedge fund managers who speculate in whizzy derivatives and use arbitrage to fashion returns which can be exceptional but rarely last, Armitage makes money the old fashioned way. He earns it by buying undervalued shares. Some of his thinking about individual investments is apparent in how Armitage sees investing – which is as a highly competitive industry and a very difficult business.

"Most investment managers make mistakes habitually. If you get 60 per cent of what you do right consistently you will have an excellent record so you have to compete at the point of your greatest competitive advantage. If you take a position in a security, underlying that must be an assumption that there is an inefficiency in the pricing. So you have to ask yourself, 'What do I know that the market does not know, and am I really sure about what I know?' This is true whether you are buying or selling."

Given this assessment of the vagaries of the investment business and his own experience base and background, the focus Armitage brings to Egerton is not surprising.

"The only thing I know about is Europe and stocks. So we are simply not interested in trying to compete with people in other areas or other investment media."

That said, the performance Armitage achieves and the way he realises superior returns contains lessons for investors considering a much wider range of investments than that which falls within the remit of Egerton Capital.

TRULY A HEDGE FUND

"One of the themes of the way we invest is that we try to have long/short positions in a portfolio of uncorrelated businesses so that the fortunes of the fund don't rise or fall with the trends or sequence of events in any one industry group.

"My whole thrust is rather than having a panorama with all the trees visible, I'd like to know about every twig and branch of a few. I'd rather know a lot about a little than a little about a lot. It's critical that what you know about must be *worth* knowing. We try to focus on market inefficiencies, rather than companies which are correctly valued."

Portfolio management and stock selection are interlocking but separate functions at Egerton. There are several strands here which need to be considered separately, as each makes a quantifiable contribution.

1. Market Exposure

Armitage and Bollinger work very closely in determining the overall exposure of the funds they manage. The funds' net long and gross (combined long and short) exposures measured as a per cent of net equity are generated by current absolute and relative performance.

"We do not like to invest and lose money and if we consistently underperform rising markets we are not doing our job properly, so we cut back."

2. Portfolio Concentration

"Concentration is something we've increased. When I was at Morgan Grenfell, I was restricted by guidelines, and the biggest position we could have in any one stock was 5 per cent of the fund. We can have 10 per cent at Egerton, based on the *book cost*, which means it could be more. So far, the most we've ever had is 8 per cent, but typically we have between 65–80 per cent of our net assets in the top 20 long and short positions.

"It is a higher risk strategy, so you have to be more confident. It's also important that these are businesses which are not correlated with each other."

3. Variety is the Spice of Life

Armitage has no particular predilection for one sort of business versus another. He is predisposed to look for good opportunities across all industry groups.

"We have looked at and have held major positions in businesses ranging from the software sector to life assurance to distilled spirits to food retailing, banking and pharmaceuticals, from capital goods, to oil field services, consumer products and airports. I tend to find that I look at a very diversified range of companies in different industries. We consciously aim for lack of correlation between the main holdings in our funds. Look at our current ten largest holdings. None of them are in a similar industry. This is something Egerton as a Firm strives to achieve."

This emphasis on the need to avoid correlation in the key holdings is one of the most central creeds which influence Armitage in picking particular stocks. Take the oil or banking sectors, both of which are relatively homogeneous across Europe with similar factors affecting the industry environment and where there are international drivers which can to an extent determine performance in the business, and he'll look to own *one* – one of the *best*. He would rather not own the cheapest if it is not amongst the best as the security of quality is important. Companies where national or even local competitive factors influence the industry performance, rather than determinants across a wider geographic sphere, provide the latitude to own several even within one country. Building contractors or software companies vary across countries. There are more company specific factors at work here so owning several is an option. With retailers, you can even own multiple holdings in the same country, as long as they are not carrying competitive product lines.

> *We consciously aim for lack of correlation between the main holdings in our funds.*

"If you are looking at different companies in the same sector around Europe, provided the valuations are within a certain band, it would always make sense to go for the best company – the one with the best market position, the strongest management, the best balance sheet and most cash generation. Of all those, management is most important. I wouldn't say British Airways has the best cash generation or balance sheet, but it does have the best management."

4. Long and Short

"We try to short to make money rather than simply to hedge and thus offset long positions, although we hope that our shorts will serve as hedges if the market as a whole comes down.

"If you need to hedge an individual position, perhaps you shouldn't be in it. If you like Volvo, but there's something so wrong with the automotive industry you need to hedge it by shorting another car company, you probably shouldn't be in Volvo. We have short positions in anything from retailers to transport to information technology companies. Actively looking for shorts is a good discipline.

22

"Show me a bad business to short and I'll like it. Show me one which is highly leveraged and cash flow negative and I'll really like it. If it has creative accounting as well, that's the cream. Even good management coming to do a turnaround can't cope if the financial structure is entirely inappropriate. If the next six months of trading are likely to change the debt to equity structure substantially, then that is an opportunity for a short.

"We don't short good companies with rising earnings, even if they are very highly rated. Fundamentals are easier to understand than valuations. When you talk about valuation, you're really talking market psychology and what causes the next buyer or seller to emerge. Well, who knows? So we won't go short if there's good earnings momentum, even if we think the valuation level is wrong we try to wait for the fundamentals to deteriorate. The converse is also valid. My partner (Bill Bollinger) has a phrase: 'Every time you short a security where there has been a bad earnings release, you are making a sale which someone else would like to have made.' There's a lot to that."

Armitage has a big advantage over managers whose brief or whose abilities restrict them to the decision 'invest or not to invest'. Most managers are fully invested all the time. Since he can go both short and long, the issue of valuation becomes much more open ended. Overvaluation or undervaluation can be equally attractive. What he shies away from is fair valuation. This is strictly stock specific analysis and does not apply to markets. Shorting *markets* is for hedging only and anything else is speculation. Theoretically it is never possible to make as

> *If things are going against you, you have to get out of the way and protect capital.*

much money going short as can be gained going long and for that reason if for no other Armitage is more at home in the long side; look back and observe the obvious. Over long periods of time stocks have gone up as an asset class, and only a subset go down, but at least this option increases his alternatives when the market is clearly weak.

"There are periods when it pays to be aggressive and there are periods when it pays to stay out of trouble. If things are going against you, you have to get out of the way and protect capital. If the market is moving sideways you can do better by being mostly long but selecting a few stocks to go short."

We can see this philosophy at work. In 1995 the year started with circumstances which were difficult with rising interest rates, a strong Deutsche Mark and stock prices which were under pressure on most European exchanges. Egerton had cut back to 35 per cent net long by early March in that environment. 35 per cent net long consisted of 90 per cent long, offset by raising the number of individual short positions to an effective 30 per cent short, and then adding protection through hedges in the futures market. By the end of April as interest rates started to slip and a more benign environment emerged the exposure was rapidly reversed to reach 100 per cent net long. For the next six months Egerton's portfolio remained at or over that threshold.

The strategy is not so much actively trying to short stocks. What drives Armitage is the search for deviations from fair value, positive or negative. Instead of trying to decide if something will go up, Armitage asks questions which are double edged.

"I start out looking at a stock and asking myself if it could go down a lot or up a lot. Is there an inefficiency in the price? Is it a good business which the market underrates or is it actually terrible and the market rates it more highly than it deserves? You can always tell roughly what the consensus thinks the company will make and, hence, the valuation.

"First of all, you have to decide on what you believe the realistic medium term growth prospects are for the company. Then you have to ask: are those growth prospects worth more or less than the market is willing to pay?

"One has to look at every aspect of valuation. You have to assess the assets and see if there are not strategic businesses which could realise a higher value elsewhere. You have to look at both earnings and cash flow, though I'm always suspicious of companies selling on permanently low cash flow multiple but which never produce any earnings. Different businesses deserve different multiples. A high cash flow multiple can be entirely appropriate if the business isn't capital intensive."

The net long/short evaluation introduces some more macro level issues into Armitage's investment calculus.

"We were as low as 35 per cent net long in February 1995 because we didn't like the market. There were plenty of good long ideas around, but the US dollar was weak. The implications of that for Europe were deflationary and also indicated a strong Deutsche Mark. Therefore, rising rates would be required on the periphery of Europe, and how would countries cope with that?

"The net position is a result of being tactical about markets, but strategic about stocks. What we look at is interest rates, currencies, and the market direction. There's nothing unusual or scientific. We like rates to be going down, not up. Declining long rates are positive for stocks and the reverse is true. A weak US dollar is bad for Europe."

5. Portfolio Turnover: A Necessary Evil to Stay Ahead

Armitage believes that a good manager must constantly be looking to improve the portfolio. Turnover is, therefore, inevitable, even if a lot of the best gains come from stocks held the longest. An analysis of how the holdings in his portfolio have changed suggests he is very much at the upper end of the spectrum in terms of turnover. Compare the Morgan Grenfell EGT portfolio at the end of November 1993 to its composition two years earlier, and you could be looking at two separate entities. Only 13 out of 95 holdings survived that long. These represented 18.5 per cent of the total value in 1991 and only 11.6 per cent of the 1993 year end balance.

I take, very strongly, the view that you shouldn't sit with something which you no longer like – and a lot of people do.

Perhaps this should not be so surprising, given that Armitage has only a one year time frame in mind when he buys into a stock.

"I take, very strongly, the view that you shouldn't sit with something which you no longer like – and a lot of people do. You shouldn't hold positions in things which you can't justify quite well. It's important to be proactive rather than reactive. You hear people saying, 'We own X because we want something in Germany,' or 'We own Y because it's part of the index.' These are not good reasons to hold a position."

Part of Egerton's philosophy is to review and rebalance the portfolio each month as if starting from scratch. The aim is to have a combination of stocks which should move in the short term and sleepers which will pay off substantially longer term. "I think of it as a bakery where you sell bread every day but make extra profit from selling wedding cakes every so often."

THE PORTFOLIO TAKES YOU ONLY SO FAR

Analysing individual companies and choosing specific stocks is as important a part of the investment process at Egerton as managing the overall portfolio. Extract the essence of the portfolio thinking, apply it to a business and you can see the start of how Armitage selects his individual investments. As goes the portfolio, so goes the stock with certain specific factors leading the way. The story so far goes something like this. First the growth.

"Management must be able to explain their financials from the top line downwards: will the business grow? If so, why? What about it will make it grow? Does that answer seem logical? Do I believe and accept it? What could prevent it happening?"

Then the focus moves onto margins.

"We place particular emphasis on the cost structure of a company and its operating leverage – which works both ways."

Finally and inevitably, Armitage comes back to cash flow.

"Has the company got the ability to self finance? Management's attitude towards its capital and use of shares is critical. We dislike companies which are promiscuous with their equity and tend to avoid companies that can't grow through their own free cash flow on a sustainable basis. Management shouldn't tolerate dilution of any sort, unless they absolutely need it."

> *We dislike companies which are promiscuous with their equity.*

One factor which does not seem to feature in Armitage's approach is country weightings. Most managers of regional or global funds are very conscious of how they are positioned relative to a reference benchmark of the right geographic split. Armitage is so cavalier, he does not even know the exact mix in his funds.

"We tend to look at markets from the bottom up, not the top down, and our market exposure is, therefore, a function of the number of investment ideas we have in any particular geographic locale.

"There are several obvious themes which can make one country more attractive than another at a given point in time. If a country has just had a devaluation or has voted in a government pursuing pro corporate/stock market policies those things are positive. It's clearly an advantage for certain sorts of companies in Italy and Sweden to operate with a weak currency. For example Natuzzi, based in Southern Italy, manufactures leather seating. It didn't even have a business in Italy until recently but produced there with a really cheap cost base for global exports. Still, these are exceptions, for the most part. It may lead you to look more closely at certain sectors in a country, but I would not weight the country more unless I could find good ideas and the right companies in which to invest.

"A lot of these country level themes don't pan out. I never followed the German unification boom with the theory of what opening up the east would do for the profits of many companies across Germany. I couldn't see the opportunities in the equity market there and, with hindsight, it didn't move much more than other markets."

In the same vein, Armitage does not focus much on industry weightings, except to ensure he does not create too many correlations within his portfolio. He does, however, actively search for sectoral themes which can throw up companies likely to exhibit unusual earnings momentum. This exception made a contribution to the first half of the 1990s.

"We did very well out of the telecom and cellular related theme. I believe that cellular telephone is an enabling technology. It really does change the way people live. We have been very heavy in those stocks for a long time. As someone with a very large monthly bill even so I haven't cut down because of the convenience. More use is inevitable. It is rare to see such a major technology unfolding in front of your eyes.

"We have owned the infrastructure providers like Nokia or the network operators like Vodafone or TIM in Italy, and companies which have part ownership like Kinnevik. I have always thought this theme would run and run. If the price of a cellular service is right everyone would want one. The price elasticity on the downside is enormous. There are whole new uses still to come like cellular data. Hewlett Packard has teamed up with Nokia to integrate a phone with a computer."

His experience in striving for exceptional profit through following a theme is more mixed. The offshore service boom, for instance, never materialised, and Armitage highlights that as one of his big busts. This, and other observations, have lead him to stick close to a one stock at a time strategy as the overriding principle which guides his investment philosophy.

"One sector where you have to take a view on the industry not the company is bulk carriers. There it's more important to get the big picture right than the little picture. You have to time the cycle and as long as the fleet is good there is not so much management can do, one way or the other to impact the numbers.

"I find on the whole sectoral analysis for me doesn't work whereas analysis of a company gets to the right answer. Acerinox, a Spanish stainless steel manufacturer, is a great company. It has conservative accounting, good plant and strong management. However, the issue of whether Chinese stainless steel import tariffs will rise or fall, which could have a great impact on the stainless steel market is something I am not qualified to evaluate; but Acerinox will do well whether that happens or not.

"In mid 1995, paper company share prices were saying the cycle is going to end very soon yet, when you talked to the companies, they were not at all sure. Capital spending was actually running at quite low levels, relative to existing capacity. With earnings multiples of 5 or 4.5 times, that left a lot of room for things to go wrong."

So the best way to get to grips with how the investment strategy at Egerton actually works is to discuss specific stocks. Armitage is at his most eloquent talking about why he likes one company and why he is willing to short another. As his reasoning unfolds, you can pick out the criterion he uses to make investment decision. What emerges is:

A. First and Foremost: Strong Management

Armitage does not subscribe to the Warren Buffett dictum that, when a good management meets a bad business, the reputation of the business always prevails. Preferably, one finds good management *and* good businesses; but good management can sometimes make money out of bad businesses and, if push comes to shove, Armitage would back the management.

"The UK clothing market is difficult. Consumer spending in the 1990s has been weak. The retailing sector is mature and competitive. The UK is overshopped. Yet we have had a major holding in Next, the retailer run by David Jones, who is one of the best managers I have ever met and the stock price has come up from 9p when he arrived in the late 1980s to 550p now."

B. A Clear Competitive Advantage

This usually, but not always, translates into some sort of Market Leadership. It's harder to get a handle on how this dictum can be encapsulated into a single sentence that will work across vastly different industries. Not every company can be number one in its market, but a nice niche will do. What all this is leading up to is a proxy for sustainable growth, because only if growth is sustainable can earnings grow and good cash flow follow. A few examples should help:

- British Airways dominates Heathrow.
- Hamleys has the best brand name in toy retailing in the UK.
- Misys has a near stranglehold on software for insurance brokers.
- Bic's name is now synonymous with pens and disposable razors.
- Finnlines dominates import/export in and out of Finland by sea.

It is important to stress that this commentary represents Armitage's views as of April 1996 and that a week in the investment business can be a long time. His own portfolio could look very different as of the date of publication, and nothing he says should be taken as recommendation to buy or sell any security. The general points are what is important.

"We have a holding in Hamleys, where you have a famous brand with a flagship store, and some peripheral businesses exploiting the core brand. There had been a history of poor management at that company before Howard Dyer took control. Recently, the new group of people with proper incentives to perform are putting that history behind them. Hamleys has an unusually high gross margin for a retailer of 50 per cent plus, and thus significant operating leverage and, in good times, can generate strong positive cash flow.

"Another big position is British Airways. We think that there is a positive backdrop to the air travel industry. There's rising demand, tight load factors and limited supply of planes. I met the management of SAS recently. Their capital expenditure programme over the next few years will be taken up with replacing their existing fleet.

"BA has a dominant position in Heathrow, one of the world's leading airports, a very strong position on the transatlantic route, an extremely profitable exposure to routes which, to a large extent, reflect certain vestiges of the old British Empire in Africa and the Middle East, a management culture which is about as cost conscious and profit driven as any; and all this is at a rating which I believe is too low. It's worth more than a 10.5 times multiple of earnings.

29

Misys is a company active in the banking and insurance business. It just made a large acquisition of which the market is, and has been, sceptical. Some people have raised queries over how they have accounted for the property aspects of the acquisition, but any uncertainty is more than compensated for in a rating which is very low, given the quality of the earnings and the growth prospects. They are in growing sectors. Their insurance division is characterised by so called tollgate transaction revenues which are very high quality and very attractive. They have translated pre-tax profits into cash generation at a 100 per cent rate over the last few years. They're trading at a multiple of about 14 times, which is much lower than their real growth."

C. Cash, Cash and Cash

Cash flow is king when Armitage evaluates the financial aspects of a business. Yes, he looks at growth. Yes, he looks at profits. Yes, he looks at assets; but he starts and ends by examining the cash characteristics. Is the business generating cash: if not, can it? If not, he moves on to the next prospect. It is critical not to confuse the importance of cash flow generation with cash flow multiples. Here Armitage parts company with the investment crowd who tend to see low multiples as a panacea.

> *Cash flow is king when Armitage evaluates the financial aspects of a business.*

"Low cash flow multiples are not necessarily good. Some businesses with low multiples are just low growth or highly leveraged and all the cash has to go to the banks or they never pass cash on to their shareholders. So they may deserve to have a lowly rating. It looks attractive but the business can be stuck in a rut. You have to distinguish between the operating aspects of the businesses to see what multiple is appropriate.

"If you look in the European airline sector you can see an interesting contrast in Scandinavia. Braathens, a regional Norwegian carrier, combines a low cash flow multiple with other attractive characteristics. It has an average age of around $4\frac{1}{2}$ years for its fleet. This must be about the youngest fleet in the industry. If you ask the question does a low cash flow multiple actually translate into free cash flow? Well clearly Braathens is not going to have to spend much on new equipment. Is it well run? My answer is that it is more profitable than most in its industry; and its productivity is very high. It has a 20 minute turnaround for flights and gets a lot out of its equipment.

"So is Braathens cheap? Compared to other European airlines it is because it has a low cash flow multiple which is not deserved. Whilst SAS's multiple may be right given its need to spend money to modernise its fleet." Chart 2.1 summarises the point.

Chart 2.1 Comparative Airline Valuation

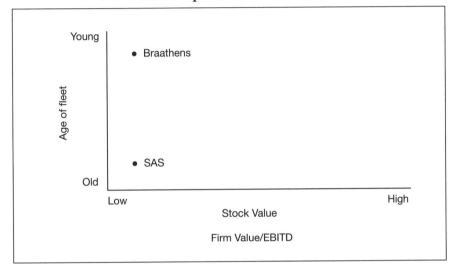

D. Growth at a Discount

Get past cash and, other things being equal, Armitage always plumps for a business which has good top line growth potential. In a way, he is a sort of value growth investor. If sales are growing, can earnings be far behind? Jim Slater has reduced this evaluation to a single index, the PEG, which is now computed for every publicly quoted company in the UK. Armitage has an approach which is rather more complex but, in essence, it boils down to something similar. He is interested in buying at a price where the earnings multiple is at a discount from its underlying earnings growth and, preferably, to the overall market as well.

Other examples of specific stocks held by Egerton help round out the story.

"Telecom Italia had a very valuable cellular business which was growing very fast. When the demerger happened, the price did not reflect the phenomenal growth in numbers of subscribers and the tariff structure. There was a several year track record, but still a lot to go for. We ended up with the Italian cellular company TIM as our biggest holding in mid 1995. The Company is very well run. TIM has the largest subscriber base of any cellular network in the world but is still growing at $2\frac{1}{2}$ per cent per month. It competes with an operator which has only just built out its network, and has a weaker balance sheet than TIM. Moreover TIM trades on a cheaper cash flow multiple than its peers. That all makes it more attractive.

"We invested in a Norwegian company Tybring Gjedde, a distributor of office consumables to business and other sectors such as hospitals and government departments. It has a very profitable domestic business which has generated circa 30 per cent compound annual earnings growth over the last few years. Prospectively, the business in Norway on its own was only on a 12 times multiple. The Norwegian side was a superb operation and deserved a higher rating; but Tybring also owned a Swedish business, a mistimed acquisition which meant the overall company was barely breaking even. The Swedish business was itself an agglomeration of poor acquisitions.

Armitage is like an archer. He has a quiver full of questions.

The excellent performance in Norway was masked by losses in Sweden. What we wanted to work out was what the value could be if the Swedish business came right? With hard work they got it to break even and then added on a distributor in a complimentary sector – educational supplies – which brought with it good management. This combination should allow for rationalisation in the distribution and lead to purchasing benefits and cross selling. In 1997 the company as a whole should make excellent profits and the Swedish subsidiary has plenty of tax losses."

The emphasis on individual stocks explains one element which is core to every investment Armitage makes. It is not the methodology or analytical tools which he uses to evaluate a company, but the totality of the process. The cornerstone is meeting and discussing both the business and the industry with management. Armitage is like an archer. He has a quiver full of questions. Every answer generates another question. He also treats all answers with an instinctive scepticism. One which got past all the hurdles was the Bank of Ireland.

"Its business is not very complicated. It's got a massive market share in Ireland, and a treasury business, and an American bank.

"I asked about lending growth and margins and costs. It's a bank which is very profitable and generates a very high return on equity, a lot of which it retains, and it has a lot of excess capital. Yet it is on a low multiple and in addition owns this US business which is non-strategic. So half the most recent meeting was about how much capital they really need and what will they do with the excess, and what is the future of the US business? That led to a discussion of how could they return capital to shareholders if they decided to do so? What were the merits of buy backs or stock dividends? We address these issues in a direct fashion.

I felt comfortable after this conversation – not because they agreed to do anything, but it's well run, management are earnings driven, and they are responsive to shareholders.

"Since then they have merged their US subsidiary with the US operation of the Royal Bank of Scotland. They now own 23 per cent of a larger entity which would lead to more capital realisation if they can sell their share.

"An open and honest dialogue between management and shareholders within the constraints of the obligation placed upon public companies is a very positive sign of a confident, well run organisation. The reverse is an indicator of the contra conclusion.

"I never invested in Polly Peck because management could never explain to me why the cash flow was less than the earnings. I met them several times. Their reticence made me suspicious. I stayed out of the Norwegian banks because they could not convince me of the asset quality."

To recap the key points again: what makes a business attractive to Armitage is:

(a) having the right characteristics:

- quality earnings growth and/or earnings power;
- free cash generation;
- a solid balance sheet;
- good management with a shareholder orientation;

(b) an attractive value relative to its:

- growth;
- free cash flow;

- competitors;
- the market;
- private value.

There is one other item in his bag of tricks.

E. The Conglomerate Discount

In the spirit of searching for pricing inefficiencies Armitage also keeps an eye open for not only what is but what could be. The value of a company is the sum of its parts but sometimes the sums add up in ways which produce results that do not make sense. What a business is worth on a stand-alone basis versus its value within a corporate structure may be more or it may be less. That latter scenario attracts forward thinkers like Armitage who can spot where managers have an opportunity to improve their share price through means other then running the operation.

One well known UK example which may not be obvious to every investor but is a name every reader will recognise is at the forefront of his list in early 1996.

"If the different bits of Boots were trading separately and if a demerger could be done without causing significant cost relative to the business as a whole then the market value of those entities should be much higher than the current valuation for the company combined.

"There are some poor performers in their current portfolio and the unsuccessful businesses mask the success of Boots The Chemists. Split off Do It All and you might manage that entity so as not to have a negative value. It would cost money to sell; but what if they spent their dividends one year recapitalising it and spinning it off to shareholders?

"Boots The Chemists is one of the best businesses in the UK. With a 75 per cent return on capital and an impregnable position what is it worth? Say, 18 times earnings. That seems realistic. The Contract Manufacturing business probably could not be demerged even though it has third party sales, because Boots the Chemists is such a big part of the total, but it is a good business. So it deserves the same rating.

"The low profits in the OTC drug business as they expand internationally with heavy investment revenue depressing the margin deserve a high multiple but it will not get that hidden within the current Boots conglomerate. On its own it would have a higher value. Look at the recent trade sale value on Childrens' World which had £2 million of operating profit but was sold for £60 million. This shows the sort of thing I am talking about for Boots."

The conglomerate discount can be a source of added value to shareholders however well run the company. Armitage has been a long time supporter of Securitas, a Swedish security firm which came public in 1990 at SwKr90 per share. He had been hugely impressed by the management and in particular by Melker Schörling, the Chairman and Thomas Berglund, the Chief Executive. Come the end of 1994 and the stock was up to SwKr200 and the Company had paid dividends, a good return for three plus years. The best was still to come.

> *I'm incredibly sceptical of book value, which is just an accounting fiction. Who knows what the real value of the assets is?*

"Within Securitas was a well run locks business (Assa) which was on a small scale. Assa merged with a larger company called Abloy and so was spun out of the group in a process which gave shares in the new entity to Securitas shareholders. Since that merger profits of the combined Company have risen substantially. As of April 1996 investors have Securitas shares now worth SwKr375 on top A-A stock now at SwKr78 and have received further dividends – an even better return for the extra two years."

While he may not be a card carrying disciple of any specific school of financial analysis, Armitage still has strong views on how certain formulae can, or should, be used and interpreted.

"I'm incredibly sceptical of book value, which is just an accounting fiction. Who knows what the real value of the assets is? What's the point of a company valued at a high discount to book which can't make a profit out of its plant? Perhaps a different management could do better, but how do I know if the plant is good? Ask two people whether that plant can be used more efficiently and you will have one saying it could, and the other saying it couldn't.

"I follow a paper company in Sweden which trades at three times cash flow and a discount to book value, but people in the know say no-one in the industry would buy its plant. So what's it really worth? Sometimes book value is just inventory, and you can look at that, but what is it worth? You may have to flog it to see what it is worth. Then you find out if you have made a profit. Otherwise it's not important. A property company has a real book value.

"If there is a remote element of a franchise to a business, book value has no meaning. United Biscuits make a 25 per cent return on capital employed in their biscuit business, but their brand has a value, and that's not on the balance sheet, so this is not a real number."

When you look through Armitage's portfolio, you won't find many businesses which are asset rich in the traditional sense of the word. What you will find are companies which are worth a lot, but where the value is not often expressed on the balance sheet.

Another way to get to the bottom of why Armitage has outperformed the market by such a wide margin is to trace some of the themes he has employed which have proved so successful for him and his shareholders.

"In 1988/9, we made a lot of money buying cyclicals which had high *operating* leverage. Hoesch in Germany and Leifhoegh in Norway are two cyclical companies, one in steel and the other in bulk shipping, which came right at that time. After the sell-off in 1987 you had rising earnings but you could buy them on low multiples so we caught that up trend.

"In Europe, you have been able to find businesses with significant *peripheral* assets which were just not valued properly.

"In 1993 we looked for companies which had come through in industries where conditions had been awful in the previous two years. There were so many factors suggesting interest rates had to come down. It was going to happen most where governments no longer needed to put up interest rates to boost their currencies. Interest rate sensitive businesses and companies which had high financial leverage would benefit. The Spanish utilities performed well. Norgeskreditt, a mortgage bank in Norway, had survived the Central Bank raising rates to 30–40 per cent which brought down two bigger banks. It had low loan losses of around 2 per cent. It was at half book value when book was made up of good mortgages or cash and it had a high capital ratio. We did well with that."

One interesting idiosyncrasy which arises from Armitage's immersion in his investment activity is that the intersection between his portfolio and his personal life is the exact inverse of the Peter Lynch shopping mall approach.

"If we own a company, then I try to use the products. When I'm in the US, I always order Heineken to find out whether it's in the bar, and when we owned SMH, I always bought a lot of Swatch products to see how they were doing."

For a manager who is so single minded in being a bottoms up stock picker, that selection process is crucial. When evaluating ideas, it is essential to use tools to weed and prune but, before you make a significant investment of time, you have to find good candidates. This is the starting point for Armitage's success. Some of what he does is sheer hard slog, but other features of the way he sources stocks are only available to professional investors or very high net worth individuals.

"We believe in working with the most talented stockbroking firms and using their really bright analysts. Why hire someone if you can pay commissions and work with the best? There are many creative thinkers out there who spend their lives visiting companies. You need to know them.

> *We believe in working with the most talented stockbroking firms and using their really bright analysts.*

"I try to look at a lot of ideas. A lot of what I do is sifting things. There's no point doing work on issues which appear to be within 5 or 10 per cent of the right price."

So how to categorise Armitage? You probably can't in any convincing way.

"We try to follow Warren Buffett's dictum 'We're all interested in capturing the highest stream of discounted cash flow.' The NPV of the growth is what counts. Whether that comes from buying a high P/E company that's growing fast, or a low P/E that's barely growing does not matter. It's more or less the same thing.

"I'm not very good at conceptualising turnarounds. I prefer to buy what I can see in front of me."

Armitage is sufficiently relaxed about his success that he is also willing to share a cautionary tale about one error individual investors should be careful to avoid.

"Many of the biggest mistakes I've made were not selling things as they've gone down. Why haven't I sold when the shares were behaving like shit? I thought I knew something more than the market and, usually, you don't. So if the market is telling you to sell, in most cases, you should sell. It's no good to say you know it's cheap. It is an emotional and intellectual habit to want to lean over backward to justify decisions we have made. The worst losses have always been not selling when the signs are there that something is going wrong. You cannot ignore evidence from the market. You can never know a stock that well however much analysis you do. The more time you spend visiting the company, talking to brokers and analysts and reading other research, then the more you want to be right. You fall in love with your own work; but you cannot. One of the things I am most proud of is that we had a big position in Volvo after much research but started to see signs it was not going that well. So when Volvo went to 125, down 20 per cent, we had already sold two thirds of our position at more or less break even.

> *If the market is telling you to sell, in most cases, you should sell.*

"There is always an element of hope, or supposition when you buy or sell a share because the assumption is that there is some inefficiency. You are making a forecast about the future price movement and forecasts are tricky things.

"In a good year you are wrong 40 per cent of the time. It is difficult to do much better than that. So an important question is how much do you make when you are right and how much do you lose when you are wrong. The key is not to lose 70 per cent or 50 per cent when things go wrong but only about 15 per cent or 20 per cent. Then when and if you win and if you make 100 per cent or 200 per cent that is a huge multiple of your losses and you end up well ahead."

When you run a vehicle whose focus is European equities, it is not unreasonable for concerns to be raised about the impact of currency movements on returns to investors. Armitage is able to put that issue to rest with ease. Returning to the Morgan Grenfell European Growth Trust, it is interesting to look at his period of management compared to the Morgan Stanley Capital Intentional Europe Index (excluding the UK) and expressed in several key currencies, shown in Table 2.1.

Shortly before he left Morgan Grenfell, *The Wall Street Journal* ran a survey compiled by Micropal which placed Armitage's fund first out of 247 ranked funds in the European Equity sector over a five year period.

Table 2.1: Annual Compound Returns (4/88 – 3/94) (%)

GBP		US $		SWFR	
MEGT	Index	MGEGT	Index	MGEGT	Index
27.1	16.8	22.0	12.2	22.7	12.8

This is the sort of exceptional record which is attracting clients to follow Armitage to Egerton, where he already has more money under management, but the outperformance has continued.

Not surprising that, with these numbers under his belt, Armitage attracts accolades galore, as can be seen from numerous articles in the financial press and commentary from top flight investment professionals around the world over the last ten years. What follows is only a small sample.

'I consider him the best European stock-picker around.'
Alan Djanogly, *International Asset Management*

'Managed by John Armitage . . . Morgan Grenfell's European Fund has performed consistently well through the turmoil.'
Philip Coggan, *Financial Times*

'Mr Armitage at Egerton Capital is one of the best. He's got the passion.' Susan Douse, *Watson Wyatt*

'It's little wonder that investors have been pouring money into Egerton.' Robert Bonte-Friedheim, *Wall Street Journal*

'He is more thorough and more focused . . . than other fund managers.' Harold Grimsrud, *Fondsfinans*

'If anyone can get out of a tricky market, [Armitage] can.'
Stuart Mitchell, *Morgan Grenfell Investment Management*

Looking forward, Armitage sees tough times for the economy in Europe, and economic cross currents which will sort the men from the boys to an even greater extent than has been the case in the preceding period.

"I think the environment will be one of low inflation and subdued growth everywhere in Europe. It will be hard for companies to grow their earnings and lead to a more severe divergence between good and bad companies. In this environment, pricing power will be very hard to get. Corporate restructuring has become a permanent part of life.

"We are in a low growth, low inflation environment. Without a special service or product where there is pricing power, or without an international element to the operation, and the ability to expand overseas, it is very hard to grow the top line. In an environment of lowering trade barriers, exports will be the other route to growth.

"Do you give a damn about the price of your timber preservatives or tropical plant service, which is partly why Rentokil works so well? Do people really haggle about the price of their security service if it is good? That leads to sustainable growth. Find a product you need where you cannot worry too much about the price.

"Some brands can travel well around the world. In Europe Heineken has such a franchise and has grown its exports. It does not have the earnings record of Coke but has performed in spite of having a base in Holland where the currency is stronger than the Dollar."

Armitage does not feel investors, as a whole, can achieve much by trying to outguess the markets on political factors. Changes in Government policy need to be assimilated into analyses of the business – no more than that. If outsourcing is on the rise, that is one extra factor that adds to the case for buying Capita but it does not clinch the decision.

To say a hedge fund manager is a conservative investor sounds like a contradiction in terms but, applied to Armitage, the characterisation fits. He is careful to minimise market and sector risk, and picks his stocks without emotion or bias, or any kind of personalised judgement. The focus is clinical and clear cut: do the financial profile and operating performance present an opportunity to make money – long or short? You can expect calculated risk aversion from a man who was once quoted as saying, "When it's easy to lose money you've got to survive. Why stand up to be machine gunned?" So, with Armitage, you get safety and superior returns, which is a winning combination.

* 'One of Europe's most powerful fund managers'
Wall Street Journal

* In his *first two years* as a manager Bolton grew his fund by
62 per cent versus the benchmark increase of 9 per cent

* One thousand pounds invested in 1979 with Bolton would
be worth £24,953 in 1996!

ANTHONY BOLTON

Finding Value Where it is not Fashionable

For someone who is generally regarded by his peers in the financial world as one of the truly great European investors, Bolton is a relatively young 46; but 25 of these years have been spent in the investment community and, as long as 16 years ago, Bolton had already acquired a reputation which few achieve in a lifetime.

Often referred to as the Peter Lynch of London, an accolade he himself would refute, Bolton is one of the few true British investment legends. He has chalked up accolades too numerous to include. A sample should suffice:

- 'A talented share picker.' *Money Observer*
- 'His terrific long-term performance speaks for itself.' *Fund Research*
- 'A fund manager to follow.' *Investors Chronicle*
- 'One of Europe's most powerful fund managers.' *Wall Street Journal*
- 'No article on great gurus would be complete without recognition of Anthony Bolton.' *Sunday Times*

We could go on and on, and we'll come back to the numbers that prove the point later, but, for now, the goal is to try and understand how Anthony Bolton came to rise to the top of his profession. Bolton's background lay in engineering and his arrival on the investment scene was sort of serendipitous. Thousands of shareholders should be thankful to an anonymous Procter & Gamble executive for steering Bolton away from industry and into the financial sector.

"At one time I thought I was going to be a scientist, and I had originally gone, when I went for my interviews at Cambridge, with the intention of reading natural sciences, but my future tutor told me it was much easier to get in to do engineering. Being pragmatic, I decided that I'd better do engineering, because the thing I was keenest on was getting a place! I was very unsure that engineering was the right career, but it was the easiest way to get in. I had some idea that the computer industry might suit me. Later I went on an external, vocational guidance course. They tested me for what I was good at, suggesting management and general terms like that.

"One businessman, who was a friend of the family thought the City would be good experience. Even if I didn't want to stay there, I would learn things I could use in other walks of life. Then I went for a sort of 'showing undergraduates a company' type day with Procter & Gamble. On the way back, the chap from Procter & Gamble who had organised it said, 'If you really want to be successful and earn lots of money, don't come into industry, go into the City!'"

Bolton took the advice and joined Keyser Ullmann, "possibly their first and last graduate trainee". Part of his initial training involved learning where the important buildings were in the City, and he started out life as a messenger walking Treasury Bill tenders to the Bank of England. "You weren't allowed to run or you got ticked off by the people in their pink coats." Wearing top hats held little appeal compared to the interest of the investment side. So, once his rotation was over, that was the area where Bolton ended up.

Bolton found he was starting his investment career at one of the less orthodox ends of the spectrum – smaller companies. Keyser Ullmann had a stable of three closed-end funds operated under the name of Throgmorton. There Bolton had his apprenticeship under the savvy tutelage of Bill Douie and Bob Seabrook.

"Two things from that period have stuck with me throughout my career. Smaller companies are, on the whole, more interesting than the blue chips and there is more chance to make money in that sector. At the same time, investing in smaller companies means you must go and meet the people who are running the business if you want to understand it and decide whether this one makes sense to back.

"When I think of what we do today, say here in Fidelity, versus what we did then – the amount of contact and the way we go about investing – has changed almost beyond recognition. Keyser Ullmann did have a fundamental analyst, an economist, and, unusually, a technical analyst. That's also an influence that has remained with me: an interest in charts and the technical side, in addition to the fundamental side.

"What I mainly did was to read through annual accounts. We had a summary sheet – some balance ratios – and I had to write a short synopsis with a conclusion. It wasn't terribly advanced – although the sort of things we were doing included stripping out exceptionals, and trying to show the underlying profits. And there were visits. I remember going to see a Welsh company making saucepans. Down one end of the factory there were piles and piles of saucepans. So we said, 'Well, what's this,' and they said, 'We had a design fault. The handle was supposed to be insulated, but the insulation didn't work, and the handle used to heat up as hot as the pan. They were all rejects.' It was pretty obvious the business was not going as well as people in the market thought! We were able to stay away from that one."

Bolton's second stint was with Schlesinger Investment Management. Schlesinger was a hive of innovation which rubbed off on Bolton. Although sceptical of some of the ideas being tried out involving quantitative models and efficient market portfolio techniques, he began to utilise some of the tools of the trade. More importantly, by seeing what did and did not work, he was able to build on his experience at Keyser and began to articulate his own philosophy.

"I realised that, to outperform, you've got to hold something different from the market. It sounds terribly obvious these days but, in those days, looking at relative weights against an index was quite a new concept, and wasn't widely done. If you've got high turnover and you're holding something near an index fund, you're almost bound to underperform by definition. To do better, you may need to accept greater volatility and even more risky investments. They've always tended to be medium and small cap stocks rather than big stocks. Risk can be measured and managed even with smaller companies."

Bolton was already making his mark. He really came into his own assuming responsibility for the Schlesinger Special Situations Trust in 1977. In two years in that role, he achieved a growth in NAV of 61.7 per cent against an increase in the UK smaller companies sector of a mere 8.9 per cent. No wonder he got a warm welcome on calling Richard Timberlake, an ex-MD of Schlesinger's who had been head hunted to start up Fidelity in Europe, after Timberlake had announced he was looking for investment people to join that innovative enterprise.

"They were a large US organisation, and had a very good reputation in the States. This was a very exciting opportunity to be involved in the ground floor."

By the time Bolton moved to Fidelity, he had already developed an investment style which was to make an immediate impact on the Special Situations fund which was launched on his arrival. That approach has been honed and refined over the years, but has stayed essentially intact, though with growing sophistication in its application. Bolton describes his philosophy, which continues until today and has survived the 1987 crash, the Gulf War and the slump of the early 1980s with an unbroken record of superior performance:

"I manage the portfolio with an above average risk reward profile concentrating on contrarian type stocks. The main area that I've always looked at is in recovery type stocks, and that has tended to be the biggest group in the portfolio. And it's recovery rather than cyclical. My ideal stock is one where things have gone wrong in the company, but it looks as if things are changing. There's perhaps been a restructuring, or a change in management. I also will buy undervalued,

> *My ideal stock is one where things have gone wrong in the company, but it looks as if things are changing.*

under researched stocks, and what I would term unrecognised growth stocks or growth stocks that are, perhaps, going through a temporary blip or something that I perceive to be growth that the market doesn't. This phrase that I use is 'finding stocks that are unfashionable and cheap, but I think there is some characteristic about them that will recapture investors' attention or interest on a one to two year view'."

There are three main factors which fashion his investment strategy.

1. UNFASHIONABLE AND UNDERVALUED STOCKS

First and foremost, he is looking to find *unfashionable* and *undervalued* stocks.

A good example of this was his purchase of £7 million in the Midland Bank at a time when the general view was that Midland was the worst of the UK clearers. "Midland was seen as the riskiest of the UK banks, but it seemed to me that it was also the one with the most potential for change, particularly given its capital structure." The fact that it took another institution, Hong Kong & Shanghai Bank, to bring out the value doesn't affect the result – for Bolton, an 88 per cent gain in just under 24 months.

Undervalued can be both an absolute and a relative term, as expressed in this extract from the Managers' Report on the 1987 Fidelity Special Situations Trust:

> In addition to Midland Bank, the Trust has also bought shares in Barclays Bank and warrants in National Westminster Bank, all of which seem to be on low *ratings relative to the UK market and to similar US banks.*

It sounds almost trite to say that your strategy is to buy unfashionable and undervalued stocks, but the beef is in implementation. Bolton has identified nine separate categories of companies which can fit within the broad parameters and find a place in his fund. This creates a blended composite approach which owes something to many different schools, but does not get too attached to one specific style. While we will cover each separately, these investment themes are not mutually exclusive categories. A decision to invest in a company can result from more than one applying simultaneously:

(i) Internal Recovery

"Internal recovery is one of my biggest areas, particularly in the UK. A number of these have involved refinancing. In some cases, like First National Finance, I have come back to something that I had owned before. What I find, with these recovery stocks, is that people generally don't want to buy things that have done poorly. Wickes and LIG were two recent picks where the core business is strong. Both went off and diversified into something that's been a disaster. Wickes went into timber importing. They bought that just before the recession at exactly the wrong time. They got over geared and got into financial difficulties. They've needed two refinancings since then but, all through that time, the basic DIY business appeared to be strong. Of course now we know things were not exactly as they seemed, but on the surface the Wickes story looked like a classic case of a refocusing which worked.

"Change of management is another thing which I often look for. WPP is another example of refinancing when they converted their preference shares into ordinary shares. They're a good business but they had too much debt. Mirror Group is another example among shares I own today.

"Perhaps I should add there should be something about the company that makes other investors uncomfortable and, therefore, they don't want to invest. My whole nature is that I want to have a second look at those. If there's something that's putting off other investors, I want, at least, to look at them.

"An example from the early 1980s is Mersey Docks, which had got into difficulties because the docking industry was highly unionised in the UK. Then the Government brought in a scheme which would pay for the redundancies of the dockers. Each year they made redundancies and the Government picked up the tab. There was a contingent liability in the balance and, theoretically, if the Government ever asked for that money back, they wouldn't have been able to pay it. But the Government was a large shareholder. It kept 20 per cent and had two people on the board. It seemed to me that it was pretty unlikely that the Government would ever ask for that back. You had unit which sold in the 20p to 30p region and, for that, you got 100p of loan stock plus one share.

"The other aspect that interested me was that they are quite big property owners in the port of Liverpool which, with other points of entry, were made free ports. This change increased the value in the property.

"One of the things that put off the investors was that Mersey Docks were also the employer of last resort in Liverpool which meant, if any other company that employed dockers in Liverpool wanted to lay off their dockers, Mersey Docks had to pick them up; but this was the early 1980s and Thatcher was changing working standards. When AB Ports came to the market, one then had another quoted port company. People started to understand the business of running ports and the attraction, because ports actually can make good margins. The properties are valuable. In the case of AB Ports, the Government wrote off 70 per cent of the liabilities that they had for laying off dockers, which was a precedent. In the end, with Mersey Docks, the Government wrote off 100 per cent. They didn't want any of it back, as I thought would be the case. The stock was a ten bagger."

(ii) Unrecognised Growth

"Unrecognised growth is more looking for companies or areas that I think have growth, where the market, for some reason, doesn't think that. I'm always looking for aspects where I think the market's view could change. It's looking forward, so a double guessing game, and a psychological game. Bulmers was an interesting one. Cider has been one of the few areas of the drinks market which has been seeing decent volume growth over the last few years. I got interested in this, particularly at the time of the MMC report into the brewery sector several years ago. It looked as if Bulmers, had been restricted and, as part of the MMC changes, the brewers were going to have to give access to more pubs where, previously, the brewers had stocked only their own brand.

"Also, Bulmers had a change of marketing strategy, where they decided to increase their advertising substantially on their brands to advertise them more like a lager brand, and that looked as if that could be successful. In the short run, doubling the advertising spend hurt profits and the market thought their margins were in decline. In fact, they were investing for increased revenues which came through later, and I was able to see the volume gains which, initially, did not offset the increased costs, but caused higher profits after a time lag.

"Casinos would be another classic example of my bigger holdings. If you look at casino companies in America and in the Continent, they tend to get fairly high valuations because of the cash generation prospects. Here people have been worried, with some reason, because it has been a risky business in the past. Casinos have lost licences. People remember the Ladbroke's fiasco, going back a number of years. Therefore, when London Clubs was floated, it was floated at a very low relative valuation. What had changed was the way that licences could be taken away. A chain couldn't lose all its licences at once, in the same way as they could have in the past, so it made an investment less risky. Plus there looked to be a relaxation in the whole environment for betting with the National Lottery. You started to see these companies revalued. I'm very interested in looking at different valuations across markets, where people in one market value them differently, compared to the others.

"Radio is another area. Only a very small per cent of advertising historically, in the UK, went on the radio. It looked as if radio could take market share from other forms. Capital Radio was the main play there. More recently I've had several computer software companies. Some have disappointed, but one of my big holdings is Misys, which has taken over ACT. The price got down to where Misys was selling at a large discount rating to the market, which I don't think is right for that sort of industry. Misys has a business which had grown to be one of the largest suppliers of computer services to banks worldwide, which was an attractive franchise."

(iii) Discount to Assets

"Another whole group is based on just straight discount to assets. Here, one of my big holdings has been an investment trust, London & American Growth, which used to be called London & American Ventures.

"It changed its policy in the early 1980s and went into mezzanine finance of technology companies in the US. Hambrecht & Quist became managers at the peak of the last full cycle in technology. Then, for about eight years, basically the net asset value went sideways, so it had been a very disappointing investment. The share went to a 50 per cent discount to assets. It seemed to me investors were giving up on it just at the time when it was getting most interesting. With venture capital, the things that go bad go bad relatively quickly, and the ones that are good tend to take a while to come through. Most of the things that were going to go bad had gone bad and you were just coming up to the stage where the successes were coming to the market.

"The American system is different from the UK, where companies that specialise in unquoteds like 3i, revalue their unquoteds up to valuations based on the quoted equivalent plus a discount. In America the system is generally that you don't revalue unless there has been a secondary transaction or quote. So what tends to happen is that you make a big gain when a holding comes to the market. London & American Growth have made one capital repayment and look as if they'll make more. Recently, the directors of the Trust have been changed and the new board is more attuned to shareholder concerns and the need to erase the level of the discount.

(iv) Undervalued Class

"There are two examples I've got of those at the moment. News International special dividend shares is a subsidiary of News Corp (see Chapter 13 on Nils Taube); and Securicor preference shares.

"Securicor and Security Services are two sister companies, and they've been a long-term favourite of mine. I've had holdings in them for over ten years. Mainly, it's a long-term story about Cellnet. They own 40 per cent of Cellnet, which, with Vodaphone, were the two original cellular telephone franchises in the UK. The interesting thing was, if you looked at the valuation on Vodaphone and the number of subscribers and then you adjusted the 40 per cent of Cellnet owned by Securicor and its sister company, Security Services, to an equivalent valuation, and put some value on their other businesses, practically all through this time they've sold at a discount of significance to that composite value.

"An added, and even more interesting way in, is that Securicor has some participating preference shares, which are unique – I don't think I've ever come across a similar instrument – where you get a fixed dividend *plus* you get a variable dividend in line with the ordinary shares. They have an unusual clause in their deed which means that they share in the income in one way, which I've described, on the dividends but, on a wind-up, they get 25 per cent of the assets of the company, which is more generous than their income rights, which equates to 13.6 per cent. Everyone looks at them purely on their income value and, because they are not very marketable, they also tend to sell at a bit of a discount just because of that. But, in certain circumstances, if the capital side was ever taken into account, they're worth more than their income value. It's obviously very debatable how much. On rights issues and such, they get their share and have a vote as a class on changes. In certain cases, their approval is needed as well as that of the ordinary shareholders, so they've got quite strong powers.

"The interesting thing is that it looked increasingly likely, over the last couple of years, as if the group would sell their holding in Cellnet back to British Telecom. It has started to be an anomaly in the UK, that the main PTT doesn't own 100 per cent of its Cellular franchise, and it has been announced, in the last month or two, that they, in fact, tried to do that. The regulators stopped it, but I think it's inevitable that, in time, a buy back will happen. The company has said, if they do do that, then they will pay the majority of the cash back to shareholders. That's the sort of transaction where the rights to a greater proportion of the distribution than the 13.6 per cent could come in. What I like about the preference share is that it tends to be valued purely on one basis. If you do your research, they're worth more than that."

(v) Corporate Potential

"This is not saying, 'I'm just buying takeover candidates.' Given two similar companies, one where there's no corporate potential because of

> **Given two similar companies I'd always choose the one where there's corporate potential.**

the shareholding structure or whatever it is and another one where there is, I'd always choose the one where there's corporate potential. It is possible to predict groups of companies where there is an above likelihood that there was going to be corporate activity. We've done very well out of owning a number of the UK television shares. The two that I've got left, Scottish Television and Yorkshire Television will probably not survive over the next three years.

"There are times where you don't pay for that extra corporate potential. Securior Group I mentioned in the context of the sale of Cellnet back to BT. Waste management – I've got a couple of firms there, Shanks & McEwan and Leigh Interests. I think that's a sector with higher than average potential.

"It's partially the industry, but also can arise from the shareholder structure. Look for companies where there is an unusual shareholding which may require a change. Wellcome was one example where a large holder and the trend to diversified assets for trusts meant, at some point, it was likely that the trustees would want out."

(vi) Industry Niche or Arbitrage

Bolton is willing to scour the globe to find these companies with added ingredients. One that he recalls with some enthusiasm was Allflex, from New Zealand, which is about as far away as you can get from his office in Lovat Lane.

"Allflex had patents, which gave it a stranglehold on the entire world market for plastic clips to put in cows' ears – an abstruse sector, perhaps, but there are plenty of cows out there waiting to be tagged. The company also benefited from a falling New Zealand dollar and from tax concessions to exporters.

"But Allflex had still more bright ideas. It wanted to add electronic chips to each tag, allowing close monitoring of each cow's movements, and to impregnate the tags with insecticide – so that the cattle would be less bothered by flies and would therefore get fat faster.

'Bolton did well from Allflex's success.' *Financial Times*

"As an industry example, look at casinos, where the valuations in one market are different from the other. Or funerals: I had a big holding in Hodgson, which became Plantsbrook. The main argument really was that the valuations in the UK were significantly lower than valuations in the US. These differences got resolved by acquisition. All the main quoted companies have all been taken over by US companies, and Service Corp took over both Plantsbrook and the only quoted European one.

"Computer games is a new area and has suffered in the short-term. If you look in the US, software companies producing computer games tend to sell on two to three times revenue and there have been a number of corporate transactions. I've invested in two. Centregold is more of a publisher and BCE is a developer. I like this change in the technology from cartridge to CD based games, which puts much more of the margin in the hands of the publisher/developer than in Sega/Nintendo. What I had got wrong with Centregold was how painful that process of change would be on a short-term basis. They've had a very poor trading situation over the last year. Now they're going into a very interesting time. They've announced they're in discussions – I think they'll be taken over, or end up with a major corporation taking a strategic stake."

(vii) Secular Demand/Supply

"I'll try and find areas where you can analyse the demand/supply and it looks as if they're getting out of kilter. Take tanker shipping – I've only got one example in the UK: that's LOFS, but own several in Europe, including ICB Shipping and Bona. I like to look where there seems to be an imbalance, or a shortage that's developed or likely to develop.

"In tanker shipping the argument is simple. There's a big fleet of tankers used for transport of Middle Eastern oil to America and to the Far East. A large number of those tankers are over 20 years old. Every five years they have to be reviewed. A number are now starting to be scrapped because of their age. There's little new building, so you get to the stage where the fleet starts to decrease, but the demand for oil is still increasing. The shipping market is a feast/famine market and, when it goes from famine to feast, you get very big movements in rates and values. So that's an industry where I've got a big exposure."

(viii) Restructuring

"Berisfords and Ascot are two that I own which were more like large shell companies. Berisfords has been transformed. Ascot will be used in the future to buy into new areas. In both cases, new entrepreneurs bought in when we bought in. I think shells can be an interesting area. Berisfords bought Magnet, the kitchen people, and now has bought a larger business, a US company called Welbilt which is in food service equipment."

Sometimes, several of these themes coalesce in one sector and, when that rare alignment occurs, Bolton will put a large amount of money into that sector. As of end 1995, Bolton was heavily overweight across all his portfolios in media – up to 15 per cent in some funds. His reasoning reveals the interaction between the single strand themes which has been emphasised so far, and a multivariate analysis that highlights clumps of value.

(a) Most media businesses have attractive *franchises*. These can be strongly cash generative.
(b) Many companies in the sector, particularly in Europe, have large market positions which give them an added competitive edge.
(c) There has tended to be a great deal of corporate activity in the sector, especially in the UK.
(d) The sector has not been generally well understood, in Europe, by the local investment community. It is usually relatively new and relatively small, and so does not justify the coverage. Commercial television is a young industry in Europe with limited history to appraise. France, Holland, Germany and Sweden all exhibit this characteristic.
(e) There is long-term secular growth in most segments of the media market. The overall market is growing, and shifts in spending patterns create pockets of exceptional growth which are accentuated by the move from paper based products to visual media.

It is interesting to contrast these categories with those utilised in the mid 1980s. There we found some of the same:

- Recovery
- Growth
- Changing business
- Discount to assets

but most of the rest are lumped in a catch call headed 'undervalued'. There has been a subtle transition, over the past eight years, as Bolton has refined his approach, and in part, his own ability to articulate these divisions has come about as a result of needing to explain his exceptional results to an always sceptical investment community.

It is also interesting to see how the emphasis on categories has changed. Take the group called 'recovery' depicted in Chart 3.1, which nearly tripled as a percentage of the total as the economic cycle went into reverse between 1989 and 1991 and doubled again by March 1992 as the economy remained listless.

'Recovery' stocks now comprise the largest single group for Bolton, which underlines the success he has enjoyed with spotting this sort of stock. Still, it is essential to understanding Bolton's style to keep in perspective that they remain less than one third of the portfolio. Meanwhile, 'undervalued' have fallen from 44.3 per cent in 1987 to 24.7 per cent as of September 1995.

Chart 3.1 Percentage of Total Portfolio in Recovery Stocks (1989–1992)

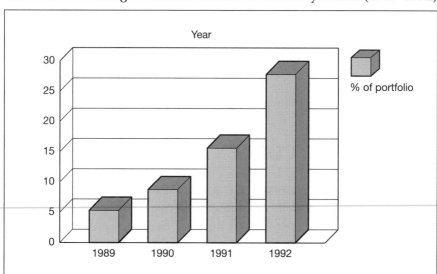

If you look at the largest individual holdings in Bolton's overall portfolio, you can see how these themes play out in practice. This reflects the situation as of September 1995.

1. Nokia: (Finland)	Cellular phone play. Area of exceptional volume growth.
2. Philips Warrants: (Holland)	Leveraged play on electronics conglomerate. Restructuring.
3. FNFC: (UK)	Consumer loans: Internal recovery.
4. Audiofina: (Belgium)	Controls Luxembourg based radio and TV conglomerate: misunderstood media.
5. London Clubs: (UK)	Casinos: Unrecognised growth and industry arbitrage vs US valuation.

Looking back over the last ten years, as captured in Table 3.1, also reveals why Bolton's favourites perform so well.

Table 3.1 Review of Largest Holding as of March in Special Situations

Year	Company	Activity	Category
1985	British Telecom (UK)	Telecommunications	Industry arbitrage
1986	Montedison (Italy)	Chemicals	Recovery
1988	Hafslund (Norway)	Pharmaceuticals	Unrecognised growth
1989/90 & 1993/4	Securicor (UK)	Security & cellular phones	Corporate potential & and undervalued class
1991	Colonia (Germany)	Insurance	Industry arbitrage
1992	Granada (UK)	TV & services	Internal recovery

2. CONCENTRATION

Having found the investment that fits his criterion, he then constructs a portfolio with a relatively high degree of *concentration*. The rationale is simple. If you have spent the time and effort to identify situations which should outperform the market, you want to own a large amount of those investments and they should make up most of your portfolio.

By *concentrating* on likely winners, you ensure a few select investments have a disproportionate impact on your overall performance. This is rather like eating filet mignon, if that is your favourite food, once in every three times when you dine out, because that meal gives you the greatest pleasure. It is common sense, and the only oddity is that more managers do not follow this strategy.

If you have spent the time and effort to identify situations which should outperform the market, you want to own a large amount of those investments and they should make up most of your portfolio.

A review of the existing flagships shows that the top 16 holdings in his UK and European portfolio make up over 34 per cent and 26 per cent of the total. Bolton is quite comfortable putting over 3 per cent of a fund in a single stock.

Concentration has always been a hallmark of Bolton's primary vehicle, the Special Situations Fund. The top 12 holdings have never accounted for less than 25 per cent, and averaged about 40 per cent in the 1980s. Concentration was highest in 1982, when it reached 51 per cent. Inevitably, as the pool of assets has grown, this becomes more difficult to accomplish but, even at the end of 1995, the level ran at 27 per cent.

3. COUNTRY WEIGHTINGS

Bolton is concerned about the country weightings, though it is less important than stock selection. When you run a regional fund like Fidelity European Trust, part of your superior performance will come from being in the right countries at the right time. Bolton does not place undue emphasis on macroeconomic factors. His weighting, to a great extent, is a result of his stock picking. He does, however, consider certain factors in checking that the bottoms up approach produces a geographic balance that is consistent with the macro trends likely to be most positive for stock markets.

"Mainly I pick my stocks and then say, 'Am I happy to live with these country weightings?' The one exception where macroeconomics can come in is looking at the flow of funds. I have a very high weighting in Norway. It's about 20 per cent of my European funds, but it rates only 1 per cent or so of the MSCI Europe ex UK index. That's mainly because there are a lot of companies that I find there; but I do then say, 'It this prudent? How big a risk am I taking, and are there some macro arguments that back up this stock weighting that I've got?'

"I think there are. People have been very worried about countries with budget deficits. The Norwegian government finances are one of the strongest in the world. I don't start by saying, 'Which country is the best? I want to put X in that market.' I don't believe in the rotational approach that other managers use for Europe. They say, 'France has really under-performed the last six months. I should be switching from Germany, which has done better, into France.' When I look at my relative weights, I feel uncomfortable if I've got the same weights as everyone else. It comes back to being contrarian. I always feel more comfortable in something slightly different. There is one thing that can make a difference. If there are big flows of funds from large institutional investors, I'll take note.

"I like to place my bets where we've got more added value. With the macro approach, a lot of other investment houses do it and do it well. Why should I have a better view on the oil price than the next guy? And there's not a huge amount of added value on that, or trying to guess when the Bundesbank is going to change its rates. I don't want to make my big bets on that. Where I get worried about the top down approach is that you start with one or two premises and then you model a whole portfolio from these central assumptions. If one of your assumptions is wrong – say 'the dollar's cheap and it's going to go up' – you have a hugely uncomfortable three or four years while it gets cheaper and cheaper before it eventually turns. Taking lots of little bets is less risky."

As of December 1995, the European pool was heavily overweight in the Scandinavian countries, and noticeably light in Italy. The breakdown is as summarised in Table 3.2.

Table 3.2 Top Seven Country Holdings (as of December 1995)

Country	% Total
Norway	19
France	18
Germany	11
Sweden	11
Switzerland	6
Finland	6
Spain	5

Go back in time, and the mix has been very different. In 1986, Bolton's greatest concentration was in Italy and, by 1987, Spain had emerged as number one. These migrations can be seen in Table 3.3.

Table 3.3 Largest Country Holdings
(1986–1995, as of 5 October)

Year	Country	% Total Portfolio
1986	Italy	15
1987	Spain	26
1988	France	20
1989	Germany	20
1990	Germany	27
1991	France	22
1992	France	19
1993	France	16
1994	Germany	13
1995	Norway	19

In contrast to country weightings, you rarely hear Bolton talk about industry weightings. To the extent he ends up with concentration in any one sector that is almost always the result of the stock selection process. Bolton has expressed preference for service oriented businesses with positive cash characteristics.

Trying to sum up these themes in one statement on investment style is impossible. There are elements of fundamental value, elements of selecting for recovery, micro elements of macro top down thinking, strong strains of growth investing, and even a bit of momentum analysis. So it's hard to say that Bolton belongs to any single camp. Superior total return is the goal and he will employ every weapon in the investor's armoury at different times.

> *Bolton has expressed preference for service oriented businesses with positive cash characteristics.*

What is clear is how well his polyglot approach works. Fidelity's European funds are consistently in the top quartile. On its tenth anniversary, Micropal ranked it as the top performing fund in the sector. As of year end 1995, *The Financial Times* ranked it as the top unit trust over ten years, with a staggering 739 per cent increase in the unit value since 1985.

The Special Situations Trust, Bolton's flagship, comes third out of 63 comparable funds over the most recent ten year period, as ranked by Micropal. One thousand pounds invested as recently as 1985 would be worth £4,729 as of year end 1995. Go back just a shade further to 1979 and Bolton's performance is even more remarkable. One thousand pounds invested then would be worth £24,953, which translates to 16 years of compound annual growth of 22.7 per cent, a truly phenomenal record of consistency. All this was accomplished with only a modest level of risk. The fund is scored as having relative volatility of 1.18 and a beta of 0.87, which means the excess risk of this fund, over and above the systematic risk inherent in the market, is tiny compared to the excess return. Shareholders who have hung around with Bolton have a lot to be happy about.

Bolton also runs two Luxembourg based funds with similar portfolios to the two unit trusts, and two investment trusts – the Fidelity Special Values plc and Fidelity European Values plc, which also have similar portfolios.

NUTS AND BOLTS

Once potential investments are identified, fundamental analysis comes into play. Bolton is cautious about how much reliance investors should place on public accounts, particularly outside the US and UK, though even those countries contain pitfalls for the unwary. He prefers not to place too much reliance on some of the familiar ratios which trip off the tongue in conversation with most fund managers, opting, instead, for a more comprehensive review of the people and the business in combination with comparative company bench mark analysis where the emphasis is on total value and cash flow.

"I think the UK is somewhat less advanced in the breadth of its analysis than continental Europe and that that's partially because, in continental Europe, you've got much more opaque accounts in a number of places. Using earnings in continental Europe can be downright misleading. People have to use other valuation measures and other ratios. In the UK, we've been spoon fed with earnings per share and, therefore, the analysts are much too ready to look at that and nothing else.

"One ratio that we find quite useful is enterprise value to gross cash flow. Take the market cap plus net debt divided by the operating profit plus the depreciation provision. We look at that on every company and, particularly when you're comparing across borders, we find that quite useful. We also find it's a ratio that companies use when looking at each other in terms of acquisitions. If companies use that in deciding whether something is a good acquisition, that makes it a fairly good ratio for us to look at. It's used a lot across Europe, and Australians use it quite a bit. In the UK it's creeping in now, but it's much less used.

> *One ratio that we find quite useful is enterprise value to gross cash flow. Take the market cap plus net debt divided by the operating profit plus the depreciation provision.*

"What I don't have very much time for, or only in certain instances, are these discounted cash flow models, or where you take the yield or the earnings and you discount them back. The trouble with those is you put so much emphasis on the later years. I find, in this business, it's difficult enough to predict the next three years. If you've got a model that puts most of the weighting in years three to ten and on your terminal value rather than on years one to three, then the prediction of terminal value becomes critical, and that's a long way ahead. Obviously, with companies that are not making money – like cable companies – you have to have used those types of measures."

One place where Bolton parts company with most stock pickers is that he respects the role that technical analysis can contribute. Looking at what charts can tell you has been one feature in his style which has given him an extra edge over managers who focus exclusively on the fundamentals of each investment one at a time. Bolton is careful not to over-emphasise the reliance he places on chart based analysis but, equally, he is open-minded about using such tools where there is proven value.

"My view now would be if I had no access to the fundamental information and just wanted one input, I'd probably want the charts, because they tell you, at the end of the day, the net effect of all the investors. The way I use them on individual companies is as a checking mechanism. They're a screening tool to identify companies that I ought to look at as buy candidates. I like to have charts, particularly on the stocks that I own. They make me really examine the fundamentals. If something I own starts to deteriorate, and show relative weakness, it doesn't mean I'll sell, but it does mean I'll say to myself, 'Am I really sure that we've got the full picture? Is there something that other people know that we don't?' Often enough, I'll say, 'Fine, I'm sure enough about this.' But, at other times, the chart might be the warning system that means that there is something else we then find out.

"I also have a view that the bigger the company is the more useful the chart. The bigger the business, the less likely it is that you know everything about it, and the more difficult it is to move the market. If for some reason big funds have turned against a share, even if it's very cheap, it can take some while for that to turn round. That will only show up in a technical view. With small companies it's slightly different. Charts are also a very useful way of summarising flow of funds – who's investing where. We have two people in the team who just look at charts. In the States we have a big chart department. It has always been part of the Fidelity ethos to use technical analysis."

> **The bigger the company is the more useful the chart.**

The importance of dialogue with company, and a personalised analytical style which incorporates a dose of chartism, should not obscure the preparation which goes on up front. The impression Bolton conveys is that he has become something of a dilettante, but that belies the rigour of his analytical approach. You can sense the amount of work going on underneath when he describes the qualification process and how he selects stocks to buy. That involves both quantitative and qualitative analysis, with one thing in common: it's comprehensive.

"Most important of all are the notes prepared by our internal analyst. We supplement their work with a number of outside services. Holt Value Service looks through the accounting to try and get at the cash and strip out the cash return on assets and then tries to give some sort of fair value model based on that. They do a lot of adjustments in terms of off balance sheet finance, finance leases, that sort of thing. So we look at that approach. Then we'll have our own analysts' notes. The analyst will do projections, P&L, cash flow and balance sheet. We use Extel Financial. I'll look at the company announcements over the last year, just to see there's nothing significant there. We then use a Z score system – Syspas. After the last recession, we were keen to bring in things to protect us against buying poorly financed business. It aids us with a double check on companies that are under financial pressure and as an early recovery indicator. Banks use it a lot."

Bolton nearly always comes back to his own direct contact with the company and the market-place. He puts his time to good use, and averages two face to face meetings a day.

"It's looking at the trade press and information; it's cross-checking with the customers; talking to competitors. If somebody rates . . . I'll always try and use the last few minutes in a company meeting to talk about a competitor or someone they do business with, and get an informed view. I find that useful."

It is always easier to find someone able to articulate why they make an investment than it is to extract the secret of selling well. Bolton is equally at ease in explaining his exit philosophy as his entry strategy. Basically, his disposals are driven by one of three events.

1. He finds *something better* which causes him to switch. There are shades of Templeton thinking here, and Colin McLean (Chapter 9) is another who is very much of this mind set. Actually, Bolton puts it differently. 'The good drives out the bad,' could be Peter Lynch's words.

2. Stocks may be ripe for sale when *something changes*. Something could be internal to the company or external, affecting the environment in which it operates.

   "Where I bought a stock for certain reasons and it's deteriorated or it's changed, then it may be time to sell. I like consistency with these regular meetings, and I do get worried where they tell a different story or they say they are going to do this and that and then they go off and do something different. That's something I'll look for."

3. When a holding becomes *fully valued*, then it no longer offers the sort of upside Bolton demands of all his investments, and it is time to part company with the position, even if it is an old friend which has performed well over many years. Stocks have to earn their entry to Bolton's portfolio and then they have to continue to justify their retention. There is no room for sentimentality.

Fully valued could mean a number of things. Selling and lack of sentimentality are clearly key elements in Bolton's success. He times his portfolio more than most other great investors, which is in line with his disciplined approach. To find something better you have to raise cash. A stock rises past fair value and it's out. If you look at the top ten holdings in each of the last ten years – outside of Securicor, which is there in one manifestation or another seven times – only two other companies appear in three years.

> **Selling and lack of sentimentality are clearly key elements in Bolton's success.**

"It's not a straight in or out decision. In essence, the portfolio is in a state of constant flux, because some stocks are being built up as my convictions increase, while others are being reduced as my convictions wane."

No-one can accuse Bolton of not banking his profits. None of which is to say he is a trader. The portfolio turns over about 75 per cent a year, high but not excessive. What it means is that he is constantly on the look-out to improve the composition of his portfolio. This is not a straight buy/sell/hold process. There is a continuity at work where fresh information means a stronger or weaker conviction which can lead to adding to, or reducing, a holding at the margin, all of which contributes to turnover.

With so much money under management as the funds have grown, Bolton has had to become very efficient in running his portfolios. Leveraging his own time to the maximum is fundamental to his ability to stay on top. He starts out by recognising the limitations of his own position. He cannot go to all the company meetings. He cannot review all the accounts. He has cultivated a team of individuals who have the same investment view and, in a sense, could be said to operate in loco Bolton. There is a team of 40 analysts and ten managers, all of whom share ideas and can be used as a sounding board. One who stands out is Sally Walden, who runs the other Fidelity flagships – European Opportunities and UK Growth.

Looking forward, Bolton has a view that continental Europe is likely to offer the investor who likes equities a more rewarding ride longer term than will be available in the UK. He makes an all too convincing case. The force is with Europe when it comes to stock momentum.

"One of the very interesting processes, I think, which has been going on in Europe for some time, and still continues, is the opening up of those markets. The increasing ownership of equities by individuals and, in particular, by European institutions' pension funds and insurance companies, should have a positive impact. If I have to pick one thing, I'd rather bet with that trend. A typical German or Swiss company will only have 10–15 per cent in equities. Here, it's 70–80 per cent. In America it's 65 per cent. A lot of Europe has only 10–15 per cent. I think that will change over the 1990s and into the 21st century.

"One of the driving forces is demographics. The funding of social security and pension schemes will lead to higher equity ownership, so you've got that on your side in Europe which, to some extent, has been played out in the UK. In the UK, equity ownership by pensions funds might even go down a bit.

"And, on the Continent, you've got an environment where companies are opening up – at different rates in different markets. It's much more advanced in some than it is in others. These are the sort of things that excite me. Kuoni, in Switzerland, is one of my big holdings. I had a holding in it for the last few years, because we thought it was interesting, and mainly because one of the drivers is the UK Kuoni business, which is long haul travel and very successful; but it was a very difficult company to analyse. They gave you very little information and they would see us once in a blue moon. The catalyst was when a German store company had bought a big stake which they always felt uncomfortable about, and they managed to get that stake back but needed to replace it in the market.

"We said, in meetings at that time, 'We like the company, but our big criticism is you're very shareholder unfriendly . . .' They took that all on board and they have now substantially improved the information we get. They've also explained the profits and, what we've now found is, that some parts of the businesses are making losses and other parts profits. They've told us of plans to turn around the loss makers. There's substantial cash in the business. Part of that's prepayments, but part is completely surplus. They see us regularly now. This opening up is one of the most significant trends and is very good for investors who are there as that process happens."

Bolton seems to be indefatigable. One day, no doubt, he will follow Peter Lynch's example and move to a more consultative role suitable for an elder statesman who has done it all. For now, he seems to relish the formidable challenge of continuing to maintain his top of the table per-formance, while managing a much larger pool of money for more shareholders than ever before. He sees almost endless scope to expand across Europe, exploiting inefficiencies with his careful and clinical approach to identifying clusters of value which will produce superior returns. Clients of Fidelity can look forward, with confidence, to the benefits of Bolton's expertise deployed on their behalf.

* Hong Kong based manager who specialises in Asia

* One of the first people to buy stocks like San Miguel
and Siam Cement

* Has made shareholders 13× their money in
only 14 years!

PETER EVERINGTON

Value from the Top Down

Britain has a long history of investors with wanderlust who search the globe looking for opportunity. It is, perhaps, surprising then that only one of our top British investors is based outside the UK. Peter Everington, Chairman of Regent Fund Management Limited, is following in a well trod tradition, but he has carved a new path. Before investing in Asia became as popular as smoked salmon sandwiches on the cocktail circuit, Everington was already active in Asian markets and, by the time owning shares in Hong Kong and Singapore had become recognised as a 'good thing', he had moved further afield, alighting on Taiwan and Thailand.

Today, with Asia now an accepted part of any global portfolio, Everington is still pioneering new ways to stay ahead of the investing herd. Having learnt his trade in the hothouse that was GT Management before moving on to Thornton, he jumped at the chance to go to Hong Kong in 1984, showing that impeccable sense of timing, which would stay with him through the following decade. He quickly positioned himself at the forefront of the expanding financial services sector in South East Asia. Thornton Management soon became synonymous with innovation and performance. Have you ever wondered where the Tiger fund concept came from? That was one of Everington's ideas, proving he is not a one dimensional number cruncher, but has marketing flair as well. The Tiger family spawned no fewer than ten derivatives over six years, including Little Dragons, Tiger Evolution, Lux Tiger and Tiger Opportunities. Behind the 'Tiger' concept lay Everington's view that the collapse of the US dollar and fall in the price of oil in 1985 would trigger Asia's longest and strongest economic boom in over thirty years.

It was not, however, his skill in packaging product which attracted all the attention, but the outstanding outperformance of markets, in themselves doing well, which caught the eye of hard nosed investors. Prior to arriving, he had done well managing to make 83 per cent on his managed funds versus a rise of only 34 per cent in the Morgan Stanley Capital International World Index during the period October 1981 to December 1994. (Note: all returns are calculated in US$.)

71

Chart 4.1   Everington – The Early Years in Asia (1986-1990)

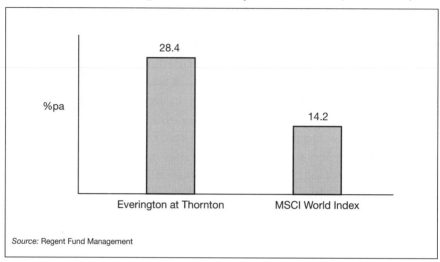

Source: Regent Fund Management

Once he had his feet under the desk in Hong Kong, returns took off as Everington exactly doubled the annual progress of the MSCI World Index. Chart 4.1 shows the result.

In 1986 alone he made his investors a staggering 68 per cent and, in 1987, during which Hong Kong went into free fall and several regional stock markets suspended trading, he held his losses to 5 per cent. Everington comments that the Asian Tiger countries are like young children – they grow rapidly but have a tendency to higher volatility. Making money in Asia is easy but the skill lies in holding on to the gains when the periodic typhoons blow through.

An important feature of Everington's career and progress has been his association with Jim Mellon. When Everington moved to San Francisco for GT in mid 1982, he worked for Jim. In their first year as a team, the GT US and General Fund won *The Money Observer* award for the best American Trust and ranked fourth out of all 470 UK authorised trusts at that time. Mellon and Everington were also co-founders of the Asian side of Thornton Management. In 1986, Everington won the Lipper Award for the best performing offshore Australian equity fund. There is more to Asia than just South East, and Everington can coin a profit in more mature as well as the emerging markets of popular imagination. More Lipper awards followed, and even Barrons had picked up on him by 1990.

When Mellon moved on to found Regent in 1991, Everington was not far behind. Regent has been able to attract, as shareholders, not only Equitable Assurance of the UK and Tokio Marine and Fire Insurance Co of Japan, but also Daewoo Securities in Korea, who you might think would know a bit about Asian equities. That is a major vote of confidence from some blue chip names in a start up whose credibility consisted entirely of the reputation of the key principals.

Once underway, they wasted no time. In 1994, the Regent Pacific Hedge Fund was ranked number one out of 28 comparable vehicles by Micropal in the Offshore Funds – Actively Hedged Sector: not by a slim margin, either, but by 25 per cent versus an average decline of 5.5 per cent across the group. During the first four years, Everington averaged gains of 31.7 per cent pa. Not surprising that funds under management soared to $2 billion as clients beat a path to Regent's door.

As with any good story to understand the ending you often need to go back to the beginning. Everington made his management debut onto the investment scene, after only a 12 month apprenticeship, on 24 August 1981, when he started with the GT Capital Fund. The timing proved interesting, as Everington learned all about market cycles in his first six months. More importantly, he got a lasting lesson in humility, which is why, 16 years later, he still remembers the precise dates.

"I inherited this fund just before going on holiday. I got back on 9 September. 22 August proved to be a peak in the market and, between then and 29 September, the UK stock market fell by something like 23 per cent. The fund was invested 105 per cent when I took it over and the market was plunging. I took it at once to 50 per cent cash, which meant we were outperforming as the market went down. I thought, 'I'm hot. I've obviously got tremendous talent.' Then the market bounced, just as I was in full bearish mood and, over six months, climbed a wall of worry while I gave back most of my relative outperformance."

But not all; and, by 1982, Everington was already demonstrating a flair for investing, for which there were no obvious clues in his background.

"I'm an aeronautical engineer by background, and a pilot, so perhaps I understand what makes things go up and down. That aside, it wasn't lost on me that, particularly here in Britain, the country is notorious for turning out a lot of engineers who promptly go bust. Even Rolls Royce, which makes tremendous aero engines, went down the Swanee. To set up my own engineering company, I thought I should get some business training first. Business degrees weren't really established here, but I had a friend in the fund management business who seemed to be having a lot of fun. Analysing a lot of businesses seemed a good way to understand what worked and what didn't."

> *To sell half the portfolio and sit on cash shows a level of decisiveness which has been a hallmark of his career.*

For someone two weeks into a new job to sell half the portfolio and sit on cash shows a level of decisiveness which has been a hallmark of his subsequent career. That Everington was able to take such a radical position is also a testimonial to the environment in which he operated. GT always did have quite a reputation.

"Richard Thornton [the T in GT] was very much someone who encouraged decisiveness. If you had a strong opinion, you had to act on it and shouldn't hesitate. In retrospect, you have to say there was something of the recklessness of youth in there, and I wonder whether I would have the flexibility to do that today."

After prompting on this point, Everington acknowledged that big moves are still an essential part of his approach to portfolios. "Would he do the same thing all over again?"

"I would and, probably, I would go short."

What is so remarkable about Everington, when you look over his career, is that he has outperformed from the word go starting off in the UK, but branching out to every major equity market around the world, and topping the charts in the US and Australia, as well as in so many Asian markets. Still, it is as an Asian specialist that he has established his reputation. Thus the focus of any examination of why he has shone in the region of the rising sun needs to focus on the tools he employs to invest in these markets. Everington's focus is all the Asian markets, which encompass some 15 very diverse countries from Japan to New Zealand to Pakistan. It is in this context that investors need to place Everington's approach though, broadly speaking, a similar paradigm would be applicable outside North America and Western Europe.

TOP DOWN

The essence of the Everington approach is that investment decisions have to start at the top, with an examination of what makes the market move. If you can bring together all the elements which drive overall market performance, you will make more money, because you will be investing with the wind at your back.

"Most definitely, in emerging markets, the top down approach is the appropriate one. When you talk about technically efficient markets, you cannot add value through macro analysis, and the only way to add value in the US is to pick stocks. In Asian markets, and in all emerging markets, the macro decision – the asset allocation decision – is a more important contributor to performance than the actual stock selection. This has been demonstrated mathematically.

In Asia, once you have made the country allocation, you have to go straight to stock selection. I call this approach top down, bottom up, but really, it is top down with the middle bit missing.

"The difficulty in Asian markets is how to do it. You can do the top part of the analysis and decide which countries you want to be invested in but, once you go beyond and say, 'Now we've chosen this country, which industry should we choose?', you come up against a brick wall because, in most of these markets, you don't have a choice. In Singapore, you would be attracted to the electronics sector, but there are very few companies in that industry which are quoted so you have to choose something in a sector which is not your first choice.

"In Asia, once you have made the country allocation, you have to go straight to stock selection. I call this approach top down, bottom up, but really, it is top down with the middle bit missing."

LIQUIDITY IS THE LOVE OF HIS LIFE . . .

The starting point for Everington, in asset allocation, is to determine where liquidity will work in his favour. There are two types of liquidity which have relevance, but by far the most important is liquidity that is generated by the economic cycle. The analytical approach is spelt out in some detail because, to understand Everington's success, you first have to sign on to his methodology.

"I'm a great believer that the liquidity cycle leads the economic cycle. I'm talking here about the internal dynamics of an economic system – domestically generated liquidity. The various elements that come together to form that in the Asian countries are actually very predictable and, because all of these countries are very dependant on foreign trade, the most important variable is the trade cycle.

"I start by trying to assess where the liquidity cycle is and then drive the economic cycle off that. What I'm looking for is to find countries still declining, with decelerating growth, but where liquidity is starting to build up and you can see the bottom of the cycle. The best situation is where GDP growth has reached its low point, but liquidity is expanding dramatically. Then you know you've got the start of a new cycle.

"The cycles in Asia have not changed much, which is another reason they are fairly predictable. The cycle is normally four years up, two years down. This current cycle kicked off in late 1992, early 1993, and is going to expire in late 1996, early 1997. We are into the tail end, now.

"Most of these economies are growing relatively fast. They have cycles, of course, but these are very different to what investors in Europe have come to expect. In most cases, recession means growth slows to 4–5 per cent, while expansion equals 10–12 per cent. The characteristics are the same, but the amplitude is greater and neutral is not zero as it is for many western countries.

"Coming back to foreign trade – for Hong Kong and Singapore, this is 300 per cent of GDP, which compares to 27 per cent in the US. These countries are highly susceptible to external influences. You can look fairly easily at their trading partners, at the major economies in the world, and you can derive from that what is going to be happening to these countries.

"Then you have to look at the capital expenditure cycle. In a classic cycle, you find, at the bottom, everyone is depressed, the economy is slowing down, capital expenditure has been cut and, as a result, loan demand is falling. Typically, at that stage, governments become worried and ease credit somewhat. This leads to increasing credit supply at a time of collapsing loan demand. If that converges with a time when the export cycle is turning up, you have all the elements of liquidity moving in the same direction, which is obviously the best situation you can have.

"As the cycle picks up, the local entrepreneur will still be sceptical. Business will suddenly and mysteriously pick up, but he's still pessimistic and only late on, when he's running short of capacity, will he start to spend money on expanding facilities. At the start of the cycle is the best time to be in the stock market, because the liquidity within the system is expanding, but it's not being drained off by other requirements such as capital expenditure.

"Ten years ago, all the Tiger countries used to go up and down together. They were completely synchronised, for the simple reason that most of South East Asia was within the US dollar system and America was their biggest trading partner. So America was the driver. Now some of these countries have become more dependent on Japan or Europe and differing cyclical influences are therefore at play. Countries are diverging; but, broadly speaking, in 1985–90 you had the first big up cycle. The two main variables at work were that the yen went through the roof, or the dollar collapsed, making South East Asia super competitive relative to Japan and, secondly, you had a collapse in the price of oil, which is one of the great input costs for the region. So you had business booming on the front end, and costs going down on the back end. That gave you the longest and strongest cycle in 30 years.

"By 1990 you had a lot of overheating pressure. Inflation was well up. Some countries were slipping into deficit, and the global economy was slipping towards the 1990 to 1992 recession. When there's a global recession, watch out Asia. So, from 1990 to 1992, you had poor economies and poor stock markets throughout most of the region. By the end of 1992, early signs of a pick up after a long depressing period began to emerge. It was around the third or fourth quarter that the liquidity cycle began to turn again. Korea, Taiwan and Singapore were the first ones to take off. By first quarter 1993, Malaysia and Thailand also began to pick up. In the second half, Indonesia and the Philippines followed."

THE IMPORTANCE OF SAVINGS. WHAT ELSE CAN COMPARE . . .

You can't understand the liquidity cycle without following shifts in capital formation. The focus in Asia is very much on the private sector to drive that requirement and provide the funds. The value of high savings is well understood, but its relative importance is, perhaps, less widely recognised. Equally, investors are aware that countries in South East Asia have a propensity to save at a much higher rate than in the US or in Europe; but the magnitude of the impact that this differential can cause has not been fully taken on board, save but by a few – one of whom is Everington.

"The essence of Asia is not just the hard working labour force, high levels of education and pro business governments, though all that is true. The absolute key is the high savings rates, which finance the high rates of capital formation, and that is what generates the growth in the long run. Asia can be described by the virtuous equation:

High savings = High Capital Formation = High Growth

which is why the Tiger countries have been growing at 8 per cent compound for 30 years. America would be the reverse of that:

Low Savings = Low Capital Formation = Low Growth

End of story.

"The savings rates in Asia are high, partly for cultural reasons but, to be blunt, principally because of the absence of social welfare. If you are sick, you have nothing but your family and your savings. Turning that on its head, the introduction of social welfare in the West has inadvertently, and unfortunately, created two problems. Firstly, it has undermined the family unit and, secondly, it has collapsed the savings rate and, with it, economic growth."

> *With a country, you have to look at savings in the first instance, because to ignore that would be like a company ignoring its internal cash generation.*

Not only is this an important dynamic to decipher before any asset allocator can start to place bets, but savings are also a starting point for the overall liquidity analysis that is fundamental to Everington's conception of the investment world.

"Savings are the most basic element of cash flow for an economy. With a country, you have to look at savings in the first instance, because to ignore that would be like a company ignoring its internal cash generation. That's why I would never rate the Philippines as high as Singapore so, if the P/E ratio is the same, then I'd prefer the Singapore investment."

MARKET LIQUIDITY – A NUTRITIONAL SUPPLEMENT TO COUNTRY LIQUIDITY

You can compare Everington's approach to that of a surfer searching the sea for where the currents come together in one place forming the perfect wave to ride. When the overall economic cycle and the savings situation combine to create conditions that steer money into the stock market, Everington wants to be in position to take full advantage of the surge and, by the time the tide turns, he wants to be out of the water.

"I know that, right now [February 1996] the Hong Kong economy is in recession. I know that there are some fairly bad things happening in Hong Kong. None of that is relevant, because there is a wall of liquidity blowing through the market and overcoming resistance points. When we went through 10,300, which was my mental stop, it was clear that liquidity was stronger than the poor fundamentals and that the market was headed higher.

"Investment liquidity is the most difficult side to anticipate. For instance, the recent American decision to chuck a lot of money at Asia is hard to analyse. These portfolio flows rushing round the world can be the single greatest influence on markets as recent developments clearly indicate. From 1955 to 1990, the US public put $100 billion into equity mutual funds. In the five years since that time, they have put in a staggering $500 billion. Out of this incredible mutual fund boom has come the US

> *US investors have become the most important external variable in Asia currently.*

appetite for international investing which is why US investors have become the most important external variable in Asia currently. While US interest rates fall, US liquidity will remain abundant and Asia's market will rise. But when US rates rise as they will over the balance of 1996, watch out."

IF IT'S 1988 IT MUST BE THAILAND . . .

In essence, Everington treats countries much as most investors evaluate equities. At the heart of his success has been his ability to apply

Table 4.1: Country Mix of a Tiger Portfolio (% Total)

	Country	Dec 1986	Dec 1990	Dec 1993
Original Tigers	Hong Kong	34	39	3
	Singapore	41	14	9
	Korea	10	2	28
	Taiwan	3	–	12
New Tigers	Malaysia	–	12	–
	Thailand	7	8	7
	Indonesia	–	4	5
	Philippines	3	1	–
	Subcontinent	–	–	12
	Cash	2	20	24

the liquidity analysis in such a way as to be overweight in markets within Asia when they were doing relatively well, and underweight, or even out altogether, in markets which were underperforming. A snapshot of the distribution of investment in Table 4.1 will demonstrate the degree to which these shifts can over time change the appearance of the portfolio.

Everington estimates that he spends 70 per cent of his time and effort on making the decision about country rotation; sector analysis barely gets a look in, and even specific stocks only rate 30 per cent of his attention. That reflects the relative importance in Asia of being in the right market versus picking the right stock, let alone the right sector within a market. Everington keeps on the move and rarely stays over-weight in the same place for too long. Swings can be severe. Korea barely featured in 1990 but was his largest position three years later.

In the context of confirming markets where analysis seems to give you the right answers, but the rules of investing are not always as they seem, and certainly not always the same, how is it that Everington has done so well?

"My best decision was to have been in Asia in the first place. Once you're there, you can beat the index by being in the right countries at the right time. In 1985, I was convinced that a combination of a strong yen and a weak oil price would lead to the largest and strongest boom in Asia in 30 years. That's when we decided to launch this new fund, investing in Asia ex Japan. I was reading a *Business Week* article in September 1985 which referred to these South East Asia NICs [newly industrialised countries] as like tigers. So that became the first Tiger fund. Later we had Dragons and other variations on the theme.

"In those days, any Asian fund would be very heavily weighted to Japan, 40–50 per cent most likely, whereas we would have had 35 per cent in Singapore and 30 per cent in Hong Kong, and also 10 per cent in the Philippines. Now 10 per cent may not sound like much, but it made a difference. Remember, in late 1984, Marcos was losing control and the country was going bankrupt. The IMF effectively took control of the central bank and, in 14 months, squeezed inflation from 96 per cent to zero. As the inflation rate started to come down, we could see the currency would stabilise and, once that happened, foreigners would come back and take a look.

"We came across PLDT [Philippine Long Distance Telephone Company], which was selling at 39 pesos, which we figured was about 1.6 times earnings. In fact, we were completely wrong. The real P/E ratio was more like 0.4 times as earnings subsequently accelerated far more quickly than ever we expected. We bought half a million shares and, when the revolution occurred, the market took only a 10 per cent setback. That was all. We held on and, after that, the market was off to the races. We got 20 times the price we paid for it in 1989. It was a small position, but the increase was so large it made an impact on our overall performance. We also managed to pick up a position in San Miguel, which was trading only $2,000 a day. We needed size, so we bid a 25 per cent premium over the listed price of 16 pesos, just to get a line of stock. Today San Miguel is over 100 times that price. In those days, San Miguel and PLDT were about the only shares you could consider 'blue chip' in the Philippines.

"In Thailand, we had a very big position in Siam Cement, which went up tenfold between 1985 and 1990 as Thailand was 'discovered'. The market in 1985 traded on around 4× earnings and Siam Cement was a blue chip proxy for the Thai economy as a whole. Thailand itself qualified as an 'Emerging Tiger' or 'Little Dragon' as we came to refer to those newer Tigers."

Besides quantitative measures there are certain cultural themes which temper a pure country rotation strategy. Everington has concluded there are in-built biases to the Asian approach to business which have to be factored into his country weightings.

"Asia is multi-cultural, but the true strength of Asia comes from the Chinese side. They are the entrepreneurs. They are the supreme businessmen. All around Asia, the most successful businesses are run by the Chinese."

Compare the results across countries and you soon become convinced of the validity of Everington's diagnosis, at least as far as it pertains to South East Asia.

"You don't have all the same ingredients in the Philippines as you do in Singapore. It's amazing to me that, 35 years ago, the Philippines had the second highest per capita income in Asia and now it's close to the bottom of the totem pole. This poor management is mainly attributable to the fact that the Philippines has basically spent 400 years in a convent and 50 years in Hollywood.

> **The Philippines has basically spent 400 years in a convent and 50 years in Hollywood.**

"In India and Sri Lanka, you have some of the right ingredients, but it's not the same straightforward growth story. Amongst the 875 million people in India, you do have an entrepreneurial class of perhaps 200 million, but that's still a minority. And for the country as a whole, you don't have the savings rate. They have only, perhaps, two thirds of the growth potential, but they do have the attraction as a turnaround economy."

So how does Everington see himself in the light of his liquidity driven focus? The answer is a complex mix which combines some core financial analysis with an assessment of the financial and operating characteristics of specific companies.

VALUE AND GROWTH = SUPERIOR STOCK MARKET PERFORMANCE

"I would describe myself as value orientated growth. My idea of value is not buying hard assets at a discount. I'm looking for growth companies which are selling at low prices. The P/E can be low at the top of cycle, simply because earnings are through the roof. Often, at the bottom of the cycle, the P/E can be very high, because earnings are depressed. It's not a rule, but you can almost say you should be buying a lot of these markets when the P/E is high, and selling them when it's low, because you want to be buying accelerating earnings."

RELATIVE COUNTRY, RELATIVE COMPANY

Macro analysis not only has validity in its own right, but can also be emulated with nominal modification at the micro level. What makes a country attractive is, in large part, the same combination of factors as the mix which should drive stock selection. Sectors certainly and, to an extent, even individual businesses will exhibit some of the same cyclical patterns, though with idiosyncratic modifications. Everington approaches the task of choosing one company over another for investment with a similar philosophy and many of the same tools.

"I analyse entirely on the basis of cash flow. It's the lifeblood of a country and a company, so it's far more important than earnings. For comparability, cash flow also gets rid of a lot of the distortions which can arise, as there are many different accounting conventions in the region."

There are some very specific considerations which Everington uses to whittle down his list of possible investments to the final selection. Once the market decision has been made, it's down to the company level with a brief gloss of sectoral overlay.

BUSINESS CHARACTERISTICS MUST MAKE SENSE . . .

If you want to keep the wind at your back, both at the macro and micro level, you want to choose businesses which work best in the countries you have chosen to overweight.

"The closer the business is to a commodity business, the more critical it is to have the lowest labour cost. So I won't invest in companies producing plastic toys because, quite clearly, that business needs to be resident in China and paying 50 cents for labour.

"For Asia, I like businesses which need low labour cost but not necessarily the cheapest. Software companies can get very well trained software engineers in India who are paid $3,000 a year as against $50–60,000 in the US. They are every bit as bright. They can write the software in Hyderabad at the other end of a telephone line even if the software is for the use of a company like John Deere half way across the world in the US. You have to look for businesses which can capitalise on the local advantages.

"The advantages in Asia are much lower labour costs, much lower land costs, a much more flexible labour force and tremendous production skills. Where you have both cheaper labour and cheap land, heavy, labour intensive manufacturing is appropriate, e.g. China. Where labour costs are higher, the industry must be higher 'value added' in nature or even a service industry as opposed to manufacturing. In Singapore and Hong Kong, per capita GDP now exceeds that of the UK and land is expensive. Clearly these countries are only viable as service centres for the rest of Asia as opposed to manufacturing bases in their own right."

A PROPRIETARY POSITION IS A BONUS

Ideally, you can also find something special where the company has a real competitive edge.

"In its purest form, a company which has a monopoly has proprietary advantage. Legislation can enshrine this advantage as is the case for many utilities in Asia such as Korea Electric Power, PLDT, Hong Kong Telecom, etc.

"Samsung Electronics is one of the great examples of this. It is extremely well managed, and has very different characteristics from its peer group. It has a very conservative accounting system with great cost control, which leads to high cash generation and a cost advantage. They've taken this advantage into several areas which they've dominated. In semi-conductors, they have taken on the Japanese and are now the world's biggest producer of 64 D-RAMs. They have the lowest labour cost within the context of Asia within a country where you could reasonably expect to produce semi-conductors."

While Everington has confidence in Samsung Electronics as a great long term investment as of August 1996 the stock looks particularly attractive. The share price has more than halved over the past year during a period when the Korean market has been poor and the semi-conductor cycle has turned down.

RETURN ON EQUITY AND SUSTAINABLE GROWTH RATE : THE SIAMESE TWINS OF SUCCESS

Everington does not ignore the need to look at financial performance. Here he keys in on two particular indicators as most important in a region whose culture and political imperatives both reflect an absolute commitment to growth.

"High internal cash generation translates into very high return on equity. Return on equity mathematically defines the limit on growth for a company, so high returns normally mean high growth.

"We are looking for companies which exhibit a high return on equity and have characteristics which suggest they can sustain that rate of return over time. A strong management, some proprietary technology or unique distribution conveying a competitive advantage, together with a sound balance sheet relative to the industry they are in, can all be an indicator. Management is the most important element. Samsung would be the best managed company in Korea for example."

STOCK PICKING WITH A TWIST . . .

Everington is an equity investor first and foremost, but he is not closed minded about how to acquire a position in a company.

"Essentially, everything I'm doing is looking for the equity investment. If I'm buying a convertible bond, it's because it's the better way into that equity. Once I've decided I like the company, I have to access the cheapest asset. In Asia, that can be pretty complicated, because you may have restrictions on classes of shares, or even on whole countries which you've got to deal with. In Korea and Taiwan, there are still strict limits on foreign participation although these barriers are gradually being removed. Even in Singapore and Thailand foreigners are restricted to how much they can own in banks for example. This restriction typically gives rise to hefty premiums on the foreign class of share and the trick here is how to avoid such premiums."

SECTORS HAVE THEIR SAY . . .

. . . just not much of one. Everington is aware that much of what he does logically invites more importance to sector weighting, but that is not practical in the Asian markets. As a positive discriminator, sectors can play only a limited part, but, as a negative variant, they steer him away from less desirable investments.

"It's more that there are certain sectors I'm not interested in. I've never liked construction. It is an industry which is often at the centre of corruption in the system, which is not something you can analyse. In Korea, the construction sector is very much at the centre of the recent scandal over a slush fund concerning two former presidents. That is why the whole sector has to suffer as the witch hunt proceeds. I don't particularly like property. I prefer industrial companies. I like simple businesses like utilities, and I like banks. With banks, the difficulty is to work out how conservative they are being on their accounting for bad loans. The Thai banking sector has been a great example of a proxy for the Thai economy in recent years. More importantly, financial deregulation has allowed for a huge expansion in operating margins. This theme is the prognosis for Korean banks over the next three years as Korea deregulates its banking sector.

"I liked telephone companies, but telecoms generally have become the sex appeal stocks of the world, so that's destroyed a lot of the value for now. When people start to say this is a lousy business, then I might be able to get back in. Clearly it is a growth industry.

"Good consumer electronics businesses, run properly, are very controllable. Asians are very good at producing things in bulk, a trick first mastered by the Japanese and now being copied throughout Asia."

PRACTICAL APPLICATION

A few cautionary words are appropriate, particularly for individual investors who feel inclined to chance their arm in Asia. The rationale for allocating a chunk of the portfolio is compelling, but investing is not always as straightforward as picking up the phone to one's broker. While the climate has mellowed greatly over the last 20 years, certain restrictions still apply, both in terms of choice amongst countries and stocks, and some residual limitations on overall foreign ownership.

"When I first started investing in the early 1980s, if you went to the Philippines, there were only two stocks to buy – San Miguel and PLDT. There were severe foreign ownership restrictions and foreign exchange controls. Korea and Taiwan were not even open then. In Asia, there was really only Hong Kong and Singapore. Thailand was just becoming accessible but, in all these countries, you were talking maximum top ten stocks.

"Now it's more complicated. There's still only 20 decent sized, good quality companies in the Philippines, but Korea has 800 listed companies. The market in Korea is huge, but foreigners can only own up to 18 per cent of any company, and an individual foreigner can only own 4 per cent (limits increased from 1 April 1996). A couple of years ago, the quotas got filled and you couldn't buy companies like Samsung. Then you had to decide whether to buy from another foreigner and pay a premium. At one stage, Samsung went to a 50 per cent premium; at that level, the premium decision becomes as important as the underlying investment decision. Right now, you can buy it without any premium down from 30 per cent six months ago and, with the stock over 50 per cent lower in market price, for a foreigner, you are paying rather less than half what it would have cost a year ago.

"In Singapore, with all the liquidity in the market, right now, to buy, say, DBS, which is a very fine bank and one of the leaders in Singapore, as a foreigner, you have to pay an 80 per cent premium. Singapore Press is at a 78 per cent premium, and Singapore Airlines at 87 per cent. Two years ago, they were all on zero premium. In my view these sorts of premiums are just insane."

Add premium and market timing to all the other analytical tools, and one is left thinking that, outside of Hong Kong, this is a game best left to the professionals. It's back to unit or investment trusts, where the variety at least allows for every possible permutation of country or regional selection.

WHITHER ASIA?

With so much interest in where an individual can find bargains in the world's most exciting growth region, insights from a resident pro have all the more value. Everington has been based in Hong Kong, now, for

12 years (only 10 more than he had originally intended), and has travelled extensively to every country in the area which has a functioning stock market, as well as to some that have yet to open up officially.

"First, to look forward, you have to look back. The story today is the same as it was ten years ago, and even 20 years ago. It's a very high growth region, principally based on a high savings rate. As long as that savings rate is maintained, then countries can continue to grow fast. They may make mistakes and not grow fast, but the fuel is there. The difference is that, ten years ago, the markets were relatively undiscovered, and they were very cheap. Thailand was four times earnings and most other Tiger markets sold at PEs of less than ten times. All that has now changed although the sub-continent is less discovered and the opportunity for multiple rerating of the good companies still exists.

> *The sub-continent is less discovered and the opportunity for multiple rerating of the good companies still exists.*

"Now, every man and his dog has discovered Asia. There are hundreds of Asian funds and the region is no longer the bargain it was. The theory is that high economic growth leads to high stock market returns. That appears to have been true but, if you dig below the surface, an alarmingly high part of the stock market returns over the last ten years has come from PER multiple expansion rather than actual earnings growth. You've had the once off discovery of Asia, taking Thailand's P/E from four to 18 times. Maybe the multiples can go higher, but you've substantially had the rerating.

> *An alarmingly high part of the stock market returns over the last ten years has come from PER multiple expansion rather than actual earnings growth.*

"Another point to watch for is that the earnings per share growth in Asia has never come through quite as well as it should have done."

Most people are somewhat aware of the first point, though it often gets forgotten in the general enthusiasm. Only a few people are aware of the second point, and an understanding of why it should be true – and, sadly, it is true – is fundamental to any evaluation of stock market investment in Asian companies.

"Let's look at the China perspective. China opened its doors to foreigners in 1978. Since that time, the economy has growth 8 per cent pa compound for 17 years. It's a fantastic rate of growth. This growth, in GDP and revenue, somehow never quite makes it down to the earnings line. Direct portfolio investors long-term cannot make money this way. People who do make money are the multinationals, who go in and negotiate big to big and set up facilities, often for export, and retain majority, or even 100 per cent, ownership.

"If you look at Hong Kong, the manufacturing sector has shifted its entire production across the border. It's not just the manufacturers. Even utilities, like China Light and Power, are producing a fair degree of their power in China. HAECO, Hong Kong Aircraft Engineering Company, has lowered its costs by moving some of its repair and engine test facilities across the border. Johnson Electric has shifted all its manufacturing across the border."

So Everington's prescription for the individual investor is to play China, preferably through known multinationals, or selectively via the Hong Kong market.

> *Everington's prescription for the individual investor is to play China through known multinationals, or selectively via the Hong Kong market.*

We put Everington on the spot and asked him where he thought the best returns would come from over the next ten years.

"Apart from Russia, which is my absolute favourite market, the answer is Korea. It is the one country which could be the next Japan. The Japanese have drawn the map, and the question is, 'Who is going to follow the route?' You need to remember Korea was occupied by Japan from 1906 to 1946. Many of the structures in Korea are modelled on the Japanese. The Ministry of Finance in Korea was established by the Japanese. The Bank of Korea was established by the Bank of Japan. The industrial conglomerate in Korea, the Chaebol, is exactly the same as the Zaibatsu in Japan. There are similar equity cross holdings. Every Korean over the age of 60 speaks fluent Japanese thanks to the earlier occupation.

"The parallels are uncanny. Take the financial markets, which have been the slowest to develop in Korea as they were in Japan. On average, companies are geared 3:1, which is similar to how Japanese companies were geared in the 1960s. P/E ratios were very low in Japan at that stage, as they are now in Korea.

"Put this in context. America is the centre of the world, economically. America will give up the baton to Asia, probably Japan in the first instance. Add to that, Korea is the cheapest market in Asia by a long way. For example the price to cash flow ratio of the Korean market is under five times. It has been that way for a while.

"Koreans are worried about their depressed market. That's forcing Korea to try to make the market more attractive to foreigners. The foreign quota should go from 18 per cent to 20 per cent by end 1996 and 25 per cent by early 1997. At that stage, the market is effectively open. In Japan by comparison, foreigners collectively have never owned more than 10 per cent of the market."

Not surprisingly, Korea is Everington's country of choice when it comes to overweighting a model equity portfolio, as of March 1996. Asked to take a three year view as to how he would allocate investment across the region today, starting from scratch, he came up with an answer which showed a high degree of concentration.

"Korea is just rolling up into a new cycle and is at such depressed levels. I would put 30 per cent there. I would also put 30 per cent in Japan and 30 per cent in Taiwan."

In a recent presentation to institutional investors in London, Everington emphasised several reasons for his optimism about the Korean market:

- Falling interest rates
- Bank of Korea easing credit in response to the bankruptcy of Woosung Construction
- Low CPI increase versus growth in GDP
- Market PER at eight year low on par with 1992 trough
- Maximum pessimism by Koreans – a good contrary indicator and, yes, his old favourite
- Regional liquidity percolating to Korea with revival in offshore and GDR market.

Taiwan is the other market where Everington currently wants to go heavily overweight. The reasoning here is different from how he came to plump for Korea, but contains at least some elements of the same philosophy.

"I'm not a blinkered contrarian, but I do tend to like to go where other people don't. I do not believe the political risks are anything like as bad as many people see them. Make no mistake – if Taiwan declared independence tomorrow, I have no doubt that the Chinese would invade, but I don't believe that the Taiwanese will be that stupid.

"The mainland Chinese are supremely economically rational. However, when it comes to nationalism, there is a big danger. There's five thousand years of history, but they will not push Taiwan, unless provoked in this extreme, to the point where it affects their other interests in Asia. The day they chuck missiles at the Taiwanese mainland, you'd lose 3,000 points off the Hang Seng Index.

"Right now, Taiwan is a strong buy. At 4,500, technically it's very attractive. If you look at the five year chart, you can see that, with the onset of the China crisis, the index dropped down to 4,500. That was the missile tests of July/August 1995. China has been conducting missile tests in the same place, at the same time, for the last ten years. The only difference is that, this year, for political reasons, the Chinese chose to make a big deal about it. After the initial crisis the market began to bounce. Then, as we came into the legislative elections in December 1995, which is what they were trying to influence, China started putting on the pressure again. This time, the market fell to 4,550 and, after that bounced again. Towards the March 1996 presidential elections, again, China piled on pressure and the market fell, but to 4,650. Each time the reaction led to a slightly higher low. This market is building a base, which suggests it is very cheap at this level. This is the lowest P/E for the Taiwanese market in ten years.

"What do you buy? Inside Taiwan, the domestically listed closed-end funds currently sell at a 20 per cent discount to asset value. So why bother to buy stocks? The market is cheap, at 4,600, but you can buy it at 3,800 through the funds such as the Fu Yuan, China Growth or Kwang Hua. This is as good as it gets, because the Taiwanese have introduced legislation to say if the discounts go to more than 20 per cent, then automatically these funds open end, in which case their discounts fall to zero.

"If you do get into a bull market, and I believe we will see one, the discounts narrow. My Taiwanese exposure, in my hedge funds, is entirely through these closed-end funds."

Again, Everington cited several specific factors he thinks make early 1996 a favourable time to buy the Taiwanese market:

- Increasing current account surplus
- Inclusion, as of first half 1996, in MSCI Pacific Index

- Good GDP growth relative to inflation
- Biggest investor in China
- 1996 PER of 14 times lowest since 1986

These views arise from a number of considerations but, bearing in mind Everington's focus on the liquidity cycle, it is useful to see his view of where each country is as of March 1996. This is depicted in Chart 4.2.

The best time to buy a market is in the months before the relevant economy reaches its low point. At this stage liquidity is rising as loan demand is depressed and, typically, the Government is actively stimulating liquidity. At the same time, most of the bad news on earnings is to some degree discounted in the price. At this point you are well set to catch the upwave of earnings acceleration as the new cycle unfolds. That is where Taiwan appears to be as of April 1996.

Chart 4.2 Economic/Liquidity Cycle

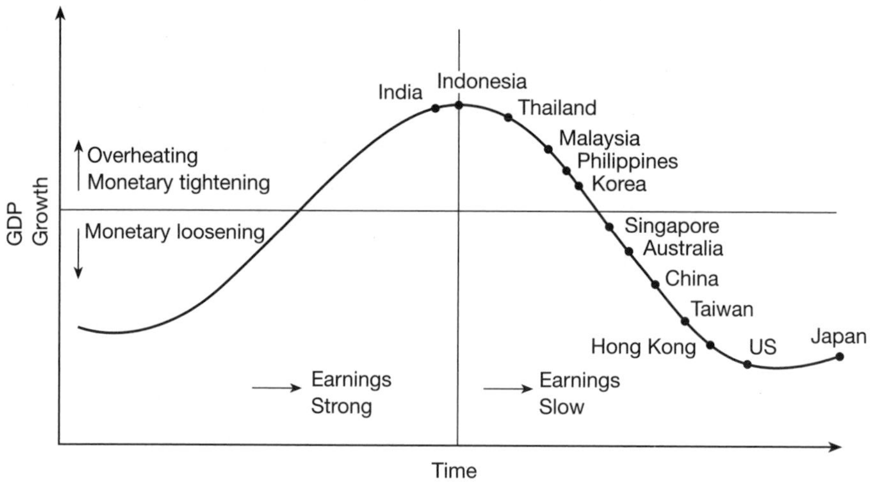

Source: Regent Fund Management Ltd

CLOSED-END FUNDS

This highlights one other aspect of Everington's activity which is noteworthy as a separate item. Concomitant with a philosophy which emphasises a more macro interpretation of markets and draws its strength from market allocation Regent, as a firm, has developed expertise in exploiting the inefficiencies of the closed-end fund market. Taiwan is a classic case in point, but there are other examples where extra value can be created for investors by a willingness to take an indirect route into markets.

Nor is Regent necessarily a shrinking violet if traditionalists stand in the way of realising superior investment performance. Asian culture commands respect for an older generation, but also places great emphasis on business and financial success. Regent has taken on board the culture of the countries in which it operates, but shows the greatest respect for its own shareholders. If change does not lead to performance improvement, it will go to bat.

The following extract from one of Regent's corporate brochures elaborates on this philosophy:

> Both market intelligence and fund construction know-how are brought into play in pinpointing and acting on suitable closed-end funds; usually this means those trading at a discount of at least 15 per cent, and with relatively liquid investments in their portfolios.
>
> While the bulk of these funds are listed on international stock exchanges, we also buy into unlisted closed-end funds to a limited extent.
>
> A significant amount of specialist funds investing in the Pacific Basin have been set up in recent years, and we believe a number of these are both small and trading at wider than average discounts, leaving them open to corporate activity.
>
> We seek out closed-end funds where corporate activity is likely with a view to taking advantage of changes being made to the structure, which could involve liquidation, unitisation or, less commonly, a take-over bid, thus narrowing or eliminating the discount at which its shares trade.

In this arena Regent has been active in initiating the unitisation of funds such as the Malaysian Capital Fund and GT Chile Fund and has also made profitable aggressive corporate moves in funds such as China Assets and Thai Asia Fund.

ASIAN INFLUENCE AFFECTS OTHER ASSETS

1996 finds Regent and Everington in unfamiliar guise with a commitment to gold. From his position in Hong Kong, he has a slightly different slant on the forces at play in this specialised commodity sector.

"I do not subscribe to the view that inflation is down and under control. Liquidity has been ripping through the system. I believe inflation has been running rampant over the last five years but, instead of manifesting itself in consumer prices, which is what everyone tends to associate with inflation, these forces have been manifesting themselves in financial assets. A general pick-up in inflation, if it gets going, will be very damaging for equity markets. Inflation is like drinking. Initially, the first effects are very pleasurable, and only subsequently do you suffer the hangover. The first signs of inflation often manifest themselves in stock markets which do rather better than they should.

"My concern is that, because the major economies are rather depressed in 1996, I see countries all around the world trying to get away with easier and easier credit, and trying to get away with less than justifiable exchange rates. You've got competitive devaluation and competitive expansion of liquidity. You can see it in the US and now, add to that the Japanese are printing money like it's going out of style because, if they don't, for them it will go out of style.

"So everywhere I look I can see the printing presses burning. That means to me that, if – up to now – inflation has been confined to financial assets, there's a good chance it's going to be spreading. There are so many forms of inflation. In 1995, commodity prices picked up immensely and so, if the question is, 'Where does inflation move to?' It seems to me that commodities are next in line. That includes gold.

"For the last three years, the fundamentals of the gold market have been moving severely out of balance. Jewellery demand has been going through the roof and now exceeds long-term annual gold supply by about 20 per cent. The equation only balances because of unprecedented forward selling by producers and massive selling by central banks.

"In December 1995, the price of speculating in gold reached unprecedentedly low levels. The implied volatility in option pricing on gold had fallen to just 8 per cent. At the same time, the contango in gold, the forward price over the spot price, had come from a $26 per ounce premium to $12. The third element was that the cost of borrowing physical bullion had risen to 3.5 per cent pa, which is a very high cost. Add all those three elements together, and you know that the producers are going to stop forward selling. There's no advantage any more. So, unless central banks increase their selling, the market will be out of balance and the price has to go up."

The story of successful investing in Asian markets is still in its infancy, as far as stock markets go. The best is almost certainly ahead, and Everington will be busy making sure his clients are in the right countries at the right time. With a wide range of specialist vehicles available, investors can easily become confused about the right choice. What is clear is that a static approach – staying in Hong Kong regardless – is not the best. The leading market is rarely the same in two consecutive years. Everington's experience has demonstrated the immense importance of rotating through markets, and he has an exceptional record in picking the top performing places year after year.

It's comforting to stay home and build up a nice nest egg of blue chips with recognisable names; but investors have to be aware of the need to seek superior returns in other parts of the world, and backing a manager of Everington's calibre is a short cut to financial security. The net returns to an investor on Everington's managed funds have been phenomenal.

Taken as a whole, Everington has done extraordinarily well for his investors. Anyone who had handed him $10,000 in October 1981 and followed him to each new home would have a holding, as of year end 1995, worth $130,520, or over 13 times their initial investment in only 14 years. Such is the power of superior compound performance from an investment grand master.

Peter Everington was a contributor who wrote the section on Convertible Bonds in *The Financial Times Global Guide to Investing*.

* King of fixed income investing and a leading
global asset allocator

* Consistently wins awards for performance from
Micropal as best in sector

* Not just an investment manager: Flight is an author
(of *All You Need to Know About Exchange Rates*) and active
in politics (Prospective Conservative candidate for Arundel
and South Downs)

96

HOWARD FLIGHT

Investing in the Common Stock of Countries

Everyone who knows anything about the investment history of the UK since the Second World War knows that you would have been better off investing in equities over the last 50 years than in any other class of financial asset and as a result most people assume equities will always be a better investment than bonds. Try telling that to Howard Flight. Flight was one of the first to identify the turning of the post-war inflation trend and its positive implications for bond investment, when combined with successful currency management. Guinness Flight's performance record in bond and currency investment and, in particular, that of Guinness Flight's flagship fund, the Managed Currency Fund, over the last 16 years has been such as to put many stock pickers to shame.

Over the last 15 years, Guinness Flight has soared above the average, offering relatively low risk returns, and has outperformed against deposit yield benchmarks in all five major currencies. Looking at Chart 5.1 overleaf you can see that the Guinness Flight Managed Currency Fund (GFMCF) has outperformed sterling cash deposits by an average of 3.3 per cent per annum since 1980. For UK shareholders, the 14.7 per cent annualised rate of return has delivered a total sterling return of 744 per cent since May 1980.

It has been possible, over the life of GFMCF, to make deposits in SDRs – the world's only fixed currency basket for those wishing to spread their currency risk on a globally neutral basis. GFMCF has provided more active strategic currency management, and has outperformed SDR deposits over the fund's life to date by 281 per cent. (Measured on the basis of reinvesting gross interest.)

The JP Morgan Global Government Index is normally reckoned to be a good industry benchmark. Over the last ten years, the Guinness Flight flagship Global Bond Fund has beaten that index by 44 per cent.

There are other ways of looking at Guinness Flight's performance, but all of them tell a similar story over both a three and five year period. Through to year end 1995, the main Guinness Flight funds turn up in the top two quartiles, measured in both dollars and sterling: for the larger Guinness Flight Global Strategy umbrella fund, 80 per cent of the sub funds have been in the top two quartiles over five years, and for

Chart 5.1 Fifteen Year History of Currency Management

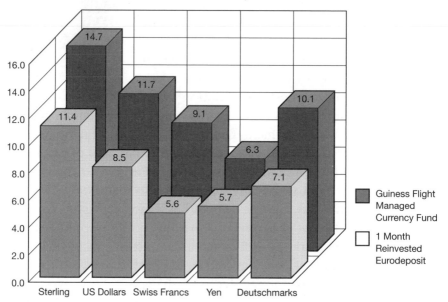

Guiness Flight Managed Currency Fund vs 1 Month Reinvested Eurodeposit
June 2nd 1980 to January 1st 1996

Returns are shown net of fees.
Past performance is not necessarily a guide to the future. The value of this investment
and the income arising from it may fall as well as rise and is not guaranteed.

Sources: Guinness Flight based on data drawn from Micropal and Datastream

Guinness Flight's Roll Up International Accumulation Fund, all of the sub funds have been in the top two quartiles over five years. Since the Micropal Awards started in 1991, through to 1994, Guinness Flight has won either the Best Large Offshore Group award or the Offshore Fund Management Group of the Year award, or both, every year. Guinness Flight funds have won awards in virtually every category. Guinness Flight was placed second by Micropal in their recent 1995 larger group five year awards and, in 1994, won the Micropal Best Offshore Equities Manager award.

Flight does not necessarily want to be thought of only as a currency and fixed income guru though, in fairness, that is where he has made his mark historically. Guinness Flight now manages money across a spectrum of asset categories and countries, including their recently launched Madras Indian Equity Fund, Asian Small Companies Fund and China Fund. Still, any conversation with Flight inevitably begins and ends in the world of currencies and bonds; and understanding the achievement of the Guinness Flight group is substantially about Flight's insights into the world of government, economic policy and other rather rarefied subjects that leave many money managers floundering.

The Guinness Flight group has existed in its present incarnation since 1986. Its business goes back to 1979, when Flight joined Guinness Mahon and when subsequently Tim Guinness and he took over the management of the small and unprofitable investment division. Flight is always at pains to acknowledge that he has been only one ingredient in Guinness Flight's success, and points out that he and his partner, Tim Guinness, are very much a pair in tandem where, in some ways, Tim Guinness is the senior partner. Their relationship stems from both having rooms in the Pepys Library at Magdalene College, Cambridge in the 1960s.

A little history sets the stage for the story of Guinness Flight's success. Flight's first own investment was in an 8 per cent Land Securities convertible bond when he was 16. "I invested £200 and it was yielding about 8 per cent at the time. The investment was made on a mixture of yield and capital growth potential grounds. I had saved that sum from holiday jobs to buy a scooter and was bribed by my parents that, if I refrained from buying the scooter, I might get an old car when I was 17. So I looked for something with an attractive, low risk return to invest my savings. Then, as now, the convertible can have its uses. It panned out very nicely."

Proving the point that good old investments never die, it is interesting to find a Land Securities 10 per cent debenture dated 30/9/2027 as one of the larger holdings in 1995's Guinness Flight Corporate Bond Trust – comprising 3 per cent of the current portfolio!

To appreciate why someone so young would choose a sophisticated and somewhat esoteric security, a bit of family background will help.

"My father ran the trustee department at Nat West (then Westminster Bank), so I grew up knowing what financial instruments were about. Also with phases of prosperity and also lack of prosperity, you'll find the Flights have been a City family since about 1640. They're all buried in Bunhill Fields and were part of the Baptist, non-conformist, City mafia, active in the eighteenth and early nineteenth centuries."

This is not the only early indicator of financial prowess. When he was 12, Flight showed an entrepreneurial streak, developing a small business to fund a record collection.

"I got turned on to classical music. There was a record series called Ace of Clubs. They cost a guinea (£1.05) each which, in today's terms, is the equivalent of about £15. Near where I lived there was a stream where I used to go and cut watercress, wash and weigh it and then take the bundles along to the WI stall on a Friday morning. I used to make about 30 shillings a week (£1.50) out of this throughout the season."

Arriving at Rothschilds in 1971, after US Business School, Flight soon found himself in familiar territory, dealing with specialist instruments and special situations. While some portfolios with which Flight was involved were invested for the most part in equities, others consisted primarily of, respectively, fixed income securities and convertibles.

"I was thrown in the deep end, taking over from a very interesting man called Tom Daniels who, within six weeks, joined de Zoete and Bevan. I was part of the pension funds' team and my investment responsibilities covered Hong Kong; UK convertibles and warrants, and take over situations; and the financial and paper sectors in the UK."

'Global' has always been integral to Flight's thinking, even before he was involved in investment activity. At Rothschilds, he got an early opportunity to apply that approach. He was instrumental in pushing for increasing exposure to the Far East, particularly Hong Kong; but, also, he found a number of external factors were forcing a reappraisal of investment thinking in the currency area.

"It was the era of organising loan finance for international investment in such a way as to avoid the UK exchange control, premium costs. It was also the period when the dollar went off the gold standard. That was the end of Bretton Woods. I asserted myself aggressively on the likely result of floating exchange rates, which had been my main area of focus at business school. I had done work with Ford's Economist as regards the outlook for sterling ahead of the 1970 UK election, and also for one of the main Detroit banks, on what was happening in Singapore and Hong Kong regarding the development of the Asian Euro markets."

Flight credits his time at the University of Michigan Business School as being one of the formative periods which has had a profound and long lasting influence on his investment style.

"There was a talented young German professor of international finance called Günter Dufey who's still at Michigan, and advises the US and other governments. He shaped my thinking and was my mentor.

"One area on which we focused then was the European currency snake and the arguments for and against a common currency. I've always been against it from what I soaked up at Michigan, although I flirted with believing it was inevitable and workable in the late 1980s. Professor Dufey made the point to me, over 25 years ago, that the southern states of America had suffered since the Civil War from having a common currency when they had a backward economy in comparison with the rest of the country. As a result, there was massive population migration and a relatively depressed economy for a hundred years. The adjustment of the exchange rate is the least socially and most economically, cost effective way of addressing the issues of different economic regions having different social and economic characteristics and different growth rates, different costs, inflation and so forth. This central point and the US case study seem to me to be fundamental in the European context today."

Returning to London from Asia in 1979, it was this broader interest, combined with a spell as an expatriate overseas, which lead to Flight spotting an opportunity in the investment funds' marketplace which prevailed at that time.

"I perceived, from my own experience and needs as an expat, the demand for what became known as the Managed Currency Fund (MC). When Mrs Thatcher wisely abolished exchange controls, this also opened up a domestic demand in the UK. In part, the Managed Currency Fund was also intended to deal with the investment management of smaller, low risk accounts in Switzerland and Guernsey, which were impractical to handle as individual portfolios. The Managed Currency Fund was set up in May 1980."

The first advertisement for this vehicle inauspiciously appeared in *The Financial Times* on a day when, on the opposite page, the headline ran to the effect 'Guinness Peat in trouble'. In spite of adverse press comment, the strength of the concept pulled in a total of $5 million. The Guinness Flight team was up and running in the business where it was destined to rise to the top.

Flight was, and still is, very entrepreneurial, and his career is sign-posted with moves which mark him out from the crowd. While Rothschilds was as traditional a starting point as any in the City, Flight left after only two years to join a boutique merchant bank – St Mary Axe Finance – run by James Heyworth Dunne and set up to operate in parallel with Gartmore. This was subsequently renamed Cayzer Bowater (CB). It had an investment trust called Ralli Securities. Flight's activities at CB spanned the spectrum. He was involved in managing the invest-ment trust's portfolio; handled corporate finance projects and some lending, and was responsible for the money book. In the latter context, this gave him an insight into the Bank of England's 'lifeboat operations' during the secondary banking crisis of 1973/4. Then followed a stint with Wardley in Hong Kong in corporate finance and Hong Kong Dollar Eurobond issuance, before being seconded to Bombay to estab-lish the Hong Kong bank's merchant banking operation in India. The reason for what may appear to be something of a digression is to under-line that Flight:

(a) has a broader financial background than most fund managers;
(b) has credit expertise;
(c) has direct working experience in several countries.

This basket of experience and skills, reflecting a rather eclectic experi-ence base, was, perhaps, the best possible lead up to developing an independent business.

Flight today operates at a nexus as amongst industry, capital markets and politics. He plays an active role in all three areas. His investment acumen is comprehensively covered in this chapter. Less well known is his involvement in the political process. He has used that expertise to benefit his investors and the investment community at large. One recent example has been his campaign, to secure the inclusion of bonds within UK PEP tax benefits.

Flight's political activities are broadly based and have been part of his life for the last 30 years. While at Cambridge, Flight was the Chairman of the Conservative Association. Subsequently, he stood twice as the Conservative Parliamentary Candidate in Southwark/Bermondsey and has been active in Conservative politics ever since – including, among other assignments, membership of HMG Treasury Tax Conservative

Committee for several years. Flight's involvement in politics, and his interest in all matters political, is integral to many of his insights into investing, and persists to the point where he has recently been adopted as Prospective Conservative Parliamentary candidate for the new constituency seat of Arundel and South Downs. Next stop Westminster?

"I was always very political. At Cambridge I ran the Tories and was the senior committee member of the Union. At the close of my Cambridge undergraduate days, I faced the issue of whether to look to enter politics at Tory Research department, where there was the promise of a job, and where all aspiring Tory politicians should start; but I didn't want to be an importunate politician and wanted a career first, so I went off to US business school."

Flight continued to rub shoulders with budding politicians. The investment division at Rothschilds has long been a cauldron of political talent. "It then included Norman Lamont and Tony Nelson." Other curious coincidences pepper Flight's progress. In his Cayzer Bowater days, he worked with Alastair Goodlad – now the Chief Whip – in setting up and monitoring a merchant bank in Singapore called Temengong (subsequently Hill Samuel Singapore).

The interaction between Flight's political interests and his financial career has had tangible benefits for shareholders in the Guinness Flight Funds. He has been able to translate his understanding of how political events can impact financial markets to reposition portfolios. Reacting ahead of the crowd who were slower to see the implications has often been rewarding. One fairly recent example of how this can work in practice were the currency moves Guinness Flight made around the time of the Iraq war.

"When the US declared war, I was sure they would win and this would benefit the dollar; their expected success would counteract the negative legacy of the Vietnam War, while the Middle East states and Japan would have to contribute to the cost."

One of the most interesting parts of Flight's personal portfolio of skills is his ability to synthesise the *long-term* financial implications of political change and economic development. An early example stemmed from a visit to China made in late 1977. Flight managed to crash one of the first western tour groups in the immediate post Red Guard period.

"Everyone on the tour was supposed to be a travel journalist writing up China, but we were all something else, including two Catholic priests in disguise! We spent much of our time going round factories and talking to managers, drinking green tea. What they all said was: imagine trying to run production when standardisation was a political sin; many of their 'bourgeois' friends and relatives had been sent off to the remote countryside and beaten up during the Cultural Revolution. Their great hope was that Chairman Zhou and Deng would steer China down a course of successful economic development and people would forget political dogma.

"In Shanghai, I found the only foreigners resident were the Hong Kong Bank and the Standard Chartered Bank managers, a Polish shipping consul and a few Japanese; that was all. After coming off that tour, I reported back to the Hong Kong Bank that I believed China was now likely to go through a period of major economic advance."

Flight's spell in India, in the late 1970s, confirmed an initial interest sparked off by reading history at Cambridge. His long-term enthusiasm had to be tempered by an awareness that the timing was premature for any major move into a market which had enormous potential, but serious tax and structural barriers for outside investors.

"I love India. The people are inherently entrepreneurial and capitalist and there are many common traits in our two cultures. But India also had many of the failings of Britain. It is very difficult to make things happen. At the time, India was obsessed with requiring majority domestic ownership of foreign companies – then the cause of Coca Cola's celebrated departure. Since 1947, India chose to follow a protectionist, socialist/nationalist set of policies imbibed from the British Fabians at the turn of the century. Edward Heath had further damaged the position by driving India into the hands of Russia when he ratted on Britain's treaty obligations to provide arms during the Indo/Pakistan war of the early 1970s.

"I formed the view that India was waiting for the right ingredients to move forward and that the British businesses which hung on during the bad times would reap great rewards in the future. Now many are doing just that. The good quality companies such as Hindustan Lever, Glaxo, ICI, Cadbury, and the three British banks, Grindlays, Standard Chartered and the Hong Kong Bank, who stayed are all now making and remitting fast rising profits. Hindustan Lever could contribute as much as a quarter of worldwide Unilever profits, and the Hong Kong Bank's Indian business is very valuable. The primary problem then was that you couldn't remit profits without ridiculous taxation. This has now gone away.

"My only son was born in Bombay and has the opportunity to choose Indian citizenship when he gets to the age of 18. I remember thinking, at the time, that India would advance a great deal before then, almost whatever; but whether Europe would move forward much was questionable. In 1996, looking forward 50 years, I believe the opportunities for British and Indian collaboration are fantastic."

In 1996, looking forward 50 years, I believe the opportunities for British and Indian collaboration are fantastic.

To understand the way Flight translates theory into practice and to get a window into his thinking, you can read the quarterly Guinness Flight *Currency and Bond Review* and the *Monthly Market and Funds Bulletin*. They are fascinating documents which discuss macroeconomic and political prospects and down to earth prospects for particular markets. The quarterly *Currency and Bond Review* focuses on changes in the factors driving exchange rates and interest rates. All the complex factors which affect the international supply and demand for a currency and, therefore, its exchange rate, are weighed and evaluated. Flight calls his approach to assessing and anticipating future exchange rate movements 'fundamentalism'. In addition to interest rates and other monetary factors:

> Fundamentalists argue that subjective factors such as politics, general momentum and sentiment are all influential, but are incapable of statistical monitoring or statistical deduction. Furthermore, the factors affecting exchange rates themselves continually change. The relative importance of the factors alters from time to time; seemingly established patterns and types of behaviour change of their own accord, and new factors come into prominence. In addition, the past behaviour of particular influences, such as current account surpluses, cannot form a reliable basis for assumptions about their future course. (*All You Need to Know About Exchange Rates*, (1988, Flight, H. and Lee-Swan, B. All extracts included with the kind permission of Macmillan who own Sidgwick and Jackson, the publishers of that book.)

The investment strategy which lay behind the Managed Currency Fund concept, at its inception, and still drives the allocation process at Guinness Flight today, is a combination of two separate, but interrelated, decisions.

"We seek to manage *both* exchange rates and interest rate exposure. We focus on currencies which look undervalued in all contexts and where the flows of money about the world suggest that their undervaluation will turn around. Our aim is to be overweight in those currencies. We take the SDR, as our benchmark and for our universe, with the modest addition of wholly liquid, secondary currencies to its currency basket composition. As to whether you hold short-term cash or extend maturities somewhat longer, the key question is what do you expect to happen to interest rates?"

The key fundamental *territories* for a currency are three:

1. What is the historic trend of a currency? Is it strengthening or weakening? And why?
2. Purchasing Power Parity (PPP). Is a currency *markedly* cheap or dear, as measured by its purchasing power and against its prevailing long term trend?
3. Trade Equilibrium Parity (TEP). Is an economy so structured as to have a congenital trade surplus or deficit, and how far should the exchange rate have a PPP discount to accommodate this?

Flight defined TEP in *All You Need to Know About Exchange Rates*.

> Trade equilibrium value is the exchange rate at which an individual country should theoretically achieve an approximate trade balance, either with the current account in balance or with a modest surplus or deficit corresponding to the international demand for its currency. The currencies of export-oriented countries will have higher international trade equilibrium values compared with purchasing power parity, to counteract the tendency to a trade surplus, while consumption-oriented countries will have lower (PPP discounted) international trade equilibrium values.

Individual exchange rates often overshoot their trade equilibrium value in either direction, and the currency becomes 'overvalued' or 'undervalued'.

"Undervalued currencies can be the result of deliberate policy. The Japanese Central Bank sought to keep the yen undervalued in the early

1980s for the specific purpose of building up the trade surplus and the Japanese economy. Experience shows that there is normally a considerable time lag between reaching trade equilibrium value and a subsequent change of direction in trade and capital flows, and in the exchange rate cycle. Trade equilibrium value is thus an ideal watershed 'marker' in currency cycles, indicating major changes from a bull to bear market trend and vice versa."

> *There is normally a considerable time lag between reaching trade equilibrium value and a subsequent change of direction in trade and capital flows, and in the exchange rate cycle.*

The factors to evaluate also are explained in Flight's book *All You Need to Know About Exchange Rates*.

As a general rule, the long-term assessment should always provide the yardstick by which to formulate strategy. It is based on traditional economic factors affecting flows of funds.

(a) Inflation
(b) The effect of money supply growth on inflation
(c) Current account surpluses and deficits
(d) Capital account flows of funds. This takes into account factors such as:

   (i)   interest rate differentials;
   (ii)   corporate investment reasons;
   (iii) portfolio investment measures.

(e) Productivity growth figures
(f) National savings rates
(g) National budget deficits and surpluses
(h) Politics
(i) Market sentiment and momentum

and, as always in an environment subject to unexpected shocks, there are major one-off events which have to be taken into the total calculus.

Most of these territories are statistically based. One example will illustrate the sort of analysis which precedes any formal integration into this assessment process.

CAPITAL ACCOUNT FLOWS OF FUNDS

Flight has updated this theme which is core to his investment thesis.

"The level and trend of capital flows are central to exchange rates in that they can either offset or worsen the current account impact on the exchange rate. Chart 5.2 plots the movement in Official Reserves against trade weighted exchange rates for the four main currencies. Here the cor-relationship is mostly good, although not necessarily reliable given the scope for co-ordinated central bank intervention. The best overall guide to the relative strength or weakness of private sector capital flows is the growth or contraction of a nation's foreign exchange reserves."

There is one additional pivotal factor which influences Flight's think-ing. In an era of floating exchange rates, currencies, like other financial assets, experience cycles.

The timing of cycles will vary. Their inevitability reflects a mixture of mood swings in investor psychology and, particularly, the cause and effect pressures of the interaction between changes in exchange rate trends and changes in real economies. There is much 'chicken and egg' in the process; exchange rate developments impact on real economic developments and vice versa. In the 1970s and early 1980s there was a high probability of currency depreciations, themselves, leading to eco-nomic events and cycles which would eventually lead back to further currency depreciation. Today this is less true as the result of the globali-sation of economies and the strong disinflationary impact on mature economies resulting from the rapid growth of emerging economies. There is notwithstanding a tendency for currencies to move over cycles from being overvalued to being undervalued (and vice versa) against their benchmarks.

This illustrates the need to assess currencies in both an historic and value context.

"People argue a currency is about right, or not about right, with refer-ence, purely, to the last six months, and not with reference to any fundamental basis of value or likely future trends.

"The level of a country's 'savings' rate is a major factor in the current global environment and is causing substantial deviation from PPP values.

"Economies which have a low savings rate will tend to run a current account deficit. Their currencies always tend to be at a discount to PPP;

Chart 5.2 Annual Growth in Official Foreign Exchange Reserves versus Trade Weighted Cross Rate (1976–1995)

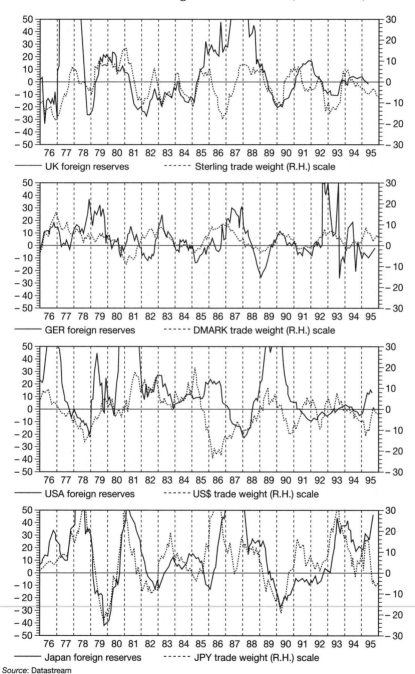

Source: Datastream

111

which is exacerbated if the private sector deficit economies are also substantial capital exporters and vice versa for economies that have a high savings rate. The discounts will move over time, but the PPP concept as a measure of cheapness and dearness is constant.

> *Economies which have a low savings rate will tend to run a current account deficit.*

"You also have to look at the factors which drive flows of money around the world. Looking back, by way of example, there was a very sharp bull market in sterling which went to over $2.40 in 1980, driven largely by rising oil prices and, in part psychologically, by the return of a capitalist administration. This was obviously a level at which the UK was not competitive. It brought recession; having had a massive industrial shake up caused by overvaluation, what got the British economy going was the consequent sterling depreciation. There are analogues today for Germany as well as Japan.

"This was followed by the great dollar bull market of the first half of the 1980s, which was both mechanical and judgemental in its causes. The judgement was that, after a period of severe currency weakness in the late 1970s, the new individual running the Fed (Volker) was pledged to an anti-inflationary monetary and interest rate policy. This both reduced US capital outflows and revealed capital inflows into dollar assets. By contrast, in Europe previous currency overvaluation led to Eurosclerosis, which we have again in the mid 1990s.

"You have to identify a difficult *territory* to monitor, which is the disequilibrium in capital flows. In the early 1980s, capital inflows to the US did not change materially, but US capital outflows collapsed, from about $100 billion to $20 billion pa. This was the main cause of continued upward pressure on the dollar. Eventually, capital flows change, but the nightmare is estimating when.

"Once a currency or other financial asset has become substantially overvalued or undervalued, you can start to look at this in itself as a potential magnet for contrarian capital flows. Timing is the difficult thing to get right. If you monitor and identify the disequilibria, you will be right for sure eventually, but you may miss quite a lot of the top or bottom. Assessing how far things will overshoot is largely in the lap of the gods."

The importance of the currency issue has never been put more clearly nor more succinctly than by Flight in the introductory section of *All You Need to Know About Exchange Rates*.

> In everyday life people use money as a medium of exchange instead of, or alongside, the barter system. What they rarely consider is that under a floating exchange rate system, money has no ultimate value. Sixty years ago, under the Gold Standard, a Pound Note was freely exchangeable for a Gold Sovereign. Even 20 years ago, under the Bretton Woods system, each currency was fixed at a given Dollar value (subject to periodic adjustments) and the Dollar had a fixed, exchangeable gold value. By contrast, in a floating exchange rate system, the currency of any individual country is only worth what you can buy with it, or what you can exchange it for. There is no support or guarantee of value; if circumstances dictate, a particular currency could become worth little or nothing. The expression 'I promise to pay', still printed on British Bank Notes, means no more than that the Bank of England will issue an alternative note or notes to the same face value. Currencies have thus become the 'common stock' of each individual country; their value, in common with other financial assets, goes up and down.

> *Currencies have become the 'common stock' of each individual country.*

> The assessment and anticipation of exchange rate movements are an unavoidable necessity and crucial to the success or failure of businesses and financial institutions. The much favoured 'discounted cash flow' approach to investment is useless without either taking into account exchange rate assumptions or hedging costs. With the growth of investment across international boundaries, and a shrinking world in terms of communications, the domestic costs of food, fuel, clothes or travel are all now substantially influenced by, and subject to, the effects of exchange rate movements.

Much of the outperformance of Guinness Flight's International Bond and Equity Funds can be attributed to currency management. Internal analysis suggests that some 70 per cent of the historic outperformance in the Prime Global Bond fund has been the result of the separate management of its currency exposure from its underlying bond portfolios. Indeed, Guinness Flight was one of the early pioneers of currency overlay. It is, however, intellectually difficult to attribute performance as between bond security and currency management – as, without the currency overly, expected exchange rate movements would have to be factored into bond allocation decisions directly, leading to very different security portfolios.

The Guinness Flight approach can, at times, cause major strategic changes in terms of the mix of currency exposure. In 1987, the dollar went from 0 per cent of the portfolio to nearly 60 per cent in the space of two months. In 1986 the Deutsche Mark dropped from just under 50 per cent to zero over four months. At other times, currency positions have been held for long periods, awaiting the expected trend changes. Guinness Flight has held an overweight dollar position for most of 1995, which is now bearing fruit. With the yen at Y100 to the dollar, it was clear the economy of Japan was in deep trouble and its recovery would require currency depreciation. The Mexican crisis intervened, and resulted in even further yen overvaluation – requiring massive monetary liquification of the Japanese economy in Summer 1995, to prevent a deflationary depression. We have yet to see the potentially large impact on the exchange rate of what is happening in Japan, which should flow through over two or three years, as the build up in Japanese monetary liquidity seeps and then flows, out of Japan.

It is interesting to ask why Flight took the plunge and staked his future on bond and currency markets in 1980 at a time when recent history had been that of inflation ravaging fixed income investments.

"I took the view that, post the 1979 oil price hike, and with Central Banks, this time round, determined not to accommodate the inflation impact monetarily, as they had done after 1973, the world in the 1980s was not going to go through another burst of compounding inflation. The pattern began to look as though post war inflation had peaked in the late 1970s, which, in hindsight, we can see is what happened. If that were the case, bonds were cheap and a long period of good performance could be expected as values adjusted to lower inflation. Add in that not many other people were focusing in this area, and that Guinness Flight had pioneered the Managed Currency Fund concept – and it was a natural move to promote bond funds in the mid 1980s. Even allowing for some overheating in the UK, and in the US in the late 1980s, and concern, at the time, as to whether the disinflation bandwagon was a false dawn; as history has shown, inflation peaks since 1979 have trended lower and lower."

That said, get Flight on the subject of asset allocation and he will admit that equities should have the edge, for the most part, long-term, but increasingly in emerging rather than mature economies.

"The last decade or so has been an uniquely good environment for bonds and bond funds to outperform. If you assume, as I do, that the mature economies are going to remain in a climate of low inflation for quite a long time, then the big value risk for bonds is no longer so great. You hold them, in the main, for income, as something which will give you a better return than cash, and as a diversification of equity risk. In the round, over the long-term, you should continue to have a better total return from equities and, if you pay tax, in many countries equities still enjoy tax privileges over bonds. If you are a reasonably cautious investor and you need income, you will endeavour to vary the cash/bond/equity mix in accordance with expected interest rate movements."

> *If you assume, as I do, that the mature economies are going to remain in a climate of low inflation for quite a long time, then the big value risk for bonds is no longer so great.*

What about the future? The environment that Flight feels now prevails for fixed income investments in the mid 1990s, and which is likely to continue for several years to come, is markedly different from that to which investors became accustomed in the 1970s and early 1980s.

"If you assume a 30 year period of relatively stable inflation, the total return on equity investment in mature economies should be better than the total return on bonds – but nothing like to the extent that prevailed from 1950 to the mid 1980s. Price volatility should be potentially greater on equities than bonds, and the running dividend yield lower. I do not expect the reverse yield gap to disappear or reverse but it should certainly reduce. We are back to the environment of my grandparents' youth. The motivation especially for older people in holding financial assets is no longer largely to protect themselves against inflation, which is unlikely to be a major risk. It is actually to secure a decent income.

"Bond yields, over the next two or three years, are likely to fall further. Bonds should return more than merely their running yields, because real interest rates are still excessively high for economies with very high unemployment, especially in Europe. I expect both inflation and short-term interest rates to fall to lower levels than are generally anticipated. The climate is not yet into a stable equilibrium. The question of how to measure the real rate of inflation is very difficult. Should you include fixed assets as well as consumables? In focusing purely on consumables, we do not yet have zero inflation. It is trickling along between 2 per cent and 3 per cent. If property and other tangible assets were included, inflation has already ceased."

"The major changes in the 1990s for investors are that:

1. The world has become global as in the late 19th Century, but in a much bigger way than ever before.
2. Exchange controls have gone.
3. The closed economies of several important developing countries have opened up. Three quarters of the world are moving from being command economies to demand economies. Their markets are coming within the pale. These are the countries were you can find profits rising at 20–30 per cent pa and where equities will outperform significantly the equities of mature economies over time, although with a lot more volatility.
4. Investment management and, in particular, the retail side, has emerged as a major area of financial intermediation. In the US, the $3,000 billion mutual fund total is already about equal to total bank deposits. Investors in the US have got used to chequing accounts attached to their mutual fund holdings. The networks of banking branches are becoming redundant. Banks require a difference between the average cost of funds borrowed and lent of at least 3 per cent to cover their costs, but the more centralised and efficient mutual fund industry operates on fees averaging around $1-1\frac{1}{2}$ per cent per annum. In the future, banks could become a relatively minor, wholesale part, of financial intermediation.
5. A global disinflationary climate exists. This is to be expected. If you look back to the second half of the 19th century, for comparison you will see much of what is now happening, has happened before (see page 559 of the *Financial Times Global Guide To Investing*: 'Emerging World Impact on Global Asset Prices' by Richard M. Young and Peter Sullivan of Merrill Lynch). A hundred years ago, money was raised and invested globally. The big emerging economies at that time were the US and Russia, analogous to China and India today; and then, as now, parts of Latin America as well. There were massive investment

projects financed by Widows and Orphans from Britain. Gilts were the main investment medium, but people would buy riskier international bonds for higher income.

"An open, global financial market encourages the financing of investments where costs are lower and profits higher which, together with worldwide competition, put downward pressure on the costs and prices of manufactured goods. This, in turn, feeds back to the domestic economies of mature countries by increasing unemployment and constraining wages, even in the services sectors. It is no accident that the power of trade unions in the US and UK has declined so much in recent years.

"In the second half of the 19th century, the main, internationally traded goods were foodstuffs, and the real price of food fell dramatically. In the UK, food production and land costs were high. In North America, there was cheap labour and land was virtually free; the key factors which enabled the markets to operate were the abolition of Britain's protective Corn Laws and the advent of steam ships. Textile manufacturers also started to move to India for cheap labour. The whole process of moving manufacture to where goods could be made cheapest goes back a long way, but became a driving economic force in the second half of the 19th century. It produced a period of price deflation and volatility in financial markets though, by and large, with very good overall investment returns.

"At that time, it was very much the Anglo-Saxon countries which were the free traders, while Continental Europe turned to protection. So history really does repeat itself! *En passant*, after the Franco-Prussian war of 1870/71, there was a ten year move to create a common European currency but, (as is arguably still the case), both the substantial differences as amongst the economies of Europe and market forces rendered this impractical.

"Both the investor and the consumer were winners during this period. If you stuck with equities and rode out the rather large falls and rises caused by the volatility in interest rates, you did well, because of high growth in profits. On the bond side, provided you had enough spread of investments, when some went bad it didn't matter too much, and yield premiums on higher risk were wide. The biggest risks were wars; it was the First World War which ended the last golden age of the global market, unleashing the Russian Communist revolution and mistaken monetary policies in Europe and the USA in the 1920s."

Back in 1996, Flight feels there are lessons for the astute investor of today to monitor from the experience of investors of 100 years ago.

"The key question is, 'What percentage of your equity portfolio should you have in emerging markets?' You have to take an investment view, not a trading view. Then should it be a mix, or should it be weighted to Asia? I would not now regard it as excessive to have 25 per cent of an equity portfolio in emerging markets, and would weight this to Asia. Asian countries are more politically stable; they have massively bigger economies than South America or Eastern Europe; bigger growth potential; more capital and less debt. Asians are generally astute businessmen.

> *I would not now regard it as excessive to have 25 per cent of an equity portfolio in emerging markets, and would weight this to Asia.*

"You could justify more than 25 per cent but, five years ago, no-one would have dreamt of saying that and also remember that many major stocks listed on the mature markets have rising exposure to emerging markets. If you buy Unilever, you're now buying towards 40 per cent emerging markets in terms of profits. There are issues of volatility and liquidity, which are still a problem if you need to realise an investment at the precise moment emerging markets are on a sharp bear phase. Notwithstanding, I expect the percentage of emerging market exposure which is deemed natural will rise further."

Flight is able to go into more detail on precisely where he feels equity investors should increase their focus over the next ten years.

"I'm a committed bull on India. As of early 1996, it is the cheapest market in Asia in P/E terms, at around ten times projected 1996 earnings, but has one of the fastest corporate profit growth rates, of around 22.5 per cent. India is well behind South East Asia and China in its economic advance, but I am convinced that, in ten years' time, the market capitalisation of India will have increased more than any other Asian market cap, and foreign involvement will be much greater.

"The issue with China is that it doesn't yet have the commercial law and professional institutions to support the capitalist process, but this will develop. It has been slow, because no-one in China has experience and understanding of Anglo-Saxon financial structures, laws and mechanics. Chinese state businesses which have gone public have frequently disregarded representations made in their prospectuses, such as that they will not lend money to other state companies.

"In Hong Kong, corporate earnings now have less to do with property prices. Earnings are increasingly real commercial profits, arising, largely, from intermediary roles dealing with China. The small companies' sector in South East Asia is also markedly cheap. In Singapore and Malaysia, markets are more mature, but still well placed, and are typically held as the blue chips in the region. Looking out further, Taiwan, Korea and Vietnam should also open up to foreign investment. India and China remain the two economic giants in which international portfolio exposure is still relatively minor."

In parallel to Asian equities, Guinness Flight has also focused on Asian currencies and bonds. Asian economies are not yet, in Flight's view, particularly appropriate for the currency overlay approach in management security investment, which has worked well for the more mature economies. He believes a different focus for Asian currencies is more appropriate.

"Currency overlay is not really worth the candle as regards managing Asian equity portfolios. The Hong Kong dollar is US dollar pegged. Most other Asian currencies operate as formal, or informal, managed baskets. Where there is a currency play it is that, for those countries which are successful, while they tend to start with currencies which are, in a PPP sense, dramatically undervalued; as they develop into mature economies they end up with a PPP premium. The yen has led the way; the Singapore dollar is already more than halfway up this ladder. It is quite a long-term process; but the economic arguments for both real, and in due course nominal currency strengthening, as these economies develop are convincing. Those economies functioning with a low rate of inflation comparable with the mature economies will experience relatively lower interest rates, but should expect nominal, as well as real, currency strengthening."

In pursuit of this philosophy, Guinness Flight was the first to establish a non-equity, currency and bond fund, focused on the region, to exploit these trends. The Guinness Flight Asian Currency and Bond Fund, started at the beginning of 1994. Over the last two years, it has achieved US dollar returns in excess of 17 per cent, compared with 10.7 per cent on reinvested dollar deposits, and outperformed the global bond index by approximately 5 per cent.

"Successful, emerging economy currencies should appreciate. While they are struggling and competing in global commodity markets, a cheap currency helps. As they develop, the position changes, both because of market forces and because it suits the countries in question. Their middle classes want to buy more foreign goods more cheaply; their governments don't want to have to pay for major infrastructure project imports in a cheap currency.

> **Successful, emerging economy currencies should appreciate.**

"For long-term equity investment, the conclusion is that it is normally sensible being unhedged in developing countries. Often, there may not be an adequate forward market, anyway. In India, the rupee is extremely cheap in PPP terms, currently at around an 80 per cent discount, reflecting India's historic position as an exporter of primary produce and of low value added goods. As with other Asian economies, as India develops, the rupee is likely to strengthen in real terms, but may weaken further in nominal terms.

"My view is that emerging bond markets, generally, are not as attractive as emerging equity markets but, in Asia, they are low risk and attractive. Both countries and companies in Asia are typically under-borrowed; yields are comfortably higher than one price dollar bonds, and the currency play is likely to be in your favour. Unfortunately, the main emerging market issuers are in Latin America. The yield premiums there are not as generous as they were 100 years ago in providing insurance against higher risk. The risk of default is quite high. Below B grade, it is about 40 per cent, although a default does not mean you lose all your money. That isn't to say that there are no attractive opportunities in Latin America. Most governments, private utilities, and companies which are part of multinationals typically offer reasonable credit risk and worthwhile yield premiums over mature economy bonds."

As a global asset allocator, Guinness Flight integrates insights at a macro level – economic, political and social – to form a view on both the relative attractiveness of different asset classes and of their respective domestic markets. This is interwoven by Flight with the currency perspective in both a protective and enhancing context. Combining all such analysis, Flight comes up with a carefully considered set of recommendations for the decade ahead.

"I believe a relatively low risk global portfolio, where tax factors are not material, should have around 30 per cent to 50 per cent in bonds and, of that, presently about two thirds in higher yielding bond funds which concentrate on economies and government borrowers with interest risk premia above where they ought to be, and whose currencies are already relatively cheap. These include the UK, Canada, Italy, Spain, Australia and the Scandinavian countries.

A relatively low risk global portfolio, where tax factors are not material, should have around 30 to 50 per cent in bonds.

"Someone of 60 or more years of age in need of income may need the bond element to be higher. The equity/bond mix will also depend on where you live and the relevant tax distortions. If you are a resident of Monte Carlo, you will normally have more in bonds, as neither interest income nor capital gains are liable to tax. Outside nil or low tax areas, typically the equity element will be higher, because of the tax bias against income.

"Of the balancing 50 to 70 per cent exposure to equities, I believe about a quarter should be invested directly, or indirectly, in emerging markets, which means 12.5 to 17.5 per cent of the overall portfolio. Personally, I have a higher exposure than this (approximately 20 per cent) but, for a more cautious investor, I suggest around 15 per cent presently represents a reasonable exposure."

Looking at equity markets as a whole, Flight feels Continental Europe will be constrained by poor economic and profits growth, although likely to benefit from lower interest rates for some time to come. European bonds presently offer real yields of 3 to 6 per cent, and are likely to produce returns commensurate with or better than European equities, through to the end of the century, and with less volatility risk.

"In Germany there are so many metallurgical based businesses which still have to contract. In France, the government has subsidised too many industries for too long. Germany has had a wonderful position in capital goods/machine tools, because it was the only supplier of good quality, but this will erode over time as Eastern Europe and Asia advance in these areas.

"Continental Europe is not addressing its economic challenges. It continues to price people out of work with excessive taxation and over-generous welfare expenditure. For example, Brown Boveri cut its labour force by 43,000, predominantly in Western Europe, in the early 1990s, but created an almost identical number of jobs in Asia and Eastern Europe. Over the last 15 years, the USA has created 30 million new jobs; Europe has lost 20 million jobs. In France the add-on welfare tax costs of empolyment are 41 per cent of pay. Core Europe now suffers the problem of overvalued currencies, which has killed off recovery. In the new technology areas, apart from the UK, Europe is well behind the USA and Japan. In many ways, it is remarkable that Germany has done as well as it has over the last two years. Long-term, I would weight mature equity exposure in favour of North America."

There is one overriding theme for the future which emerges from Flight's view of world events, and which can be a very valuable guide to global asset allocation for the individual investor, particularly those thinking long-term to build a proper pension plan.

"Crudely, what is happening in emerging economies feeds back to reduce inflation, or even cause deflation in mature economies, because of its effects on the labour market. This tends to produce an environment which is favourable for mature economy bonds and for emerging market equities. Since the start of this decade, you would still be well ahead, relative to most balanced alternative investment approaches, from having been overweight in emerging market equities, and holding a relatively higher bond versus equity weighting in mature economies."

> *What is happening in emerging economies feeds back to reduce inflation which is favourable for mature economy bonds and for emerging market equities.*

Anyone who wants a test of Fight's forecasting ability can look back at past comments on the relative likely future performance of currencies. In his 1988 book *All You Need to Know About Exchange Rates*, the prognosis for sterling was bleak:

> If British industry is to sustain its recovery over the long-term, a further depreciation of sterling, particularly against European currencies, is inevitable. In overall terms, sterling has been the weakest of the major currencies over the last 30 years, and is likely to remain relatively weak against, for example, the yen.

He also forecast the yen appreciating a further 50 per cent plus from its level at that time, to yen 100 to the US dollar. And so it proved.

More recently, Flight called the turning point on the strength of the yen. In April 1995, he wrote in his internal newsletter:

> Markets are now forcing Japan to change more aggressively. In due course, this seems likely to lead to a substantial bursting of the Yen bubble. When this happens, the financial risks now facing Japan (and, consequently, the world) will ease as the enormous recovery in export profit margins should drive up the stock exchange.

Again, Flight argued, in the spring of 1995,

> that the Japanese Authorities should take the initiative and drive down the Yen to prevent a major deflationary depression. Something had to give. The Showa depression between 1927 and 1932 – when 44 Japanese banks went under and a tenth of the nation's bank deposits proved irrecoverable, when consumer prices fell 25 per cent in 1931 alone and manufacturing employment fell 20 per cent – provided an historic case study of the extent of the economic risks being faced.

Later, Flight noted,

> The Japanese Authorities appeared to have realised the danger by the summer of 1995 and, for the last two months, have been pursuing the appropriate policy options of increased currency intervention to drive down the Yen, and cutting interest rates, virtually to zero, to help the banks and to encourage a recovery of private sector outflows. Assuming these policies are adhered to, they should stave off the risk of a major deflationary depression (*Guinness Flight October Market and Funds Review*).

And the conclusion:

> That makes Yen bonds particularly unattractive, because the currency has to drop and as a result deflation will end. On the other hand, it is positive for Japanese equities.

Flight is also uniquely well placed to comment on a number of trends which could have great significance, specifically for the UK investor over the next decade. It is hard to improve on the introduction to a new Guinness Flight product entitled *Why Corporate Bond PEPs could Transform the UK Unit Trust Industry*. An abbreviated extract follows:

In comparing the UK unit trust industry with some of the world's major mutual fund industries it soon becomes apparent that the UK is unusual in its equity base. Bond funds have a far greater share in Germany, the USA and France. Since the early 1980s, the overall household penetration of mutual funds in the USA has grown significantly with over 27 per cent of all households with mutual fund investments (this figure stood at only 7 per cent in 1980).

Germany and France – Low inflation stimulates bond investment

In Germany, bond funds dominate the mutual fund industry, with over 55 per cent of total net assets. In a low inflation environment, such as Germany, bonds have provided good returns and within a risk/return profile between equities and cash, bonds are a natural first step from cash deposits.

In France, bond funds represent 28 per cent of total net assets. Investors are eligible for FFr 8,000 of tax-free income from any Societé d'Investissement à Capital Variable (SICAV) per year – analogous to the UK corporate bond PEP incentives.

UK – New investment opportunity

In the UK, bond funds still represent only a small part of total unit trust assets. Why has the UK developed so differently? Taxation and inflation are two important influences on investment patterns. One of the key contributing factors is the UK's inflation record. As inflation rises, real total returns from bonds suffer badly. Consequently both equities and cash deposits have proved better hedges against inflation. With the UK now, arguably, in a long term phase of lower inflation increasingly, investors are becoming dissatisfied with the returns from cash deposits.

Until now, fixed interest investments have not been Pepable in the UK, except when they constituted less than 50 per cent of a unit trust. In the 1994 Budget, the Chancellor introduced the concept of tax-free bond investment. The reasoning behind this was twofold: to benefit corporate borrowers by encouraging new and wider sources of finance for these companies and to broaden the range of instruments which PEP investors can hold in their portfolios.

What will be the way forward for the unit trust industry in the UK? Conditions to encourage a more balanced asset base are now in place.

Corporate bond PEPs should be in a good position to win significant market share. In the UK, building societies are still used overwhelmingly for retail savings, and have, to date, paid very generous retail rates of interest. I believe that will fade and they will not be able to afford so to do, to the same extent. The addiction to building societies will weaken, though I do not see them going bust.

The relative risk of particular types of units trusts and funds can be assessed through Micropal volatility figures. For UK unit trusts, the Gilt and Fixed Interest sector has a three year volatility figure of 2.19. This compares with 0.15 for the Money Market Fund sector and 4.41 for the UK Equity Income Sector. (*Source*: Micropal, offer to bid, net income reinvested over 2 years.)

There is another aspect to the whole issue of asset allocation which Flight believes will be material in terms of the UK investment scene, and is a function of demographic forces at work in an ageing population.

"The increasing maturity of a lot of established pension funds where they are inappropriately wrongly positioned, with 85 per cent in equities, will have to shift. They have been slow to change, but they will change and, in net terms, the percentage invested in bonds by these pension funds will increase over the next decade. That means a larger supply of funding for bond markets, which is positive for bonds. The percentage of non sterling bonds is small in these portfolios, and this will also widen.

"The supply and demand for these securities is important, though I would not over-stress it, as a determinant of yield or prices. Much more important than this is the macro effect of real interest rates going up and down with global economic activity. As we saw in 1994, when economic activity shot up, real interest rates moved up sharply, albeit briefly."

Interestingly, for someone who focuses on bond and currency markets, where traders live and die by their charts, Flight, who is an investor and not a trader, has relatively little time for the chartist approach.

"Charts can be useful in telling you how markets have been behaving, and can work for limited time periods. But they are no more than a graphical presentation of past behaviour. Their intellectual weakness is that, for predictive purposes, they assume the same behaviour continues, where behaviour tends to change over time.

"Also, you cannot ride two horses at the same time. If you are a fundamental value oriented investor, then you should pay no more than cursory attention to charts as a quick way of seeing what has been happening over the recent past."

So what makes Flight able to anticipate moves in markets that many people miss?

"Firstly, I'm a lover of economic history. I'm also a lover of historical comparisons. I believe you can learn a great deal from looking at past analogies, even if history doesn't always repeat itself exactly. I find monitoring what is going on in economies, of which real prices are most important, is extremely interesting. I'm always looking for reference points for value, and believe you can't evaluate assets unless you have some sense and knowledge of historic prices. So history is an important ingredient.

> **I believe you can learn a great deal from looking at past analogies.**

"Secondly, I think about the future in terms of the probability of economic and political events happening. The fact that I've been politically involved for 30 years is helpful. I believe I have quite a good intuitive understanding of politics, and exchange rates are where finance and politics meet. As those are my two great interests, it is no surprise that I follow currencies, which are 'the common stock' of a country in a very real sense."

> **Exchange rates are where finance and politics meet.**

Economic history, relative values and political influences make for a heady investment cocktail. The resulting collage may prove too opaque for most investors to follow, but the historic, long-term returns for investors in Guinness Flight's Funds are clear enough. Finally, there is a way for non politicians to make money out of politics, and Guinness Flight continues to show that, in the right hands, a well managed bond and currency portfolio can outperform stocks and should be part of every investor's portfolio.

* Manager of the oldest public investment trust in Britain

* An investor who put £1,000 with Hart in 1970 had a
holding worth £33,000 by the end of 1995!

* One of the pioneers in making the investment trust sector
of the London market so popular and so accessible to
the average investor

MICHAEL HART

Nibbling his Way Around the World

It seems only appropriate that the very first public investment trust ever launched in Britain should, 127 years on, still be one of the best. The Foreign & Colonial Investment Trust (FCIT) rises above its peers not only because of its distinguished history and superior performance record, but also because it has secured the services of a succession of dedicated managers who mastered the complex and volatile markets in which they operated. The latest in the line, and one who has continued the legend for the last 26 years, is Michael Hart.

Hart does not come across as someone who sees himself as one of the great money masters of the last quarter of the twentieth century but, by any objective measurement, he is. Hart sees himself as a guardian of wealth: someone who puts safety first.

Safe does not sound exciting but, when you are Michael Hart, appearances can be deceptive. Under his guidance, the Foreign & Colonial Investment Trust has been one of the most exciting investments anyone could have made in the last 25 years. A thousand pounds invested in 1970, Hart's first full year of management, with income reinvested was worth £33,000 as of the end of 1995.

Compare that to the returns available elsewhere, for example, from the FT-SE Index over the comparable period and Hart's performance is enough to set the pulse racing and the bank balance rising! Savers who shunned shares altogether and settled for a building society, the so called 'safe' option, had only £7,300 to show for their selection. Chart 6.1 shows this story of success.

To put his extraordinary achievement in context, it is fair to say that no-one else in the industry in England has matched Hart's level of consistency over such a long period. That consistency reflects his own career, as he has shown that you don't have to move around to move ahead. Hart has given a lifetime of service to Foreign & Colonial and its clients, and the clients who have shown reciprocal loyalty to him and F&C have been rewarded with a lifetime of ever larger nest eggs, and 24 consecutive annual increases in the dividend. Not only has the rise in net asset value trounced all benchmarks, but the dividend has also grown in real terms.

Chart 6.1   FCIT Share Price versus FTA All Share Index (1970–1995)

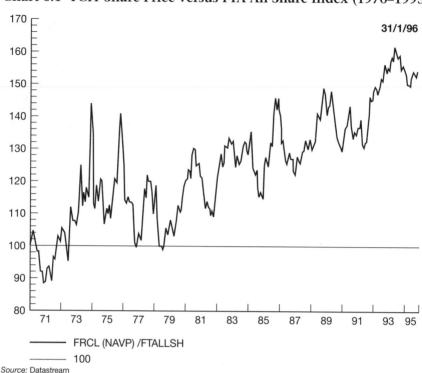

FRCL (NAVP) /FTALLSH

100

Source: Datastream

The importance of this achievement can hardly be stressed too strongly. Many small investors need income as well as growth. People who have £500,000 to play with may not care about this year's dividend, but a pensioner with £20,000 invested in FCIT needs every penny. The objective of FCIT is, 'To secure for shareholders long-term growth in net assets per share and regular increases in dividend which will beat the rate of inflation.' The evidence is clear. The jury is in. Hart has done everything he has set out to do, and more, with 25 consecutive annual increases. You can see the result in the dividend growth in Chart 6.2.

The investment business has turned a touch more glamorous in the last ten years. Leaving aside 1987, times have not exactly been tough since 1981, and risk has been handsomely rewarded in equity markets around the world. What sets Hart apart from his competition is that he has risen to the top of his profession without taking the level of risk that other fund managers have accepted in their pursuit of superior profits. Chart 6.3 contains an interesting comparative history of Hart versus the rest.

Chart 6.2 FCIT Dividend versus RPI (1970–1995)

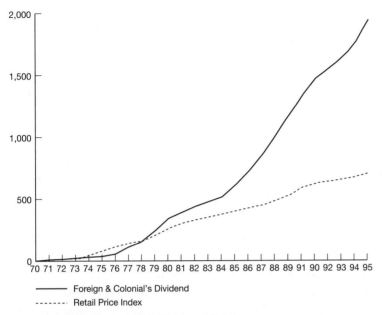

Foreign & Colonial's Dividend
Retail Price Index

Sources: Datastream and Foreign & Colonial Management Limited

Chart 6.3 FCIT Net Asset Value versus International General Trusts (1970–1995)

FRCL (NAVP) /AITINGN (AP)
100

Source: Datastream

133

This convincing outperformance, measured against a peer group, is even more remarkable than it seems, because several of the weaker brethren have vanished over the years, closed down, broken up or merged, leaving mostly better managed trusts in the rump. Hart continues to lead this tougher pack.

If there is an analogy worth making between Michael Hart and any global guru elsewhere, it would be to that other Michael – Michael Price of Mutual Series. Price and Hart share that special appreciation of risk, and emphasise the need to deliver superior returns, while protecting against too much downside exposure. Both have extraordinary insight into the definition of real value, and an instinct on how to find those elusive values in the stock market. While Price trawls his net mainly in the US, Hart fishes around the world.

Conjuring up a less likely candidate for the title 'top fund manager in London' than Michael Hart would be tough. There is nothing about Hart's background, education or orientation which shouts 'investment expert'. Hart was the son of a policeman who went to a state school. There is nothing remotely relevant in his early jobs to suggest that one of the all time great investment minds was waiting to be unleashed. Hart left school even earlier than John Major at the age of 15, and only when he was doing his National Service did he give any thought to a career. When he did, the chosen field was not investments.

"It all happened by accident – a stroke of luck. During my time in the RAF I started a correspondence course to train as a company secretary. That was my objective. I then had a couple of dead end jobs in rapid succession which weren't working out. One was a clerk with a London firm of overseas merchants, the other a book-keeping position with a third grade merchant bank. Then, in 1953, I answered an ad. from Foreign & Colonial to work in the general office. I got the job because I was studying to be a company secretary and there was potential to move into that area."

Hart duly passed the required exam in 1956 but, fortunately for many thousands of shareholders, his career as company secretary called for him to help along other aspects of the firm's business.

"The company was quite small in those days, so someone in the

Company Secretary's office had to do a bit of investment analysis. And then I got involved in dealing for the firm."

Hart could have gone on to spend his career in some kind of a support role, but an unexpected turn of events in 1969 shoved him into the spotlight and set the stage for him to become an investment star.

"The managers at Foreign & Colonial at the time were Tom Griffin and Richard Thornton, who went on to start up GT. They wanted to develop the management company and there was a bit of resistance by the old guard. There was also an argument about the Foreign & Colonial Investment Trust dividend policy. As a result, Griffin and Thornton presented the Chairman with an ultimatum. He said, 'OK – you go!' To my amazement he came round and said to me, 'Would you like to be the manager? You have 24 hours to decide.' I said, 'I don't need that time – I will do it.' With the help of three young investment managers, Eric Elstob, Duncan Fitzwilliams and Anthony Baring, I set to work."

The new manager of the flagship fund at Foreign & Colonial might not have been the most obvious successor, but the choice proved to be inspired. Hart had exactly the right temperament for F&C and for that most testing of investment times, the early and mid 1970s. Hart has always been conservative, even thrifty. That has stood him in good stead in shaping a risk averse approach to investing which was necessary as he became the navigator of FCIT.

"I was very savings conscious right from when I was a small child. During the war I had a book and put postage stamps in it. Going into the RAF there was a voluntary savings system. Pay, at first, was about 28 shillings a week (£1.40), anyway, next to nothing, but, in two years' National Service, I did save £100!

"My very first investment, once I was at Foreign & Colonial, was in Canadian and English Stores. My analysis of the situation was very qualitative. I had only held it a day or two before some bad results were announced. It proved to be a disaster. I've always been a fairly conservative investor and that experience made me doubly cautious."

Michael Hart and Foreign & Colonial Investment Trust have become almost synonymous over the last 25 years. A short detour delving into FCIT is illuminating, not only because that trust has an unique story, but also because it sheds a lot of light on Michael Hart as well. As he is the first to say, "I have been very influenced by the Foreign & Colonial history." The themes which were present back in 1868 when FCIT was launched do seem to flow seamlessly from one generation of manage-

> **'being entrepreneurial and trying new things within a world of diversified portfolios'**

ment to another, and Hart has a reverence for his inheritance. When he describes the culture at Foreign & Colonial as 'being entrepreneurial and trying new things within a world of diversified portfolios,' he really does capture the essence of the trust and his own stewardship.

It is instructive to quote chapter and verse from the original deed published in *The Daily Telegraph* on 19 March 1868:

> The objective of this Trust is to give *the investor of moderate means* the same advantage as the large capitalist in *diminishing the risk* of investment in Foreign & Colonial Government Stocks, *by spreading the investment over a number of different stocks*, and reserving a portion of the extra interest as a Sinking Fund to pay off the original capital.

While imitators soon sprang up, FCIT was one of a kind from day one. Holding true to its mission of managing risk through diversification while seeking superior returns, FCIT prospered even as several specialist funds failed.

Forty-five years on, Lord Eustace Cecil was able to articulate their tried and tested approach: "Our policy has been a *conservative* one throughout and, although the board has always been ready and *open to consider changes*, where changes were required, we have been, as I said, very conservative . . . The Italians have an old proverb which says that, 'He who goes slowly goes healthily.' That has always been our motto throughout."

> **The Italians have an old proverb which says that, 'He who goes slowly goes healthily.'**

Fast forward on another 80 years to 1996, update the vocabulary, but maintain the integrity of the philosophy, and this could be Michael Hart talking.

In 1969 Hart took the helm. He inherited a portfolio which, while solid, was not what was needed to achieve the objectives of FCIT.

"I was succeeding two highly professional managers. The problem that faced me was one of income. We had to pay a dividend, so the immediate objective was to get the revenue account on an even keel.

One of the things that I, and my colleagues, set up was a systematic review process. As results came out, we reviewed and assessed them and, as a result of that, changes did begin to take place."

Through that early period, Hart's style started to assert itself and his imprint on FCIT began to make an impression. The shift in the core positions between 1969 and 1970 is striking. No fewer than 10 of the top 20 holdings changed. Out went companies like Xerox, a gung-ho nifty fifty stock which never regained its 1970 level. In came some safer stocks with better total return prospects like Scottish and Newcastle and Lubrizol.

The fund Hart inherited was heavy on engineering (19 per cent), oils and mining (22.5 per cent) and food stores (9.1 per cent). Over time Hart moved to de-emphasise the mining sector, although he has always retained a reasonable weighting in oils. Financial services became the second largest category in the Trust, representing 16.9 per cent by 1984. The other big theme of the 1980s was consumer products companies, and Hart stepped up his holdings to 14.1

This geographic spread of investments has always been one of the great strengths of the Fund, and of Hart as a manager.

per cent in that year. By 1994, the balance had shifted again, reflecting Hart's perceptions of more and less attractive areas. The rose was off the bloom for consumer products companies and FCIT had reduced its weighting to 11.6 per cent. Financial services had moved up to 22.3 per cent and utilities emerged as a stand alone category with 10.1 per cent.

A critical ingredient of a diversified, balanced portfolio is in the mix of sectors. Combining, as he does, elements of allocation and bottom up stock picking, Hart has his own picks and pans among industry sectors. Financial services is one area of which he is fond. It has done well for FCIT and continues to be an area of emphasis. In contrast, he is somewhat suspicious of the high-tech rage which was so in evidence in 1995.

Another characteristic of FCIT throughout its history which has been continued under Hart is geographical diversification. Foreign & Colonial has resisted the temptation to accept the restrictions necessary to make FCIT an approved vehicle for PEPs, arguing that such a move could compromise the integrity of a global search for the best value for its shareholders. This geographic spread of investments has always been one of the great strengths of the Fund, and of Hart as a manager. While the emphasis has altered over the years, the theme of diversification around the world has been retained. The UK has always been the number one core country, though its importance has been cut, under Hart, from close to 60 per cent when he started to nearer 40 per cent now. Other important changes were a large weighting in Japan in the early 1980s, which soon extended to other countries in the Far East, and the inclusion of European stocks, which became a more important element of the mix in the late 1980s. Table 6.1 contains the geographic distribution of the FCIT portfolio for the years 1970–1994.

Table 6.1 Geographic Distribution of FCIT Portfolio

Year	UK	USA	Africa	Australia	Canada	Japan	Europe	Other	Latin America	Far East
1970	57	31	3	3	2	3	–	1	–	–
1974	35	32	5	3	4	16	5	–	–	–
1979	58	21	–	–	–	15	5	1	–	–
1984	39	35	–	–	1	18	–	4	–	3
1989	41	26	–	–	–	15	14	–	–	4
1994	44	20	–	–	–	13	14	1	2	6

This sort of diversification is not for show. Hart knows his way around the world. "I've been to everywhere that's got a stock market – almost." Recently he was in China testing the water. When it comes to foreign markets, analysis from afar is no substitute for on-the-ground observation. This interest in spreading the investment overseas does not mean that every emerging market is suitable for FCIT's shareholders. Hart recalls a trip in 1989 to Taiwan.

"There was a great boom on at the time. I was out there with Eric Elstob and we were shown round this broker's office and it was just amazing, really. It was absolutely packed with people who were punting on the stock exchange. Taiwan is extremely well organised: everyone had credit cards and they could put the credit cards into the machine and choose their stocks. There were women with babes in arms punting on the stock exchange. We were shown the VIP rooms, going into smoke filled rooms and these worthy individuals would spend their whole day in the stockbrokers' offices punting on the stock market. One came away feeling, 'This market is due for a big tumble soon.' So we did come back and sell a lot of shares on that market." Taiwan markets have since tumbled.

A search for the best geographic spread meant that Foreign & Colonial in general, and FCIT in particular, as part of the group, benefit by being early into new markets. Hart is not a pioneer in the sense of, say, a Dr Mark Mobious, but he is a believer in the advantages of being one of the first investors on the scene. As early as 1961, FCIT had gone into Japan at a time when most other fund managers still thought of that country as one no self-respecting investor would consider. Hart continued to build that position, leading the company into Brazil in 1972, a decision considered wildly unorthodox back then, but looking very smart in 1996, as it marked the beginning of the Foreign & Colonial's successful emerging markets business.

"The entrepreneurial background of the Trust dating back to 1868, how Foreign & Colonial started up the investment trust industry, embedded in everyone the idea that one should be more entrepreneurial and be prepared to try new things. That was the reason Foreign & Colonial, before I took over, was the first UK investor to get seriously involved in Japan and we were certainly one of the first to get involved in Latin America in the early 1970s. Time and time again, Foreign & Colonial has been prepared to try new things.

"The fantastic growth in Japan must be one of the things that really helped our performance over the last 30 years or so. Hong Kong has also been an enormous success story. Being early in those other Far Eastern markets has helped us. We bought an investment in Bangkok Bank in the early 1970s. This helped us to get to know the area and gave us important contacts. Then we switched into a Bangkok Investment Fund where we had someone on the board. BIF rose eightfold.

"If China gets its act together, that's going to have great repercussions all over that area and create the most tremendous opportunities. Amazingly, the political change that has happened in Latin America has meant a move to a belief in private enterprise and privatisation.

"Certainly Mexico and Latin America recently have had a hiccup, but we are great believers in the potential to be had there. Even Russia, which is a bit of a basket case at present, if the government can get its act together, could attract our interest. I'm a firm believer in private enterprise – millions of people beavering away, looking after their own interests, are going to transform the economy, so Foreign & Colonial has got be ready to put more and more money in that area."

The other advantage of this spread is that it allowed Hart to mix and match his investment objectives. "The way it's evolved over the years was that the UK portfolio had to produce most of the income. This was more tax effective; and the overseas portfolio produced the capital growth." The spread is also rather wider than appears on the surface. "The UK portfolio has got a high overseas content through companies which are large exporters and have overseas subsidiaries." The result has been that Hart has beaten indices around the world on a currency adjusted basis. So overseas investors have been happy, as well as those in the UK.

Of course, occasionally one can be too much of a pioneer. Even outstanding investment managers can stray beyond their areas of competence. Hart, who is essentially a very modest man, is one of the first to admit a mistake.

"In the 1970s, and through to the early 1980s, investment trusts were under quite a lot of pressure from predators, and share prices often reflected discounts of 25–30 per cent from the actual net asset value. Critics of investment trusts were saying they were dull and boring and institutional holders were saying, 'We don't want investment trusts to have lots of blue chips, because we can do that ourselves,' so we were being forced, to some extent, to look outside the conventional. We financed a film: *Biggles*. That turned out to be a flop! A colleague of mine had contacts in the film industry and these film people are always looking out for someone to back them. Somehow or other we got involved. An experience we wouldn't want to repeat."

In spite of his cautious approach, Hart is also not averse to spicing up his portfolio on occasions. He does this in three ways. The first is nothing more than a play on the interest rate spread, but that can be a nice source of profit, if you know how to do it right. Hart does. The 1984 report to shareholders refers to 'a sizeable dollar bond portfolio which has given us a useful revenue turn over the cost of financing.' To be precise, Hart had bet 13.4 per cent of the gross assets on this play: not exactly George Soros, but pretty gutsy, nevertheless, and certainly unconventional in the context of London financial markets in the mid 1980s.

"Borrowing, over the years, can play quite an important role in the management of the Trust, using an investment trust's ability to gear up or leverage, as the Americans say. This has been very important. It's something that has been done more often in my time. In the old days, investment trusts would gear up using a 25 year debenture with a 3 or 4 per cent interest rate, but then long-term interest rates went up and a tremendous number of investment trusts gave up the ghost, as they couldn't continue that type of gearing, but Foreign & Colonial didn't give up. It was impossible to borrow long-term, so we borrowed short instead. We could borrow one month, three months, six months, or one year money and put it into bonds or equities, if we thought the outlook was good. In a way it was breaking all the rules of investment. Borrowing short to invest long, but Foreign & Colonial had a very strong balance sheet." Somewhere along the line, Hart's definition of safety became a bit more elastic!

With gearing, timing can be everything, that and picking the right investment climate.

"The maximum we have ever taken the gearing up to is 30 per cent and we divided our gearing up into gearing employed in equities and fixed interest. We never take the gearing in either equities or fixed interest to much above 15 per cent. So, in total, 30 per cent. When stock markets are rising and there is inflation, gearing up can be quite a successful policy, and is relatively safe. Other trusts talked about gearing but did not do it. Foreign & Colonial continued to gear up, even though it was impossible to get long-term money at a satisfactory price."

> *When stock markets are rising and there is inflation, gearing up can be quite a successful policy, and is relatively safe.*

Finally Hart extracts a little extra from his diversified portfolio through judicious use of arbitrage to borrow in one currency and invest in stocks and bonds in another.

"This other aspect to gearing proved to be quite useful, particularly after 1979, when exchange controls were lifted. We began to use gearing to manoeuvre our currency positions. We would borrow some sterling, if we thought that sterling was going to be weak over the next few months, and we would transfer the money into an area where we thought we'd have a strong currency. Depending on how we felt about the stock market, we might transfer sterling that we'd borrowed into US Treasuries, or the US equity market. I'm certainly not claiming that we got it right all the time, but we had a fair amount of success doing that.

"Taking currency positions has been a feature of Foreign & Colonial's management ever since then, really. We've been manoeuvring these currencies around, trying to gain a bit of advantage. If you analyse, through our accounts since 1979, some years we made currency profits and some years we lost but, overall, we have made quite a few millions of pounds – I can't remember the latest figures but, since 1979, it might be £35 million. That's actually only about half the story because, when you borrow a foreign currency and repay it later, that is thrown up as a currency profit or loss, but when you borrow sterling, put it overseas and then bring it back, that doesn't show up as a currency profit, it shows up as a profit or loss on the investment. So when I talked about the £30 or so million, in fact it's been quite a lot more than that. At the time sterling left the ERM in 1992, we borrowed sterling, reduced our overseas loans, and were well positioned when sterling fell. It gave our performance quite a boost."

The benefits for shareholders of judiciously exploiting discrepancies between the currency composition of assets and liabilities within the portfolio can be considerable. While some profit from a strong dollar came from hedging in yen, the Trust also made handsome net gains in 1984 by being long currencies other than sterling. Since sterling has endured a long-term cyclical decline against a basket of world currencies during the entire period Hart has been in charge of FCIT, his understanding of the currency opportunity has been an important element in enhancing total returns. In 1992 Hart was betting against sterling, along with George Soros. His clever currency mix made $15 million profit and added one full percentage point to the performance of FCIT that year. Not only has this been a constant in his investment approach, but also Hart was involved in unorthodox currency transactions well before most of the investment community recognised the *investment* potential. A decade before SWAPs became standard tool kit issue for hedge funds, back in April 1978, Hart had entered into a ten year £/$ deal with Joseph Seagram. For a Corporate Treasurer this might have been seen as business as usual, but it was pioneering stuff for a fund manager.

Another feature which has added some spice to the FCIT cocktail is a sizeable dash of unquoted investments. This is a recurring feature of the company and something Hart himself has supported.

"Robert Fleming has been in the portfolio for donkey's years, really, all my time. We also had shares in Save & Prosper, that Robert Fleming took over, which involved negotiations with Robert Fleming about price. We consciously decided that we would take additional shares of Robert Fleming. We realised we were incredibly overweight in the merchant banking sector, but we did believe that Robert Fleming was an extremely good situation, with its valuable Far Eastern connections. It also had a first class investment management business. Another unquoted investment is our own management company which we began to build up in 1985. All the credit for this goes to Jamie Ogilvy, the Chief Executive. He really got the thing going after he arrived in 1989. The management company has built up successfully and is an important asset of the Trust. It is part of the Foreign & Colonial success story."

It is hard to pinpoint Hart, or stick a label on him that characterises his investment approach. Perhaps that is another of his great strengths.

"These days it's fashionable to be a stock picker or a top down allocator, but I've used all the weapons in the investment manager's armoury. Sometimes it has been good stock picking. Sometimes it's been getting the asset allocation right, sometimes the gearing. Sometimes it's simply been having the nerve to buy shares when the market was collapsing. That has usually worked out well two or three years later on."

This last point cannot be overstated. Hart has embraced Rudyard Kipling's dictum, 'If you can keep your head when all around are losing theirs . . .' and embedded it into his management style. He demonstrated commitment and nerve in only his fifth year as manager during the stock market crisis of 1974 and then again in 1987, when most other managers headed for the exits.

"Foreign & Colonial has had a history of having the nerve to buy at difficult times. My first real experience of that was in 1974 during that collapse. Everyone was absolutely terrified. It went on and on but, eventually, got to the stage where the yields were so high and P/Es were so low we got out a list of top quality stocks – GEC, Bass, ICI etc. – and said, 'Surely, in five years' time, these stocks are going to be much more valuable than they are today. The whole world's not going down the drain.' It was a question of nibbling away, putting a bit of money to work in those last months of 1974. Then the tide turned. One example I give is £300,000 put into GEC in 1974 which, six years later, was worth £3 million. That experience was very influential on me and we were able to apply it again in 1987 and during the Gulf crisis in January 1992.

"During 1987 there was tremendous panic and stories of people going bust and banks calling back loans from stock brokers. So the first thing that crossed our minds was to try and get an extension of our short-term loans. We phoned the banks and they didn't bat an eyelid, because our balance sheet was strong, although the bankers didn't quite appreciate how much the stock market could fall. Anyway, having got them to extend our loans, we then asked them, 'Would they increase our loans?' Again, they were quite happy to do that, and we put that extra money into the market. That proved to be terribly successful.

"The great successes have been the 1974, the 1987 and the Gulf crises, when one had the nerve to nibble away. Investment managers instinctively know that's the right thing to do but, in a free fall situation, it just gets more and more terrifying and everyone gets too frightened to do anything. Also, the investment trust structure has helped us here – we don't have to worry about redemptions – and I had a very understanding board of directors who didn't panic and demand that I reduced the gearing. They've always been prepared to increase the gearing in bad times, so one has been able to weather the storm and take advantage of major falls."

> *The great successes have been the 1974, the 1987 and the Gulf crises, when one had the nerve to nibble away.*

This line of thinking leads to a logical deduction that Hart is, in part, a market timer. He would refute any such label, as he refutes all others, but it is there in the mosaic which makes up his investment style – a little bit of this; a little bit of that. The facts confirm his outstanding ability to judge just when to bulk up his holdings. The week after the 19 October crash in 1987, Hart borrowed millions of dollars and snapped up stocks such as Telefonica de España at the bargain basement price of $5.50, not much more than half of its pre-crash value. Following the outbreak of the Gulf War, Hart again took out sizeable loans and placed a number of big bets on stocks depressed by that 'bad news'. Among them was ICI, at an average cost of £8.70. Within a year he was sitting on a gain in excess of 35 per cent.

This sort of phlegmatic approach to turmoil in the markets comes naturally to a man who describes himself as 'even-tempered,' and says that one of this great virtues is that 'I generally manage to keep my cool'.

A good way to understand what has made Hart so successful is to look at some of the specific stocks that were big hits for him and which have contributed to his outperformance. One that stands out is BTR. Interestingly, the corporate philosophy of BTR could almost be adopted verbatim by FCIT. 'Growth is the good, profit is the measure, security is the result.' Again, the starting point was being in early, which gave him a great advantage.

"A broker we knew, Jack Whing, who was not at one of the big houses, was a great friend of Richard Thornton's, so he had done a lot of business with Foreign & Colonial. In 1972, he said to me and a colleague, Andrew Barker, who is still with the firm, 'Will you come with me one day and visit Owen Green and have a chat?' So we went to BTR's offices. It was quite a small company in those days, but we came back so impressed by Owen Green, with what he'd done in turning round the company, his personality and enthusiasm. We still laugh about a couple of things in that meeting. Owen Green, at the time, said he was moving away from industrial to consumer products, and he opened his drawer and whipped out a rubber dog bowl. This was his latest consumer product! His enthusiasm for this rubber dog bowl was remarkable. Then Owen opened up another drawer and there was an enormous wodge of cheques that he was personally supervising and which wouldn't be paid to the last possible moment. His financial controls were that tight. He made a great impression; but, really, it was meeting Owen on a regular basis, probably six-monthly, for several years afterwards that convinced us. He would tell us what his plans and hopes were and he always delivered."

Hart pinpoints the essence of Foreign & Colonial as its belief in being a long-term investor. The second string to this particular bow is longevity. Once Hart had latched onto BTR, he kept it in the portfolio for a long time. BTR was bought first in 1972 when the company was a mere minnow (compared to £12 billion in market capitalisation as of

January 1996). Hart did not sell once the price doubled, nor did he flip BTR after the stock went up 300 per cent. Hart still holds a large position in BTR 23 years later for a total gain of over 1000 per cent compared to the original cost basis. Back in 1984, it was his largest holding.

Hart is always on the look-out for investments where he can take a different view from the market. There is a strong streak of the contrarian running through his approach and since, unlike so many managers, Hart is willing to wait for the market to come round and recognise what he saw first, he can make a success of this strategy. A good example is BAT Industries, where FCIT began to build up a holding in the 1970s. The stock market gave the company a very lowly rating because a large part of its earnings came from 'Third World' countries and its attempts to diversify away from tobacco were not always successful. Despite its dull image, BAT increased its earnings and dividends year after year. After it demonstrated above average growth for several years, the market finally took notice of its enormous profitability and great capacity to generate cash and rerated the stock. That resulted in a return of 600 per cent over the period.

Hart reckons his average holding is about five years or, putting it another way, the FCIT portfolio only turns over 20 per cent each year. That is a very low level of change. Many funds run at rates of 100 per cent or more. Hart is reluctant to read too much significance into this holding period, but it does ensure he gets to know his companies and their management, and is able to judge their performance over time, which has to be a plus when you have 250 stocks to follow. By coincidence or, perhaps, by design, that is almost exactly the same number of securities the Fund carried 80 years ago.

There is also the benefit that transaction costs are lower. This is consistent with a man who has the mentality of an investor, not a trader. No holding period need be too long if the story stays the same. Allied Colloids, one of Hart's favourites, has been in his portfolio for over 20 years and made a lot of money for his shareholders. Hart likes it because it's a niche manufacturer in the chemicals sector. Management scores well, too:

"They seem to be batting on a very nice wicket providing a specialist service. Their basic business was manufacturing chemicals to be put into water to make things come to the top or go to the bottom. Over the years, they have diversified into various other chemicals, but all specialties. One area which is growing fast is making chemicals for super absorbent, disposable nappies. We were meeting the management year after year, and they kept on delivering what they said they were going to do. That gave one a lot of confidence."

The same theme occurs at BAT Industries. Year after year, Hart and his colleagues interviewed the management team and they delivered on their predictions. During 1984 the team met with the Chairman or Managing Director of 79 of the 102 companies in the UK portfolio.

"The secret of long-term success in investment is backing good people who, more often than not, achieve what they say they will do."

This philosophy should come as no surprise. Hart places such high importance on the promises and predictions he makes to his own shareholders, promises he has consistently met and even exceeded.

It may seem old hat in 1996, but Hart was one of the first people in the

> *The secret of long-term success in investment is backing good people who, more often than not, achieve what they say they will do.*

investment business to appreciate the importance of management *and* to act on his appreciation by dedicating a significant amount of his time to meeting and following the progress of management.

"Foreign & Colonial was, thanks to the influence of Charles Wainman, the Chairman, the first investment trust to have an industrialist on the board. Previous to that, we had financial people, political people, City people. Also, in those days, back in 1969, there was a bit of a feeling that the broker would get the information. Institutions would be invited to stockbrokers' lunches. It wasn't usual for institutions to have the companies in for meetings. I like to feel we were one of the pioneers. Colin Corness recently retired from Redland, but is now Chairman of Glaxo. I'd known him ever since 1969. He told me that Foreign & Colonial was the first institutional visit that he made. So we were well to the forefront in that way.

"We systematically began to have meetings with companies, trying to get them to come into the office for a meeting or lunch. What with systematic reviewing of results and the management relationship, we got to know the companies very well. If we liked what we heard, we would nibble away and add in difficult markets. That was the way we built up a big holding in BTR. We got to know them well and then just looked for opportunities to buy."

If you examine the reasons that Hart gives for his large investments, a few key themes recur. The companies themselves may be a mixed bag covering a broad cross section of industries and countries, but that one or more of these key themes is present appears to be a prerequisite for every holding of substance in the portfolio:

- strong balance sheet
- strong cash flow
- market leader/world leader
- good international diversification
- fast growing markets/long-term growth business.

It is worth repeating that BTR corporate philosophy: 'Growth is the good, profit is the measure, security is the result.'

Trying to pin Hart down on the secrets of his success from an analytical perspective is even harder than categorising his investment approach. He professes rather a low key, old fashioned stance on the tools of the trade and is almost sheepish about admitting that yes, he does employ some of the same ratios as the rest of the investment community.

"A definition of value is a moving target. It's just the yield and the multiples and the highs and the lows and where the stock has been. There is no single measure. We've been reviewing these companies systematically every time the results come, in the case of American companies, quarterly, and all the usual yardsticks that investment managers use will be on our papers. Also, we list what the bull points are, and what the bear points are. There is a tremendous amount of thought going into whether a company's cheap or dear at a particular moment. When multiples get very high, one is wary. If any of the yardsticks seem to be excessive, certainly we are more cautious. During the nifty fifty period we were very careful not to get over-enthusiastic."

This should not be taken as suggesting that Hart's analysis is, in any sense, sloppy or casual, because nothing could be further from the truth. Hart is, in fact, fanatical about understanding his companies, and making sure that he and his team are up to date on every aspect of their operations and financial performance. He understood the importance of rigorous analysis before that was fashionable. He was one of the earliest members of the Investment Analysts, number 741, to be precise, and always assiduous in attending their meetings.

Another trait which is distinctive and important is the way Hart approaches the purchase of a position. In keeping with his overall cautious philosophy, he does not dive in when he finds a company he likes. He buys a bit. He waits and watches. If the company (not necessarily the stock price) performs up to, or above, expectations, he buys a bit more, and a bit more, and maybe even a bit more after that.

"It's always safer to nibble. That's the way I've operated over the years in investing in the stock market. Especially when the market is a bit gloomy. Part of our success has been because of that approach. With core stocks, when things were going badly, we'd take a little bit more or, if the price got a bit euphoric, we would reduce a bit. The holdings went up and down. The whole thing has been a series of gradual moves rather than wham bam."

A discussion of selling leads to a somewhat different view of Hart's investment style.

"I'm a chap who, 24 hours of the day, thinks about investments and investment situations but, despite reviewing these things, it is possible that one has gone on hoping the situation will turn, and a number of times it hasn't. One has had successes through that policy. We have been stuck with things and, all of a sudden, they've surged forward again. Still, the idea is that, if one loses confidence in the management, then one clears out. The trouble is, these things aren't all

> *If one's had confidence in the situation – nibble away at it.*

that obvious and, a number of times, one made a mistake and stayed in too long.

"One has read a number of books where people say, 'When something's going down you should get out,' but my inclination has tended to be if one's had confidence in the situation, to nibble away at it. That has led me to a number of successes and to only a few disasters."

Always a good test of the theory is to find out in what great investors actually put their own money. In Hart's case, it is very much a case of the chef eating his own cooking. His largest personal holding is in FCIT. He keeps on building up his position each year through the savings scheme: and why not. He could hardly do better anywhere else! Even so, he keeps to his own view of diversification. His personal portfolio includes a spread of top investment trusts, a few blue chip shares, and some index linked and government stocks. The latter are only in for balance, and in case he needs liquidity during a poor patch for the equity markets.

You might think that, with such a stunning success story to his credit, investments are all Michael Hart has time for, but that would be to underestimate the vision of the man. When Hart finally hands over the reins at FCIT, he will have a performance record without compare, but the thing he will be remembered for most is that he made sure many thousands of small investors were able to benefit from his expertise.

It would not be stretching things very far to credit Michael Hart with playing an important role in restoring the respectability and reputation of the investment trust industry. He believes in making capitalism popular and in spreading the benefits as widely as possible. You cannot win hearts and minds without putting something in people's pockets. His own record was the first essential ingredient of this transformation, but an insight in how to open up the trust to the saver in the street was a revolutionary move at the time in England.

"One of the things I'm extremely proud of is that the investment trust industry went through this incredibly difficult time: discounts were rising, the small investor was being driven out by high taxation and institutions were building up their own investment departments, saying they didn't need investment trusts. There was all this predatory activity which came to a climax when the biggest investment trust of all, the Globe Investment Trust, was taken over. We were constantly thinking, 'What on earth can we do?'

"In the 1970s and 1980s, I started doing something which hadn't really been done before. Investment trusts tended to rely on brokers to sell their shares. I read criticism in *The Financial Times* that investment trust managers never bothered talking to the press or institutions so, having read that, I started doing it. Gradually, I built up this presentation talking about how good Foreign & Colonial's performance was. The aim was to try and counteract all the bad things that people were saying about investment trusts.

"Looking at this presentation with sheet after sheet on performance, you might get the impression this is over the top and, if you listen to it, one does bang on, but, in those days, it was very necessary. Comparing ourselves with the 30 share index and all its constituents just to get that message across that Foreign & Colonial hadn't done at all badly against the index and all these blue chips was of vital importance. We impressed institutions that Foreign & Colonial should be the last trust to be attacked, because we had a jolly good record, but we still hadn't solved the problem of the high discounts.

"In 1984, Foreign & Colonial hit on the solution to the investment trust industry's problem. This arose from a visit I made to the States. I called on a few investment managers, including managers of closed-end funds, and one of them, Tricontinental Corp, ran a savings plan for its shareholders, who could send some money along to the Registrars and the Registrars would buy Tricontinental shares and then distribute them to the people that had sent the money. I thought, 'That's a jolly good idea, I wonder, could we do it over here?' No-one thought that it was possible in the UK. In fact, people thought that it was impossible because of the Company's Act, and against the Prevention of Frauds Act.

"We didn't really consult our lawyers at the time. We took a hell of a chance and introduced the new savings scheme initially to our shareholders. When it was well received by the press and shareholders, we opened it up to investors generally. The press liked it, and people began subscribing. I then had a phone call from the Department of Trade & Industry about the Prevention of Frauds Act and asked, 'Can I come round and see you.' The chap said, 'Just alter this and just alter that and it will be all right,' so we managed to get over this regulatory hurdle. One can't imagine that happening these days. We were just incredibly lucky with that window of opportunity. The idea of investment trust savings schemes proved to be an enormous success and, again, this was a continuation of the Foreign & Colonial philosophy of trying new things. As a result, the discounts have been transformed. They have gone up from 30 per cent to next to nothing, and this move proved to be the salvation of the investment trust industry."

The savings scheme received due prominence in the 1984 annual report and underlines Hart's commitment to reaching out to anyone willing to invest. Purchases started at a minimum of £25 for existing shareholders and only £250 for new shareholders. This sort of subscription structure may seem obvious today, but it was a breakthrough at the time. The same modest levels still apply ten years later, with loyal investors who put in the minimum £25 per month enjoying shares valued in excess of £7,000 by the year end 1994.

It is interesting to note that, even in this, Hart is showing a loyalty to the tradition of the torch he carries. His mission to expand the shareholder base is altogether consistent with the original objectives of the Trust as laid down back in 1868. The results have been a spectacular success in meeting the objective of widening the shareholder base of FCIT. From just under 12,000 shareholders in 1984, the register has risen and now records comfortably in excess of 100,000. Each and every one has enjoyed a really good rise. There have to be 100,000 fans of Hart out there! On that basis, he could give Wet Wet Wet a good run for their money.

Michael Hart has a generous spirit. He did not confine his efforts to promoting his own Fund He went to bat for the whole industry.

"In 1989, I was asked to be chairman of the Association of Investment Trusts. I was helping Philip Chappell, the Director General of the Association, with this tremendous battle to convince people that investment trusts were a great way for a small investor to get into the stock market."

Michael Hart is also the first to give credit where credit is due. He is the only constant through the last 25 years at FCIT, but is at pains to emphasise that the accomplishments arise from a team effort. In particular, he credits Eric Elstob, who was officially joint manager in 1971–1994. Others who have made important contributions include Andrew Barker, Ian Wright, Steven White and Jeremy Tigue.

"Investment is a collegiate affair. A lot of people have played a part. In a way, it doesn't quite fit into the theme of the book. There is no star who makes wonderful decisions. At FCIT, it has been rather different."

In the financial environment of the 1990s, with technology and the availability of data changing so much about the way people invest and trade, Hart stands as a beacon of security in a stormy sea of risk and uncertainty. His principle and policies have stood the test of time. His cautious common sense, combined with the courage to make controversial calls about the direction of the market, has prevailed over whichever fad produced top returns for a year. Hart will continue nib-

> **Even leading money managers call FCIT 'their sleep well fund'.**

bling away and investors who like dependable returns and a low tolerance for risk have found a home with Hart. Even leading money managers call FCIT 'their sleep well fund'. There can be no higher compliment.

No wonder *The Sunday Telegraph* saw fit to publish possibly the only positive cartoon on an investment house ever in a leading national newspaper.

"And of course, this is the most valuable of my collection"

First published in *The Sunday Telegraph* on 10 August, 1986. Copyright held by Foreign and Colonial

Cartoon caption: "The most valuable of my collection." An apt comment not only on Foreign & Colonial's enviable track record of financial sucess, but also on their own lack of a pictorial record of their chairmen and their directors. It is argued that it is not in the shareholders' interests for money to be spent on painting portraits of those who run the company.

* Acknowledged leader in Recovery Investing

* Keen on asset value, high turnover and positive cash flow

* The Recovery Fund has converted £40 per month into £27,000 over 15 years!

RICHARD HUGHES

Cash is King

The world of investing came early to Hughes. He was only 11 when he was given ten shares as a birthday present.

"I was quite keen on chemistry, so I chose Philblack which made carbon black for tyres. The shares were 43 shillings and 3 pence (£2.16½), a price they never hit again. They gradually meandered downwards until they were taken over at about 30 shillings (£1.50). Still I used to read the annual accounts and got quite interested and was not discouraged.

"My next share was a local North Wales company called Kwiksave, which Albert Gubay developed into one of the first discount retailers. You could see the queues of people and how popular it was, and that it was a winning formula."

These shares rose 62 per cent in just under two years and by 300 per cent over a total seven year holding period.

The fact that Hughes' father and grandfather both had small private portfolios added to his general interest. While he did not head for the City upon graduation, Hughes always had an affinity for things which were investment oriented and his career quickly took an unexpected turn which allowed this inclination to surface.

"On the very first morning after I had joined Derbyshire County Council, the person in charge of training mentioned, in passing, the fact that Derbyshire managed their own pension fund. His words were, 'It's very unlikely that any of you will end up in that particular section, because it's such a specialist area.' As he was speaking, a little bell was ringing in my mind: 'That sounds much more interesting than the other ten things he's been talking about.'"

Needless to say, that is precisely where Hughes ended up. He had his stint as trainee accountant and worked his apprenticeship on capital budgets for fire engines, but a small move sideways was soon on the agenda, with his desk strategically located adjacent to the pension fund manager.

A local county council sounds like an unpromising start for a high flying financial career, which only goes to show how appearances can be deceptive since, in less than 15 years, Hughes became a main board director of M&G. Leaving that for later, the point which is easy to overlook is that even a middle ranked local government organisation handles a relatively large amount of money. In Derbyshire's case, they had £50 million in 1978 in a pension fund. That £50 million had grown to £300 million by 1986 when Hughes moved on to M&G, a sum significantly more sizeable than almost any unit or investment trust. Responsibility was split amongst a very small team – three, to be precise – so, from day one, Hughes was involved in all aspects of the portfolio. As an added bonus, he was in a surprisingly entrepreneurial environment. The investment parameters encouraged the managers to invest in smallish companies and to take quite large stakes, and even to experiment with unquoted securities. To cap it all off, the range of investments handled was much broader than a relatively young and inexperienced manager could expect to get his hands on in a more traditional environment.

"Initially I was involved in the money market and fixed interest side, managing both borrowing and lending with quite large sums. In my first proper job I could lend someone up to £10 million of the council's money, yet I couldn't authorise the purchase of a pencil sharpener. That's how low the position was in the hierarchy.

"It was a great place to train. The standard at Derbyshire was very high. The people, for the most part, were excellent. You got used to dealing with large sums of money at a very early stage in your career. You learnt how to make quick decisions and you also learnt that you were going to make a lot of mistakes. You had to come to terms with making mistakes.

"Focusing on fixed income markets, you began to see the links between the economy, government policy and interest rates. I can't imagine a better place to be before moving into equity management.

"Matlock (in Derbyshire) is a surprisingly good place to be to learn about equity investment. We actively tried to visit the management of companies we invested in to get to know the businesses. When you think about it, you've got cities like Manchester, Leeds, Sheffield, Bradford, Leicester, Nottingham, Derby, Birmingham – all within an hour or so's drive."

Hughes still follows some of the companies he got to know on his travels while at Derbyshire, though he is pleased to note that "there is only one in the Recovery Fund". The M&G Smaller Companies Fund, where Hughes was involved between 1986 and 1992, has more overlap in its investments. Its portfolio holds EIS, an engineering conglomerate, and Matthew Clark, which is the drinks business and which owns Stone's Ginger Wine, among other interests.

One reason why the transition was so easy is that Hughes feels the philosophy which prevails at M&G is not so very different from the one he operated under at Derbyshire. In fact, the reason he made the move arose from a common holding in a company called Neepsend. Neepsend had got into difficulties in the early 1980s with an investment in a steel mill.

"The financial state was precarious. The company needed the support of shareholders and the bank to keep it going."

Hughes worked closely with David Tucker, manager of the Recovery Fund at M&G at that time, as the representatives of the two most interested equity holders, and accomplished a complete turn around. Ironically, the one common company in the M&G Recovery Fund, as of 1995, was Neepsend,

> *We take a long-term view of performance and try not to be deflected by short-term considerations.*

now on the mend once more after a return visit to the sick bay.

The M&G philosophy is clearly and consistently articulated across all its public documents, be they reports to shareholders or marketing brochures. The following extract is taken from the 1994 M&G Year Book distributed to Independent Financial Advisors:

> M&G's investment philosophy is to concentrate on long-term value with an emphasis on income and recovery, and a general reluctance to invest in highly rated fashionable stocks.
>
> M&G funds have holdings of 5 per cent or more in the equity capital of about 250 companies. We make a point of getting to know the people who run these companies because we believe that a substantial investor should have a firm and lasting relationship with the managements of companies in which they have a large interest.
>
> We do not presume to tell the management how to run their business but, if a company's actions are likely to jeopardise the interest of shareholders, we find that constructive intervention can often be preferable to disposing of a holding. This means that we take a long-term view of performance and try not to be deflected by short-term considerations. This seems to us to be in the best interests of both industry and our own investors.

This introduction to M&G is a statement of context for the investment approach Richard Hughes inherited from David Tucker when he took over the Recovery Fund and which he refined, with considerable success, over the subsequent eight years.

RECOVERY INVESTING

The essence of what works for Hughes can be gleaned by the title of the main fund for which he is responsible. Recovery, in the world of investing, has no unique meaning. Quoting again from the same IFA Year Book:

> This unit trust follows a speculative policy: investing in the shares of companies which are going through a difficult period. The managers are continually seeking new holdings to replace those where the prospects of recovery appear to have been fulfilled or where they seem to have been unfounded. Capital growth is the sole objective and yield considerations are ignored.

"The original philosophy when the fund started was not very scientific. If you buy something that other people think is going to go bust, but there is a reasonable chance or recovery, you get a good return. David Tucker very ably and skilfully refined this from his experience.

"The key is buying cheap. For that you need a fair amount of bad news. You need other investors to be disillusioned with the sector or the company. You want the whole world to know all the bad news. That would mean the maximum negative impact on the share price and, of course, you need a solution to the problem.

"The solution could be money, management, or the passage of time. The best combination really is money and management, where the company has to raise new money to repair the balance sheet and the mistakes of the previous regime. Able new management either has come in or is about to come in.

"Psychologically, a lot of institutions and shareholders are so fed up with an investment they've seen fall from £5 to, say, £1. The last thing they want to do is put more money in, no matter how compelling the case. Managers may have had a lot of grief from their trustees or bosses on the stock, asking 'Why are you holding it? It's gone down and down and down.' Many would rather not explain why they're putting more money into such a stock.

"This means the rights issue itself is usually done at a very depressed level and does give people like the Recovery Fund a chance to go in."

What is a prototype recovery investment?

"Granada had an issue at £1.40 which wasn't particularly successful. People were thoroughly fed up with Granada and its poor record. I was able to take a pretty good holding at about that price. The subsequent arrival of Gerry Robinson made it work. He improved margins, started careful cash management and turned a dog into a recovery star. OK, he had one or two lucky breaks, like BSkyB. What happened next is apparent when you look at Chart 7.1. These shares went to £5.60 and higher almost in a straight line. What had been shunned suddenly had people queuing up to come in again, while we quadrupled our money quite quickly.

"The disillusion amongst shareholders not willing to support a rights issue and a new manager coming in and good housekeeping, more than anything else, made this opportunity for us.

"Another good example is Bunzl which, when James White was running it, was doing an acquisition a week. You could just sit there

Chart 7.1 Share Price of Granada Group (29.2.88 – 4.3.96)

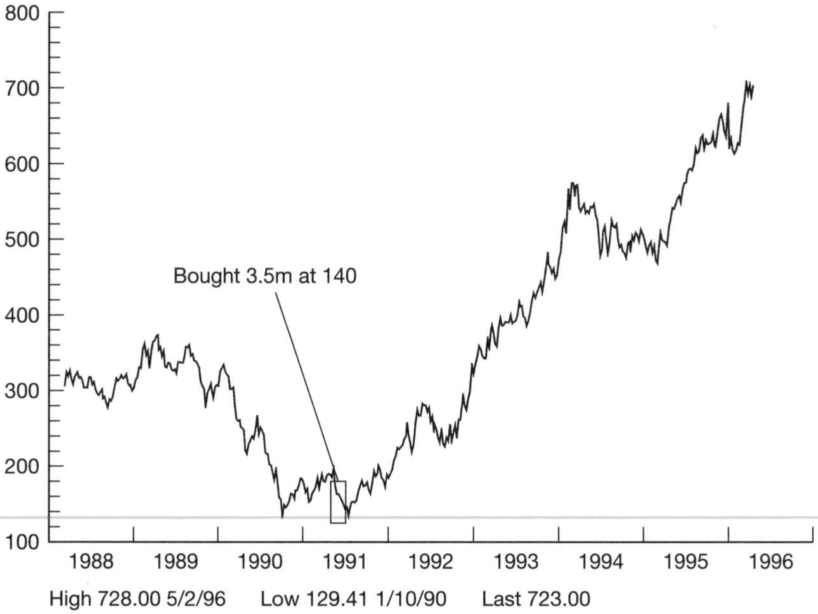

High 728.00 5/2/96   Low 129.41 1/10/90   Last 723.00

Source: Datastream

161

waiting for it to go wrong. You knew that anyone who expanded at that sort of pace could never integrate the business properly and could never be sure whether they were buying a problem business. Yet, all the time, there were some good businesses going into it.

"In due course, things did go wrong. The institutions got fed up. James White left. The shares collapsed from 180 down to 60 odd pence. David Kendall came in as the new chairman and he made a very good appointment of Tony Habgood as Chief Executive who had a brief spell at Tootal working on a turn-around there before the takeover by Coats Viyella. At Bunzl he identified the US building business as being the biggest problem area and established that before selling it to Rugby. A few more minor disposals and better management of the main divisions, and you can see the results in Chart 7.2."

It all sounds so easy but, of course, there is a lot of spadework which goes in up front before Hughes can be convinced that a company is ready for him to put his cash in. One of his great strengths is the way he has gone about identifying suitable recovery candidates. There are several clear criteria which go into the hopper for consideration.

Chart 7.2 Bunzl Share Price (29.2.88 – 4.3.96)

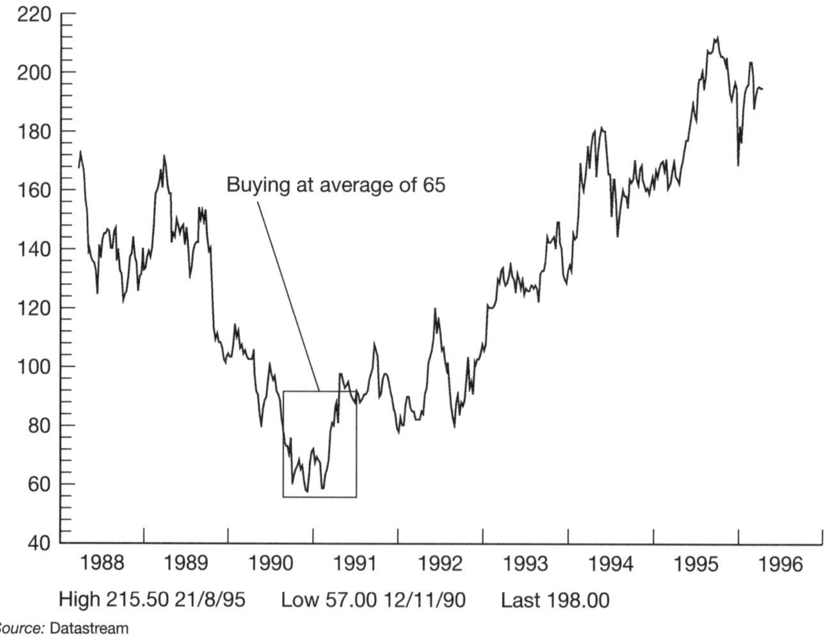
220
200
180
160
140
120
100
80
60
40
Buying at average of 65
1988
1989
1990
1991
1992
1993
1994
1995
1996
High 215.50 21/8/95
Low 57.00 12/11/90
Last 198.00

Source: Datastream

"I like to see a sound business underneath somewhere. You may find there's only one sound business and two or three not so good ones; but there has to be some sort of *jewel* in there worth saving. Once today's problems are out of the way, there has to be something people can focus on and get excited about. That is important.

"Take Philips, the Dutch giant, which was a good one for us. The disasters there were pretty thoroughly covered on the front pages of *The Financial Times*. Yet this was a company which had £25 billion in turnover and had a number of successful businesses, such as Polygram. The share price had gone down, following these stories, to about DFl 18, and it's been as high as DFl 80.

"A new manager, Jan Timmer, moved up from one division to hammer away at the whole. They were committed to going through some kind of restructuring programme. You found they were selling off businesses no-one even knew they had for millions. Slowly, but surely, the ship began to turn as the effects of the cutback came through.

"I like to see *asset value* in the business, which means you are looking more at manufacturing generally than at service. If the plans don't work out, you have a potential escape route through an asset sale. That protects your downside. Tangible assets are generally more useful. Property in the UK has historically retained its value rather better, so you have to take some account of the split. I've seen many companies who have been able to sell what looked like a grotty piece of land or an old factory, as areas change, into nice shiny supermarkets. Then something on the books at £100,000 is suddenly worth £1 million. You don't often sell old stocks at ten times book value.

"The total assets are more important. An asset can even be intangible, if it is something like a brand. You felt that, if they can't make a profit out of it, someone else will come in. There is a value which you will be paid for.

"One example, which shows how long these investments can run, is Burmah. The company was virtually bust in 1974, when David Tucker took a stake. Management has been refocusing on their core business of Castrol over time, which is a jewel. They have used their base to build a fantastic position in the Far East, are still growing in the US and are now opening up Eastern Europe. There is the making of a worldwide brand at Burmah. We still hold some stock 20 years later, and the price we paid for the first shares was less than the current dividend.

"I like to see lots of *turnover*, as long as it's capable of producing a good profit margin.

"I care about *cash flow*, so a high depreciation charge is helpful. Not making a profit never drove anyone into receivership, but a shortage of

> **Not making a profit never drove anyone into receivership, but a shortage of cash is critical.**

cash is critical. The emphasis is on the cash flow position. I'm willing to invest in companies where there's not going to be any profits for a year or two, as long as the cash flow is strong enough to stop it going bust. British Steel could be a very good example from the last recession of a company facing a severe squeeze on profits, but the cash management was very good. Once conditions improved, there was every prospect of a rapid return to profitability and for excellent cash generation. You can follow the recovery in Chart 7.3. Cash is king for a recovery fund manager. Can they manage the cash and avoid going bust? If yes, you have a possible investment."

Chart 7.3 British Steel Share Price (29.2.88 – 4.3.96)

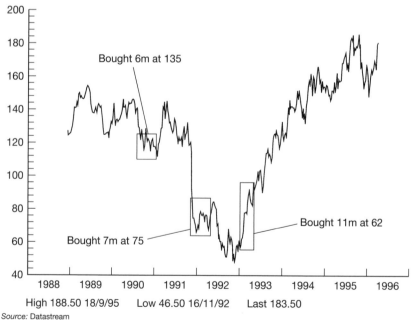

High 188.50 18/9/95   Low 46.50 16/11/92   Last 183.50

Source: Datastream

164

"The impact of *gearing* has changed. We have lived in an era with very high real interest rates for quite a while now, and I have found that to de-gear in this climate can be extremely difficult. My mistakes have been in companies which were too highly geared, so I am now more wary of gearing than a traditional recovery manager. Look at Lowndes Queensway, where the price had fallen 95 per cent, but tackling the debt overwhelmed them. If real interest rates came down, I would reconsider this aspect of my evaluation."

On share price, Hughes is somewhat ambivalent.

"I wouldn't buy 20 companies whose share price has gone down by 90 per cent. Usually there's a good reason for a 90 per cent fall and, if you did buy the 20, you'd probably wish you hadn't. I might buy three or four where the shares have fallen 90 per cent, three or four where they've fallen 75 per cent, three or four where they've fallen 50 per cent and 25 per cent. It's to try and have a balance."

The first step is finding companies to evaluate. Some of Hughes' process can only be replicated by organisations with depth of personnel and resources, but the proliferation of lower cost databases and on-line current information means the individual

> *People make the difference in a recovery. The degree of turnaround is usually attributable to the quality in the changing of the guard.*

investor willing to put in the spadework should be able to follow a not dissimilar path.

"Usually I follow hundreds of companies – almost like a vulture waiting in case something goes wrong. Suppose, subsequently, there is a catastrophe in one division, but knowing there is a good business elsewhere that can be a trigger. I'm almost waiting for an accident to happen.

"Look for a rights issue, because then you can often get a great deal more information than usual about plans and more detail on the operation than in the normal course of business. That is often a stimulus."

People make the difference in a recovery. At the end of the day, the deciding factor can often be management. The degree of turnaround is usually attributable to the quality in the changing of the guard.

"You get overshoots in everything. In a depressed company, there tends to be a culture of despondency and failure. With changes in management, the dog can become the best performer, because the potential is there, with margin improvement to treble or quadruple the value more quickly. When someone is going in to turn around a business, then it's important to meet and make a judgement as to the real values and the ability of new management to make an impact."

Hughes is acutely sensitive to how this most elusive of considerations enters into his calculation of whether to invest or leave something alone.

"Differentiating between someone you can trust and picking out the manager who knows the business from one who merely presents well is the toughest part of the investment decision. The report and accounts are our primary document, and you have to believe the figures, even though, in some highly publicised disasters, the figures have turned out to be highly dubious. So you have to trust the people producing the figures rather than putting too much faith in the numbers themselves.

> *Differentiating between someone you can trust and the manager who merely presents well is the toughest part of the investment decision.*

"The strongest factor is knowing them in a different company. If I've come across them before and they've done a good job somewhere else, that gives the greatest amount of confidence in a recovery situation. There do seem to be people with that knack. It doesn't have to be the same industry."

Hughes has seen more or less every manager with any pretensions to be an expert in this area. He picked out a few he feels are the sort shareholders can have confidence in backing.

"There's a man called Peter Frost, currently chairman of Renold, who has a very good track record. Gerry Robinson at Granada has done a terrific job there. I would back Tony Hapgood. It's early days, but a man called John Allen has gone into Ocean Group and the signs are good. John Clark at BET did a fantastic job. The cash generation he was able to drive within the company was phenomenal. Martin Taylor at Barclays is not exactly a company doctor, but is very good. Christopher Hogg was one. Richard Oster at Cookson has done very well. There is a company called Arlington which is a firm of consultants that got involved in Fenner and I was impressed with them. Colin Cook, the Chairman there, is good. I would be inclined to back a company if they were going in. Knox D'Arcy is another one which has had some success in this area."

There are other aspects to assessing people, both positive and negative. Hughes touches on several of the factors which he looks for when meeting and evaluating a management team.

"The quality of the analysis of problems they have inherited, and the realism within that, and the quality of the analysis of how to get out of the hole – again being realistic – is essential. I like to see examples of lessons learnt elsewhere which can be applied.

"I also like to see a management team with a decent shareholding in the company to show their own confidence. It's a very good discipline to have your own money at risk, along with the shareholders'. It adds to the level of commitment.

"I'm looking for enthusiasm for the company and its products. If management can't be excited by what they are doing, why should I invest. I remember a company lunch with Cookson in the late 1980s before their current team came in 1991. They were unable to recognise that there was a recession around which would impact their business and they didn't seem to understand how this would affect their financial position. Yes, they had some good businesses, but I resolved not to touch the stock there. Instead, it went on the watch list and we started to follow the company, expecting things to go wrong. At the time, the price was about 200p, and had been as high as 400p. In due course, the company had problems, and the share price halved. We came in at 110p."

Recovery Stocks Attract Corporate Attention

One very important byproduct of Hughes' stock picking is that he often ends up getting liquidity because his investments are bought out. Corporate acquirers tend to be more cautious, waiting to see how a capital reconstruction works before making a bid. Hughes is involved at an earlier stage in a turnaround, so it is only natural that take-overs have been helpful in realising returns for the Recovery Fund. This comment in the September 1992 Managers' Report is typical:

> The Fund's best performing investment was Midland Bank, whose shares nearly doubled over the period, following the bid from HSBC Holdings. There were also bids for three of our other holdings, Walter Lawrence, Taveners and Cronite, all of which were the subject of agreed cash offers at prices well above those prevailing before the bid.

As you track back through the biannual Managers' Reports, there is not a period in which some holding in the Fund did not attract a suitor, and always at a significant premium to the basis in the investment. Indeed, Hughes is not unmindful of this aspect of his activity, and it is one input into his selection process.

"I like companies which a conglomerate might look at. A business which Hanson, BTR or Tomkins might look at and feel they could run better, or might fit in with one of their divisions. We're pretty sceptical about take-overs at M&G, but we have benefited when Hanson offers £1.50 for something you have paid £1 for a few months earlier. We don't buy just for the take-over, but we often do have large stakes in companies which are taken over. We had 9 per cent of Fisons and quite a large holding in Kleinwort Benson. I do try and think of how an industrialist might regard the company."

It is worth noting that take-overs were one of the key success ingredients at the M&G Smaller Companies Fund where Hughes also played a part. The year end statement in 1986 refers to a plethora of take-over bids and lists ten – not bad for a fund holding all of 83 quoted UK securities during the period. It is axiomatic that smaller companies are more likely to be bought than bigger businesses, in the same way that recovery stocks make better bites than high flying growth stocks. Combine the two and you are in the sweet spot of any take-over activity.

A Diversified Portfolio is Essential

One drawback to the recovery style of investing is that there will always be losers. When you fish in troubled waters, some boats will sink. Bankruptcy is a cost of recovery investing, but an acceptable one. The key is to ensure the spread is sufficient so that those that fail are never too material. When Alpha Estates went into receivership around July 1991, it represented only 0.03 per cent of the Fund; Clearmark, which went under about February 1992, cost Hughes only 0.15 per cent at the time of its demise.

RECOVERY CYCLES

A recovery play can follow one of three main lines: (a) the market as a whole, (b) an industry sector or (c) a specific company.

Some of these cycles can operate simultaneously and, in certain cases for highly cyclical stocks, these factors can all combine to be at precisely the same stage which makes for a particularly powerful surge. In other instances, specific circumstances can conspire to create problems that pertain only to the company which has the virtue of ensuring a benign economic environment to facilitate the recovery.

(a) The Market

There are always going to be periods when the overall market is more receptive to Hughes, and when he will find a greater choice of companies in which to invest. The converse also operates against a recovery style. In his August 1994 letter to unit shareholders in the Recovery Fund, the Chairman wrote:

> Our experience is that, in the early stages of recovery from recession, the shares of the leading 'blue chip' companies usually make the running, with Recovery Fund lagging behind, but that the situation is often reversed later on, with Recovery Fund tending to catch up and outperform the broadly based indices.

The January 1993 letter makes a similar point, though at a very different stage in the UK economic cycle:

> Recovery Fund's investment policy, of investing in companies which are going through a difficult time, is bound to result in poor performance during a recession as the recovery process takes longer than usual. Nevertheless, as soon as the general market opinion is that the economy is improving, Recovery Fund has tended to outperform the broadly based indices. This is just what is happening now.

"The Fund is cyclical and, typically, I will be buying quite a lot at times of recession when there are lots of companies in trouble and lots of choice. There are lots of sharp falls in share prices. Then I will be less active during the recovery stage. You do have to try and phase your investment during the downturn, and not buy all at once. If you buy too early, the price can fall further."

> *You do have to try and phase your investment during the downturn, and not buy all at once.*

A combination of an inflection point in the economic cycle and an event which acts as a catalyst to that change creates especially propitious circumstances for a recovery investor. Hughes describes the single most significant point in recent times as occurring in the early 1990s, but comparable circumstances will recur and provide other opportunities with similar upside; and then investors should seize the moment.

"When the UK came out of the ERM in September 1992, I was on holiday. I got back to find 15 per cent interest rates and people saying the whole country would go bust by Christmas. Everyone was running around making contingency plans. What they should have been doing was to take out a second mortgage and buy units in the Recovery Fund. We were up 70 per cent in the subsequent six months."

(b) Industry Sector

One level down come industry cycles which Hughes has been able to follow in the same way, timing his entry to a specific sector to catch a rising tide. Banking is an area where he has done particularly well, spotting recovery around the corner at Midland Bank and at Standard Chartered.

"The team at M&G was convinced that the scope for outperformance at Midland was substantial, if Kit McMahon could cut costs. There were initiatives such as First Direct and the Hong Kong and Shanghai Bank shareholding, but the UK recession had affected the performance, and Midland Bank also cut its dividend in February 1991. The shares dipped below 200p and we made an additional purchase, trebling our holding to 13 million shares. The departure of Kit McMahon proved to be the turning point which eventually led to a bid from HSBC, the intervention of Lloyds Bank and a higher offer from HSBC. The final offer, in June 1992, valued Midland at 471p. We actually ran the new HSBC shares, as we felt there was scope for further recovery. They went from 339p, at the time of the bid, to £10 before taking profits and finally disposing of the holding in June 1994.

"Standard Chartered fought off a bid of 820p from Lloyds Bank in 1986. The bank soon ran into problems. A new chairman was put in place, disposals were made and a rights issue raised £300 million in 1988 at 400p a share. The recession in the UK hit many of the bank's customers and the shares fell to 208p in February 1991, following a cut dividend. We started to buy during this period, convinced that the Far East business was very valuable. I had visited the bank's operations in

Hong Kong, Singapore and Malaysia and was impressed. In spite of losing £300 million in India in 1992, the underlying values were there, and the share price began to reflect that. The fund started to sell on the back of this interest, finally disposing of its last holding at £10 in 1994."

Not all shareholders would have a lot of positive things to say about making money out of British bank shares over the last 15 years, but Hughes has, following his recognition of the recovery potential in the sector in the late 1980s.

(c) Specific Stocks

Regardless of what is happening in either the economy overall or in a particular industry sector, there will always be companies that run into trouble, and for individualistic reasons, become attractive to Hughes.

"Texaco had filed for Chapter 11. There was a convincing case below $30. It was in litigation, being sued by Pennzoil over the Getty purchase. The court in Texas awarded damages of $9 billion and the shares collapsed. The company filed for protection under Chapter 11. The share price fall discounted the full settlement and created a buying opportunity. The eventual settlement was around $3 billion, the stock recovered swiftly and, by May 1988, Carl Icahn was willing to offer $60 a share."

The cyclical element in recovery investing activates a formative time frame, during which it becomes clear whether an investment is working out. In theory, this means Hughes expects to hold a stock for about six years – two years for the recovery stage, and then four years of good growth. In practice, the portfolio turns over about 35 per cent each year, which means his average holding period is three years, helped along, in part, as predators pick off proven turnaround successes.

When to sell is not a subject which demands as much thought, given Hughes' particular philosophy. He has developed very clear and simple guidelines which trigger that process and set off a new cycle of searching for a replacement.

"Selling is a sign that the company has achieved a great deal . . . they are no longer seen as a problem company. They are successful and everyone now likes them. It's part of a normal cycle.

"When the profits have recovered to what you might call industry average, and when the stock market rating is also average, then we become sellers. Put these two things together, and you've got very little scope for further appreciation."

The Peter Lynch shopping mall syndrome is now well known. Invest in what you know is the main message; but there is a subsidiary theme which is also important. Everyone can use their own individual expertise to advantage, because no-one, professionals included, has a monopoly on wisdom when it comes to selecting specific stocks. Hughes, who is a consummate professional himself, can point to examples along this line in his own career.

> **Invest in what you know.**

"When I lived in Sheffield, I was about 300 yards away from a Wickes store. My father was in the building trade. When we did odd jobs around the house, we used to go there to get materials and he was very, very impressed with the quality, prices and availability. He thought it looked like a very successful operation. This was back in 1982 or 1983, and that is a little fact which got stowed away in the back of my mind.

"Later on, Wickes came to the market at a very high rating and was not suitable for my fund. They then, however, made a very large acquisition from Hillsdown. They went into the timber business at the top of the cycle with too much gearing and it knocked them for six. The core business grew through recession, but they were brought to their knees by the timber side. When they had to be refinanced to rescue them from this over-expansion I knew the Wickes story and here was an opportunity to go in.

"These problems have taken far longer to resolve than expected, but the Hunter division has now been disposed of and the core business continues to do well. Personal knowledge put this company onto the watch list, and only some years afterwards, when they got into trouble, was there an opportunity for me to invest."

Although a successful investment, the failure to fire on all cylinders resulted in Hughes beginning to sell the stake in April 1996. Sadly, the emergence in June of accounting problems which explained some of the company's success, sent Wickes straight back to the recovery ward.

Don't Lose Money

One of the key attributes of every successful manager is an ability to avoid big losses. This is a recurring feature which can be observed time and time again. Regardless of asset class, geographic focus, investment style, or any other factor, this one commonality stands out. Recovery investing is a minefield of problem businesses where the potential for backing a loser is at its greatest. Hughes has the record he has, in large part, because he did avoid the big disasters of the late 1980s and early 1990s.

"British and Commonwealth, Polly Peck, Coloroll, Brent Walker and Maxwell were five big stocks every recovery fund had to take a good look at. We passed on them all. In every case there was no meaningful change which could cause things to go better. There was no new management. You cannot rely on the same people to turn things round. The person who dug the hole is not the right person to lead the company out. There was no catalyst for change, no bodies tossed out onto the streets. If the colourful entrepreneur is still there, we won't support a financial restructuring."

Management can be one red flag. Another can be found in the accounts of a company. Any kind of unorthodox financial manoeuvres when a business is in a highly leveraged position is a sign investors should stay away. Hughes remembers reviewing C H Industrial, another he kept out of.

"They had expanded too rapidly and got over-geared. In the notes to the accounts, two days before their year end, they had entered into an agreement where they sold their debtors and then reversed the transaction two days later. This sort of blatant financial engineering was a strong signal to stay away, despite there being some good businesses in the company.

"There was a situation with a textile company which had an investment on its books valued at 30p a share when the market price of the stock was 5p. That business also went bust."

When asked to pick one stock which epitomises the recovery style, Hughes zeroed in on Cookson. Cookson (the old Lead Industries) had its largest business, back in 1988, in manufacturing industrial materials, mainly for the steel and electronics industry, though, by 1996, it had grown the electronic materials part of its business. The ups and downs of the Cookson share price are covered in Chart 7.4.

"This was a terrific case study. We had a watching brief as the stock fell, knowing there were good businesses which had real value in there, to the final point of the rescue rights. I followed the company all through 1987, 1988 and 1989, sensing something was going to go hor-

Chart 7.4 Cookson Share Price (29.2.88 – 4.3.96)

High 343.59 21/8/89   Low 62.14 22/10/90   Last 317.00

Source: Datastream

ribly wrong. You could see they were paying high prices for acquisitions, not all of which made sense, but some were fundamentally good businesses, just expensive, and funding these deals with too much debt and not generating enough cash to pay down the debt. Cookson was over-leveraged with a severe recession looming. Even so there was an ability to build on the core business as well as to divest others to rebuild the balance sheet.

"When Oster took control, one of the first things he did was to sell his own family business, which showed he was a strong manager. Once the cash crisis was over, he began a much more focused acquisition programme, paying more sensible prices, keeping the balance sheet balanced, and shifting the portfolio into higher growth businesses."

Three characteristics which permeate Hughes' career both at Derbyshire and at M&G are:

(i)   a willingness to take a large position in a business;
(ii) a focus on smaller companies;
(iii) long-term holdings.

There's not a lot the average investor can do about the first, but there's a lot of merit in the second and third. Not least, management at smaller companies are likely to be more accessible and more interested in cultivating a base of individual shareholders. Long-term holders learn a lot more about their investments.

"We will go up to 15 per cent, which is very concentrated. For our type of fund, it is very sensible. The larger stake will allow you to build up a level of understanding, and even trust, with management over time. This will repay you. They will consult you on issues and are reluctant to do anything you don't want them to. Being an important shareholder and being long-term is core to our approach."

Hughes is strictly a stock picker, and has no interest in other asset categories. Given the nature of the Fund, there are periods when he will find many more attractive opportunities and others when the landscape looks barren. His refuge can only be in cash, and there have been moments when Hughes has been heavily in cash. In late 1988, he was hit with a double whammy. An unusual level of take-overs meant a large amount of money released that needed to be reinvested. At the same time, strong performance lead to a large inflow of new investors and increased investment from existing shareholders.

> *As a recovery manager, I want to see big swings and people making mistakes.*

"There was this huge wall of money at a time when you could see the UK was coming close to recession after a long period of economic growth."

Even so, cash levels in the Recovery Fund never ran above 7 per cent. The solution Hughes saw was to find stocks elsewhere in other geographic regions.

Recovery investing is likely to remain much the same, for the years ahead, unless someone repeals the economic cycle. Hughes is confident there will be excellent returns from following a similar strategy over the next decade.

"As long as you buy at the bottom, you should make money. We are betting on the ability of management to change a company and, if a stock could go up ten times, if it all works, you can still make money, even if it only is a partial success. There's a lot of margin for us to be wrong.

"As a recovery fund manager, I don't want to see 20 years of unbroken economic growth and steady government. I want to see big swings and people making mistakes."

Chart 7.5 M&G Recovery Fund Performance versus Indices

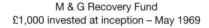

M & G Recovery Fund
£1,000 invested at inception – May 1969

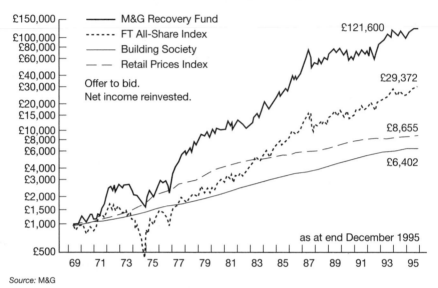

Source: M&G

"When Labour gets back in, there could be opportunities with some of the privatised sectors in the UK. It's possible investors will panic, and some of these shares will collapse. More interesting will be if they bring in various forms of control, which has a real and quantifiable impact on the business that could cause investors to overreact and drive the price down to levels below that which is warranted by the economic changes. If they put a cap on water charges and the shares fall too far, I could become a buyer."

The Recovery Fund is one of the great success stories of the UK unit trust industry. Not only has it maintained Micropal first quartile ranking throughout its life, which is an amazing long-term achievement, but shareholders have also been rewarded with the sort of exceptional growth in asset value which is shown in Chart 7.5.

If any further evidence is needed to validate the merit of recovery style investing, this sort of performance should seal the case. While each individual needs to adopt a style which they can be comfortable with, or results will disappoint, any investor following the recovery methodology articulated by Hughes, and who pursues it with the same sort of dedication and tenacity, should do well. Failing that, there is always the M&G Recovery Fund, where Hughes is likely to be in charge for many years to come.

We are not talking here about large investments. M&G Recovery is accessible to just about anyone with even a modest amount to put aside and has the added plus of being eligible for PEPs. A mere £40 invested monthly in the Recovery Fund over the fifteen year period to 31 December 1995 would have turned a total contribution of £7,200 into over £27,000. That is something to think about for the small saver, and shows the sense of starting early when you can latch onto an investment vehicle with the superior long-term performance record of M&G Recovery Fund and a manager with the steadfast hands of a Richard Hughes.

* A career out of avoiding the obvious

* "The nearest thing to Superman in fund management"
The Sunday Telegraph

* Always outperformed for blue chip clients like
Argyll/Safeway, the BBC and British Rail – by a
substantial margin

LEONARD LICHT

Flexibility is Everything

It is always interesting to see why people choose a particular profession, and even more interesting when they become a star in their chosen field. Licht claims his move into investing came from 'a lack of choice,' but dig a little deeper and you find a motivation which stems from early success in making money. In Licht's case, he collected stamps from the age of seven, specialising in the UK. Already he showed signs of recognising unusual value, which was to become his hallmark as an investment manager.

"I was always looking out for unique items and bought varieties of ordinary stamps which other people didn't understand and I did. Then more people cottoned on to this, so I made relatively quite large sums of money as their interest raised the prices. The stamp could go up £50 or even £100 as the scarcity value was understood – which, for 1970, was a lot."

Substitute the word 'stock' for stamp, and you are already part of the way to understanding what has made Licht such a success: he understands unusual values before the crowd. Licht's best deal was the discovery of some 5/- (25p) regular stamps with an inverted watermark. He bought blocks of them from the Post Office and sold them on as individual stamps to dealers for £12 each on the same day.

Warburgs seemed like the obvious move in 1963 when Licht was ready to enter the investment business.

"I suppose it was my German Jewish background. My parents were refugees, having lost all our money in the War. Warburgs was not exactly a haven, but it felt more like home than any of the other alternatives."

Licht had none of the formal professional qualifications which are almost a *sine qua non* today to get a resumé beyond the waste paper basket. For those who believe that success comes only to those who start at the very bottom and work their way up the ladder rung by rung, Licht's career provides a beacon of hope. You could not begin with a more lowly position than his first job as a clerk – with absolutely no authority to do anything but watch how other people performed. In many respects, that was a godsend. Lacking any guidance or constraints, Licht was free to experiment and learn his own lessons, encouraged by the Warburg philosophy of that era, punting with his own, very modest portfolio.

"The investment division was really rather amateur. I had the lowliest job around, filing exchange telegraph cards, which bored me, so I read them, which was much more interesting. Soon after joining I started buying and selling shares for myself. Warburgs was quite keen that its employees lost their own money and so knew how hard it was. Of course, that was a different era. I admit that I thought it was jolly good learning like that.

"My first investment was a Warburg new issue around September 1963. My grandmother started me off with £400. I had been told that a Warburg new issue would never fail. The company was a coal merchant. I tasted blood because it did go to a premium, and I cashed in for a quick profit."

Licht's meticulous records show that his very first share was Renwick, Wilton and Dobson, purchased on 15 September 1963 for £157 10s and sold on 15 November for a profit of £14 4s 3d. So coming out of the box he had booked a profit of just under 10 per cent in two months, or net 58 per cent annualised to be precise: an auspicious start. Not all subsequent trades were so successful, but net, Licht's personal portfolio grew at a comfortable clip, though it continued to be characterised by the sort of rapid turnover which is a commission agent's dream.

After about five years, Licht was finally let loose with very small bits of client money. In part, one suspects because his bosses had become aware just how good his progress was, and decided it was time to tap into a talent which was wasted on more menial pursuits.

"At this time, the investment divisions of most banks were very secondary or tertiary and many of the people in them were sub-standard. There was no concept of an investment business and most people weren't particularly interested in making money for their clients, or even for themselves. To start off I was given eight private clients. They were all demanding people whom no-one else would want, and that is probably why I got them, but I only found this out afterwards. They were discretionary, but you had to phone up on a regular basis. They were experts in their own field, while I was 24 and constantly second guessing. But I did all right for them. It was a fairly undisciplined business back then, so I was pretty much left to play the field."

He continued to demonstrate outperformance of his peers, while maintaining an above average churn of stocks in these accounts. This first experience is a complete contrast with the style Licht came to espouse later. If there is one lesson he feels that too many investors ignore, it is the importance of longevity in holding onto a strong stock.

"The great winners are the ones you hold for a long period of time. I made money at first but, with most of the stocks, I could have made more if I had held them longer. Manchester Ship Canal was a company we bought at £1 and sold at £2 after around two years, when there were questions about profit growth which proved transitory. Around ten years later, it was taken over at £30."

> *The great winners are the ones you hold for a long period of time.*

The history of the growth of Warburgs/Mercury into one of the powerhouses of the British investment management scene is inextricably linked to the rise and rise of Licht. Not that he would ever claim to be responsible. He just happened to be there; but, of course, there is more to it than that – much more. It was the performance of the funds managed, in large part by Licht in the late 1970s, that caused many long standing relationships to double up their commitment, attracted in new clients and set in motion a classic virtuous cycle.

Licht's first structured responsibility came when, in 1972, he was given the management of a very small unit trust called Tyndall Ulster.

"Tyndall had its origins in a group of Methodists out of Bristol and was one of Warburgs' oldest and biggest clients. It was very tiny, only about half a million pounds, but it doubled in 18 months. We had a big holding in Lex warrants. I was convinced that Lex was the only highly motivated, well managed garage group in an era of expanding car sales. The warrants were a geared play."

There is a chronology to the Licht story which bears recording. The investment themes in which his success has its roots form part of a mosaic which came together over a period of 20 plus years. Each was very much a child of its particular period. Having entered the business at an early age, Licht has seen many fads come and go and has hung onto a few enduring investment truths which he has used to make money for his clients time and time again.

ASSET VALUE

The first to take shape was the appreciation of assets as a long-term, reliable indicator of real underlying value.

"This came together in the early 1970s. 1974 was a watershed year. It was a great leveller, but Warburgs didn't make the mistake of selling shares, going into gold and then not getting back in, which others did. We didn't panic; and then the arrival of 1975 was the start of a 20 year bull market. This is when the discount to assets really came into play. The only question was how deep could you go. Ten pound notes in the street were either £2 or £5 to pick up in the stock market.

"The stores group, for example, had sites which had values totally divorced from their share prices, and property companies themselves had silly capitalisations. These companies were always easily understood shares with an asset underpinning. Therefore, some of the greatest investment successes in those days were the retailers. We were able to buy Burtons at a fraction of true asset value.

"Because they were controlled by the family, no-one thought the value would ever be realised; but I was confident the voting structure had to change at some stage. Our clients, who were pension funds, had long-term liabilities. So for them to own assets at a substantial discount made sense because, eventually, the value would come out."

BUSINESS RATHER THAN FINANCIAL VALUATION

The second in line was to put on a businessman's hat and see where there was a gaping gap between the market value of the public equity and the intrinsic value of the business itself.

"Take-overs were all everyone else was actually doing. In the UK you had such easy take-over rules. I was not spotting them – just doing the work of an ordinary businessman looking at the stock market. My approach is to buy a share on the same basis that someone might buy the company. You look at the enterprise value, not the price of one share in the market.

"For 20 years the great trend to follow by which you could make money was to find under-utilised assets and to trade the take-overs. One early example from the 1960s was Pressed Steel. The company manufactured steel panels for British Motor Corporation. I didn't think any other world motor company had that sort of process done for them at that time. Every other company was vertically integrated. So it didn't take a complete genius to know that, at some stage, BMC would have to buy it. And they did."

When, in September 1965, BMC made the move which Licht, and virtually no-one else, had seen to be inevitable, he netted over a 60 per cent profit for a position he held for less than 15 months.

"It may sound a bit pretentious but, looking back, what I was trying to do was to think like an entrepreneur rather than as a fund manager."

AVOID THE OBVIOUS

At Mercury, Licht started down an idiosyncratic path both in his investment style and in the way he managed client accounts.

"Increasingly, as the 1970s developed, I was given a pretty open brief. I disliked the obvious. I was not enamoured of what everyone else was doing. Back then, you could go into areas where literally no-one else was interested. They weren't speculative businesses, just neglected. Twenty years ago, these were abundant. Today the analogy would be to people in the computer sector who find new areas of software where no-one else is looking. To them this is making large sums of money out of the obvious, but it's not obvious to the majority."

Much of what Licht was doing was not so very novel though, often, he was among the first to adopt a new approach. The difference which was most notable was the result. Licht's analysis lead him to populate his portfolio with a very different set of stocks from the names which crowded the holdings of most competing managers.

"There would be no Courtaulds. The blue chip element would be replaced. Instead of Marks and Spencer you would find Burtons. Marks and Spencer did quite adequately but, compared to these companies, it did poorly. The portfolio was unrecognisable to anyone else."

One enduring theme that pervades Licht's active investment career from 1963 to 1995 is that he has always stayed away from stocks which were the household names everyone else was talking about and spent his time searching for companies no-one else was investigating.

"I've never liked ordinary blue chip shares. My first loss, which I have never forgotten, was Pye of Cambridge (a pioneer among consumer electronics companies). Pye was a virtual blue chip and, at one point, partially owned by Philips. What I began to notice about my own dealing was that a lot of the losses were in companies that other people had heard of, and this was the start of building up my long-term love, which is picking differently from other people. The worst loss of all was in Imperial Chemical Industries, down nearly 10 per cent in less than three weeks. In contrast, the Wiles Group which, at that time, was a small trucking company, but subsequently became Hanson, made a great return for me. When I acquired a new account, I would kick out many of the blue chips. They would give way to enormous holdings in unusual things."

Licht's performance is rather harder to track than that of many managers due to the structure of the accounts for which he was responsible. He has gone on record as saying, "Index linked is a cop out. You shouldn't be in the business if you can't beat the index." While at Mercury Asset Management, his specialist unit had a target return 2 per cent above the FTA All-Share Index but, in a number of years, beat that benchmark by 4 or 5 per cent. Twenty years of this sort of premium performance compounds into some pretty heady numbers, and places Licht among the very few top professionals who manage to maintain a higher level of returns for over two decades.

One actuary quoted by *The Mail on Sunday* went on the record this way:

> Between 1976 and 1986 . . . he was in the top quarter of the best performing funds in eight years out of ten. Often he was top. His record is astonishing (1 November 1992).

Take the BBC, a Licht client for the best part of 20 years. They started out, in 1974, with less than £7 million in the kitty. That account, with only modest increments of capital added along the way, grew to over £700 million during his tenure as manager. The BBC employed a sizeable number of other managers during the period, and had a policy of running six to seven of the best performers tracked by their internal watchdogs at any one time. Licht was invariably top.

At British Rail, Licht managed a large portfolio which beat the FT Actuaries All-Share Index every year between 1981–1991 inclusive. His average outperformance was 3.35 per cent pa, and the average return during this period was 23 per cent pa, which is world class by any benchmark. Commenting on these returns, David Adams, Chief Executive of the Railways Pension Trustee Company, said, "By any standards, this 11 year consecutive run of positive returns, compared with the index, is extraordinarily impressive. Leonard Licht consistently outperformed the index year after year for 11 years, often by a very substantial margin. His flair, judgement and willingness to back that judgement by taking big positions in his chosen stocks were key ingredients in this truly outstanding long-term outperformance."

If you talk to clients of Licht, they can not say enough positive things about his performance and also about him personally. Consider these comments from David Webster, Deputy Chairman of the Argyll Group which owns Safeway. "I hold Leonard in the very highest regard. His style is unique. He gives a masterly overview of the market. He is a very talented stock picker. He gets very many more right than wrong. He ran one small special situations fund for Safeway Pensions Fund which achieved an outstanding performance, coming in the first percentile of the W Universe three years running. The annualised return of the larger fund was also in the first percentile over a two year period."

All this achievement came not through handling the odd trust or two. At his peak, Licht was personally responsible for investing over £7 billion, or over £130 per person in Britain. Superior performance on this scale is really remarkable. Even rival fund managers have described him as walking on water.

The *Sunday Telegraph* called Licht: 'The nearest thing to Superman in fund management.'

The Mail on Sunday said he was, 'the nearest thing the Square Mile has to [a] . . . superstar.'

LARGE HOLDINGS IN SPECIFIC STOCKS

At the heart of Licht's outperformance is his willingness to back his own judgement way beyond where most managers would feel comfortable. "My philosophy is to have heavy bets on companies, especially those that no-one else likes." These stocks became big positions in an absolute sense, and also as a percentage of the total outstanding shares of the company. To put this in perspective, a sample of holdings where

Table 8.1 Illustrative Large Positions Held by Licht

Company	Business	Approx % of Company held	Outcome
Barham Group	Publishing	15	Taken over by IBC
Combined English Stores	Retailer	15	Taken over by Next
Debenhams	Department store	4	Taken over by Burton
Fleet Holdings	Express Newspapers	8	Taken over by United Newspapers
Foseco Minsep	Specialty chemicals	6	Taken over by Burmah Castrol
Really Useful Company	Theatrical production and musical publisher for work by Andrew Lloyd Webber	12	Went private

My philosophy is to have heavy bets on companies, especially those that no-one else likes.

he held a sizeable percentage are listed in Table 8.1. Some are recognisable companies which fell on hard times. Others are a tad more esoteric. It is interesting to note how many were taken over leaving Licht with a profitable exit.

This belief in taking very large stakes was such a pronounced part of Licht's investment philosophy that in May 1987 the *Daily Express* was able to draw up a list of no fewer than 18 companies in which Licht held 15 per cent or more of the outstanding equity.

SECTOR WEIGHTINGS

One variation on this which has worked particularly well for Licht is to go distinctly overweight in a specific industry sector. An example of his willingness to skew the portfolio came in 1984/5 when Licht's accounts had as much as 20 per cent of their holdings in the retail sector versus the overall market index average of 5 per cent. This over weighting proved to be a shrewd move, as retail stocks powered ahead of the broader market in 1986. It was in this era that J Hepworth became Next, and retailers became more aggressive in responding to a general increase in the level of consumerism. There was a feel good factor that, combined with greater growth in the economy, fuelled profits. There was a flurry of much required rationalisation in the sector which also contributed to superior gains. Inflation helped, too, giving a boost to the values of the properties. Combined with rising property values, you got two positive trends raising values in the same sector.

Of course, staking out a disproportionately big position is only a good strategy if you also pick the right stocks – otherwise it's a lousy strategy. Fortunately, in backing his own instincts and judgement, Licht has proved, time and time again, that he knows how to make the best bet. So the next question has to be, 'how does he manage to do what so few others can achieve?'

One good place to start is that Licht is focused: actually, he is very focused. He would say he has to be focused, because he is inherently lazy, which seems like a great way to turn a vice into a virtue. If you are only going to have a few holdings that really matter and make the dif-ference to the performance of your portfolio, you can afford to concentrate all your efforts on ensuring those few are right and, if you concentrate, you are likely to know more than the next manager about those few holdings, so you do improve your odds.

Sir Ron Brierley has adopted a similar approach with spectacular suc-cess over the last 30 years though, in his case, he takes the philosophy one stage further and often ends up owning the whole company, while Licht will leave a fair slice on the table for some-one else. This line of thinking also smacks of Buffett, whose multi-billion dollar Berkshire Hathway revolves around a very small number of investments which make up over 90 per cent of BH – not many more individual holdings for Buffett than you might find in a basic diversified £50,000 PEP account.

Licht talks a lot about undervalued assets, but he sees the identifica-tion of the value discrepancy as only a first step, more of a means to an end than a stand alone decision. Undervalued assets need the right con-text to justify an investment. So, trying to see how Licht has scored so well means disentangling several sub-strands within his overall approach. All have, at their core, the backdrop of undervalued assets for underpinning. We have identified:

Privatisation

Licht feels that, often, governments will price privatisations poorly, because they don't understand how the assets could be valued or could be made to perform once they are out from under government control. This led him to be a big buyer of AB Ports, which had a strong property asset base. He also loaded up on the water utilities, and has benefited from the improvement which took place once those management teams started to think like owners rather than bureaucrats.

Hold Winners for the Long-term

The point has been made earlier, but the message is so important that it bears repetition. Licht once described more or less the flip side of holding equities as akin to storing fine wines. As they mature, they get better. The point, of course, is that you should ride your winners, and stay with them as long as nothing changes. He once stated: "If you find a stock you believe in, you should be prepared to back it all the way and then wait three to five years."

Everyone Makes Mistakes – Therefore Cut Losses Fast

Licht is not one who believes in averaging down – though, on occasion, he has violated this rule. The holding in Jupiter Tyndall is a spectacular example of where he rode the dip. On the whole, Licht is unexpectedly humble about his own capabilities. He has consistently taken the view that 30 to 40 per cent of his decisions will be wrong and, more likely, 40 per cent. So, if the price is heading down, that is a very important piece of information. Rarely can even a well-informed individual know more than the market. If everyone else is bailing out, it's usually time to sell. He has gone on record as saying:

> *When a share is underperforming, there is usually some good reason, and it is always an excellent warning signal.*

"The important thing, then, is to recognise your mistake and sell . . . When a share is underperforming, there is usually some good reason, and it is always an excellent warning signal."

190

Stay with Industry Strengths

When Licht goes long on a sector, it is because he believes that is an area of the economy where the UK is strong in relative terms. Since Licht rarely strays outside the UK, his focus is on what is right and wrong with the UK economy tempered ever so slightly by where he feels the UK is in the economic cycle. Within the UK he has articulated clear views on where the relative strengths should lead an investor.

"Look at what we are good at in this country – retailing, the drinks industry, and the drug industry – and invest in those things. In the UK you can add fund management to the list. It is highly professional and very successful in the UK, compared to continental rivals. So it's not surprising that you see overseas companies looking to acquire UK expertise in this sector.

"If you want engineering stocks, generally speaking, you go to Germany, to Japan for consumer electronics, and for other high-tech companies, to the USA."

Alight Upon Assets That Aren't Sweating

Licht belongs to the school of thought which says that any company which is asset rich but performance poor is in an unsustainable situation. One important qualification needs to be noted. Assets do not *have* to be fixed, tangible chunks of plant, property and equipment, or even current assets. The definition can embrace certain intangible items. Examples abound of this philosophy at work, but some of the most successful date from the mid 1980s. Licht waxes lyrical about his large holding in Burton.

> *Any company which is asset rich but performance poor is in an unsustainable situation.*

"Burton Group had an enormous quantity of assets. Either the board was going to do something, or the whole company would be taken out but, somehow, those assets would be made to sweat. That sort of situation is a 'no lose'. We also moved money into House of Fraser on that very simple thought."

Burton got its act together and the share price responded to changes. In the case of the House of Fraser, the company was taken over; but one result was the same in both instances. Licht and his clients made a lot of money.

Invest in Nice People . . .

Licht likes to take a close look at the character of the people who manage the companies where his money is at risk. This sounds a bit old-fashioned but, if so, it is old-fashioned common sense, and the way Licht interprets character is in tune with the times. He does not feel it is any of his business if the chairman has been married three or four times, but he does prefer that the chairman should keep quiet about his personal decisions. In similar vein, he consciously tries to avoid companies where the top management has a mega ego, or where there are signs of excess in the life style.

As he said on an earlier occasion, he prefers to back companies run by nice people.

"A lot of not-so-nice people are handicapped from the start, and tend to go down quicker when times are hard. We bought David Lloyd as much because I knew David Lloyd as any idea we had about the future of tennis centres, and that turned out to be a jolly nice investment. We still had a large holding when Whitbread bought the company."

. . . And in Dedicated, Motivated and Honest People

"You must see management regularly. We like them in *our* office rather than going to *their* office. One to one, or two to one is a great help. You have to have regular meetings. That's why long-term investments are best, inasmuch as you've got to see them on a very regular basis. Two, three, four times a year over many years. You can see catalysts for change, which, of course, is what we're all after. You can see a deterioration in what they're saying, or an improvement.

"It shouldn't be under-estimated how very few people run big companies. There are two or three people who make all the decisions. The top people should be motivated, particularly in smaller companies. It's very useful if they are large shareholders. There's some old truths. I don't like corporate fountains, corporate jets, or unusual lifestyles of

192

directors. I'm not that keen on 101 per cent dedication. I think 100 per cent is enough! By and large, people should be devoted to their businesses. They should lead fairly dull private lives, and should not appear to be abnormal in any way whatsoever. Excess in any way is a danger."

Small is Beautiful

Licht has long been a supporter of the argument that, over the long run, small companies' share prices will outperform those of larger companies. The facts are with him. That influence has been one of the strengths behind his stock picking but, as of 1996, Licht may be rethinking his position, at least in some respects.

> *Over the long run small companies' share prices will outperform those of larger companies.*

"By and large, when you're in non-recessionary times, small companies do better than big companies. That's fair, but there are new elements which are causing us to make that two headed. Small companies should do well when interest rates are low. There's growth in the economy, and the banks aren't trying to kill them. That's fine. But there are also now considerably increased advantages in size in certain areas. One area that is, perhaps, under-estimated in their advantage in size is supermarkets. There are absolutely three or four operators and, clearly, no chance to enter that market; where sheer size is embellished by the problems for new companies of not being able to get planning permission, whether they want to or not. These four leaders have a stranglehold which, perhaps, is still not completely appreciated.

"I think they could increase profits, due to their amazing efficiency and to entering new areas. The latest new area which I think will be very successful is newspapers and books, all part of the destroying of Smiths. I'm very negative on Smiths. Supermarkets will take that market over. Stationery as well. Petrol has been one such new area that has not been understood.

"If you look round supermarkets, they are fantastic operators. Take Archie Norman (at ASDA). He is unbelievable. I don't think you'll find many Archies. People always under-estimate the UK's strengths. He would stand up globally against any top manager.

"It's mainly a UK story. Efficiency continues to grow apace, so the top three or four companies are changing the high street pattern and making it very difficult for Smiths and Woolworths. Those two will find life very tough in the coming ten years, because the supermarkets will take more and more on and will become, maybe unfortunately, the centre of shopping life to an even greater extent than now.

"If they were successful in translating this into, let's say, continental Europe, where I think supermarkets are fairly awful, their profits could increase dramatically over the next few years, and I don't believe there is saturation. It's an area of very great quality of management. So big is beautiful in certain areas.

"Computer technology, in certain areas, can only be used by big companies. Even building supplies, which is always presumed to be a nonsense business, is translating itself and going into the modern era. Ashtead is showing how you can apply internal controls and systems to improve profitability out of something as basic as plant hire. That's one that most people don't appreciate. Insurance is another, which should be highly computerised, and will be a market where big is beautiful. These are areas that are not assumed to be in the pharmaceutical mould.

"Pharmaceuticals are happening now. Everyone knows that there are mergers there, and you've seen the American banking merger mania. I'll just take that a bit further. Maybe our banks need to merge. Even now, there's a lot of costs that could be taken out of the banks. Big can be beautiful in creating much greater efficiency."

Licht also had a small sideline which was idiosyncratic, in investment terms, and far removed from the orthodox investment philosophy which prevailed in the past, and still, to a very large extent, continues today in the City. As always, these ventures into the bywaters proved very profitable. The challenge of transforming shell companies has attracted some of the brightest investment minds. Licht was one of the very first to see the potential, because of the value in the listing of a small company and the tax code at that time, which allowed losses to be utilised. He had been involved as early as 1969 with Bank Bridge Rubber, and the shell company story became a hallmark of his investment style even as his funds under management grew to a point where shell deals could only absorb a small fraction of his portfolio.

"I understood earnings per share and tinyness. What got me started was investigating the injection of property interests into rubber and tea companies. Some of those were spectacular, and were some of the great money making situations of all times. Hanipha Ceylon Tea and Rubber was one. I purchased it as low as 85p. They became Halcyon Investments, a property company. With a 10 to 1 split, the shares then went to £1 and returned a profit of 12 times the initial investment in just 18 months. Others were Narakuta Karama, which became Thomas Jourdan, and Bangawan Estates. Today, shells still have value, but there are so many more professional people about, you can't make that sort of money."

When asked to described his own style, Licht's response is rapid and precise: "Flexible." The best way to see how these ideas translate is to illustrate their practical application with examples from Licht's investment history. Fortunately, the pickings are rich.

"I bought Kensington Hotels, which became Securicor, at the very early stages when it was going from hotels into delivery services. Not many understood how big Securicor was becoming in terms of parcels. This was well before Cellnet, so you're talking 20 times your money.

"I made a great deal of money out of Ferranti before it went bust, and didn't get caught with any of them. Ferranti was actually a Rule 163 company, which is a precursor of Ofex. It had enormous sales and was capitalised at nothing. The market value to sales ratio was unbelievably low. You'd laugh. It was capitalised at nothing, and still had a massive business."

There is also an element of sheer opportunism which peeps through when Licht talks about the multitude of ways in which he made money. He has always demonstrated an eye for the main chance and would never allow rigid thinking to stand in the way of the opportunity to lock away a gain. A couple of examples serve to illustrate this aspect of his approach.

"Gearing was something I learnt early on. To play the nil paid game was a way to make a lot of money quickly. On a Royal Exchange issue, I was able to apply for £20,000 nominal of shares, even though I had virtually no money. That was done with only £100 down and gave me £58 profit for holding the stock for one day. Town and Commercial Properties issued a $6\frac{3}{4}$ per cent convertible due January 1990 at 100. There were three weeks where you could buy at the premium, which was only £3, before you had to meet the call on the full amount and, within the window, were able to sell at £14."

One of the smartest investment decisions Licht ever made was to leave Mercury, a really astonishing move on the surface after 28 years at the firm, and one which was commented on in the financial community with large amounts of scepticism and criticism in equal measure. Licht was unfazed, though this could have reasonably been characterised as a career gamble, even for a man who has the gall to make big bets. Two and a half years later, Jupiter Tyndall was bought by Commerzbank in a deal which valued the company at nearly four times the level prevailing when he joined. John Duffield, the founder and chairman of Jupiter, is justifiably credited as having negotiated a good deal for all parties including, as the business continues to flourish, a good deal for the buyer. Licht was an important ingredient in making Jupiter an attractive acquisition for Commerzbank. Duffield and Licht had proved the doubters wrong.

The thing which strikes you most about Licht is that he enjoys life and has an enormous sense of humour. Investing has to be fun. What then becomes remarkable about this departure from Mercury is not that it happened, but that he lasted there for such a long time. Licht needs several degrees of freedom in which to flourish. Mercury were wise enough to understand that, and give him more latitude within the organisation than anyone else. Even so, Licht increasingly found himself removed from doing what he loved most. Picking stocks. He regained the flexibility to stick to his strengths by moving to Jupiter, where he could focus on looking at companies rather than fine-tuning, and second guessing the efforts of others.

> *The recent theme which has dominated Licht's thinking can be described as 'taking advantage of governments' idiocy.*

The most recent theme which has dominated Licht's thinking over the last seven years or so can loosely be described as 'taking advantage of governments' idiocy.' This theme is more or less played out in Britain as of 1996, but is likely to be replicated elsewhere as the privatisation bandwagon gathers momentum in many of the more forward thinking countries all around the globe.

"In the UK we have just finished an era where a great deal of money has been made out of privatisation. That was the last enormously successful thought process. Most people didn't understand what the Government was doing or why they had to do it. At MAM we had very large chunks of water and at Jupiter, we have built up large holdings in electricity and have very big weightings in that sector. The investing public didn't understand the earnings potential, so missed out at first. Most governments don't normally understand anything about money and this lot are no different, so they've given away the electricity companies. You can see the real values emerging now.

"For me it started with AB Ports. We bought 18 per cent of AB Ports. You can't build ports that easily. If you are given most of them and you can bring in much better management, and stop the union process, you should start making money. Before privatisation, the whole sector had been highly unionised. This was at the time of the start of an era of deunionising. Management, when part of Government, had not been free to run the business efficiently. They brought in Keith Stuart at the time of privatisation. He is an excellent man, and did all the right things; and they had assets to work with. They had a site in Southampton which had tremendous value.

"There can be more than one way to make money out of the Government. Governments constantly create value for some within the private sector by decisions where consequences are not thought through properly – or put another way, are stupid."

"BAA was a similar story. It was a gift. If you have all the airports in a country, you have a monopoly, and monopolies are always lovely if you can make them efficient. We didn't touch Eurotunnel, because that was much harder. There is blindness in understanding value by Government and, actually, by their advisors, as well. This Government could have hired people to help who knew all about stock markets and values, but they didn't. They hired people who were looking for fees, and that's all they were interested in.

"I would think that rail privatisation, if it occurs and is structured in a sensible way, could offer similar scope for shareholders. British Rail has the opportunity to make an enormous amount of money, if run right."

Like so many of the top performing investment managers, Licht is drawn inexorably to equities, where his style of searching for specific securities has more scope. He has been particularly leery about the bond market in the UK in the past. Although there are structured shifts in the economy which may rebound to the benefit of bondholders, he remains a sceptic.

"I think bonds are complete nonsense, or have been in the UK. If I was in Germany, for instance, I wouldn't bother with shares, because the currency is sacrosanct and inflation is the main bogie of the Bundesbank. It was set up, as you know, purely to control inflation. So you have bonds there, because they will create a true return at most times. In the UK, which has, by and large, a weak currency with bouts of inflation, which are clearly currently dormant, but shouldn't be forgotten, bonds are unnecessary in a portfolio.

"Something *has* changed. Inflation is not the threat it was but, unfortunately, the currency is likely to remain weak for the foreseeable future. By temperament, I find bonds utterly boring. Governments can always change the rules of bonds. So I don't like bonds. I think they're a waste of time."

He has more time for some of the other asset classes.

"My greatest love is venture capital. I was chairman of Mercury Development Capital. In venture capital you find other people providing a lot of the capital, i.e. the banks. So, if you get it right, you make a fortune, many, many times your capital. If you get it wrong, you only lose your capital. I think that's great.

"It's very similar to the quoted arena 15 years before. You get something for nothing. Bluntly, a lot of them were over-manned and under-managed. I was also chairman of the Mercury property business but, when I was involved, conditions were not what you needed. Businesses that benefit from enormous doses of inflation are clearly not in the best sector at the moment. Property needs shortages, and government interference, so it's not very interesting. Pretty dead stuff. Of course, it could come back, with a new party in power."

Looking further forward, Licht wonders whether the lessons of the last 20 years will have the same sort of applicability for the next 20. This may require him to focus on his key core strength – flexibility.

"I think the UK is a fairly low growth area and, therefore, great anomalies, great surges of profitability are probably unlikely. But, if you look – and I was just doing the exercise – it is absolutely apparent that companies die very regularly. If you look at the constituents of various industries over 20, 40, 60 year periods, very few are in the same form as they were, so things change all the time. Clearly we're in an enormous computer-led revolution for the next 20 years, and there will be complete changes. What I'm saying is that whole different groups of shares and companies will be amazingly successful, and one's just got to move from one area to another.

"This suggests one has to change investment style. Assets are not there, at the moment. My one major theme is: flexibility is everything. I think that, as an investor, you've got to be able to change pretty dramatically and, you've got to be fluid in what you think is going to happen. You see a new Government and it will dramatically alter things that may be positive and negative. Government influence, in one or two areas, could totally alter your investment perception. If the desperation of this Government increases and they do things that effectively they said they wouldn't, like massively stimulate the housing market, even though I don't think they're capable of doing it, then you must change. If housing was, again, a priority one way or another, housing stocks could double, treble or quadruple. You've just got to be alive to new themes all the time.

My one major theme is: flexibility is everything.

"Dominance by one country doesn't last long. You have to be prepared to move from area to area of greatest success on a pretty regular basis. Clearly, the Pacific Rim is the area of greatest growth at the moment. They've got the greatest advantages. They have the advantages of a highly educated population; a motivated population; an un-greedy population which, of course, will become greedy. You cannot see them failing over the next 10 or 20 years. There's nothing clever about that. And it moves from country to country. Japan moves to South Korea, moves to Vietnam. That's not terribly clever but it is manifestly true.

"It means you should have a lot of your global money in the Pacific Rim, full stop. In our balanced funds at Jupiter, we have a double weighting in the Pacific Rim. I'm jolly happy with that. It makes common sense, and I think the political background of those countries should probably be ignored. They're not in our Western thinking, in terms of democracy, but so what? They do very well. These countries will be the dominating sector in the next 20 years, and we'll become more and more peripheral. I don't mind that, because I think we have got strengths of our own."

You should have a lot of your global money in the Pacific rim.

Licht sees the UK as retaining a great deal more by way of interesting investment opportunities than is generally recognised by investors, be they individuals or professionals.

"I think we always under-estimate our considerable inventiveness. We have created many great industries: pharmaceuticals is one that's been massively successful. We're not as technologically backward as a lot of people say. We're clearly much, much more entrepreneurial than our Continental competitors. Continental Europe, in many ways, is backward. We have an advantage over our Continental competitors inasmuch as they are hide-bound by social expenses, and we've actually gripped it. British industry, through the factory revolution, is highly efficient and even, I would say, now competitive."

What does all this mean for investment ideas?

"Media is a strong area. People in the UK understand how to get large profits out of media activities. Television and computerised publishing are areas where the British excell. I think those businesses will continue to be dramatically successful. Carlton Communications is a clever company. The understanding of how the Internet can be an attractive commercial area is higher in the UK than elsewhere in Europe, though the speed of technological change means many more companies will fail than will succeed.

"The one major detractor in the UK is the poverty of overall education. The bulk of people leaving school are not educated enough. I think that is the single greatest handicap in this country. Other successes will be revitalised engineering and specialty chemical companies that are developing. You see these sorts of businesses in some of the new issues recently. Critchley is that sort of export-led, highly motivated company making things that people want. It has a niche business marking cables with some proprietary technology and manufactures a range of cable accessories."

While Licht believes in going long UK Ltd, he accepts the premise that there may be other, very attractive opportunities for investment overseas. It's just that he can't feel comfortable calling the timetable, particularly in the one place – Continental Europe – where those daunting defences to change are so multifaceted, being commercial, cultural and political.

"I never had the energy to break down Continental investment protection. I know it's going to be broken down one day, but I haven't got the energy. There are so many barriers, but I would say Europe is the last area of under-valuation. There are enormous opportunities in virtually every single country but, because of taxation, both corporate and individual, and also because of continental thinking whereby the shareholder comes last rather than first, as in the Anglo-Saxon world, it might be some time. You can't wait for 100 years. There's no point in having an asset situation that remains an asset situation when your grandchildren are grown up.

"One or two are so obvious. At Mercury I bought a holding in Holvis in Switzerland. It was basically a group of assets that lacked good management. The businesses were paper products that were in global demand. They just didn't make a big enough margin. It was undermanaged to an amazing degree [and subsequently the centre of a takeover contest]. The pharmaceutical company, Roche, was an example which has been recognised over the last five years as undermanaged, and still falls within this category."

When looking inside to what differentiates a successful money manager from the run of the mill guy who produces an average, slightly sub-index performance, Licht focuses on attitude. Attitude is a function of ability and motivation – which makes managing money not so different after all but then, having said that, the greatest downfall is to do what everyone else does. Being part of a crowd more or less guarantees mediocrity – at best.

"Making money is an unpleasant business, really. Warburgs went down hill when it employed too many public school types who didn't have the appetite and were too much alike. You can't make money by being conventional or boring. You have to seek out the new opportunities all the time. Going with the herd is just stupid. You have to know more than anyone else and find things that others can't find. That's the other thing. Knowledge is king. To get that knowledge, you have to be completely dedicated and willing to work harder than the next person.

"You've got to love your job and you have to have more art than science. Everyone's got the science, now. Computer back-up is there for anyone. You need to be able to envisage something different, looking years ahead, and not see a situation the same way as everyone else."

There are a whole generation of managers and analysts who are growing up now with ideas and strategies dominated by computer screens and sophisticated software, and who would find many of Licht's investment ideas quaint. It will be interesting to see how their performance stacks up in ten or twenty years' time – always assuming any of them survive in the business that long – but, if they are still around, the odds have to be very high that they will have fallen far short of the achievement of Leonard Licht, who understands the meaning of value in its most complete sense and who has cultivated an investing style which endures and will prosper as long as markets are made up of people making investment decisions.

* The ultimate value manager with a twist – growth

* Winner of numerous awards from *The Mail on Sunday,
Money Magazine* and *Money Observer* among others

* One of the very few people to make money investing in
other investment trusts and warrants

COLIN McLEAN

Growth at the Right Price

If you found a firm called Scottish Value Management, you should not have much difficulty explaining the investment philosophy to potential investors. The individual funds managed by SVM resonate with the theme which is central to Colin McLean's investment style. His very first entity is called Scottish Value Trust. That was followed by Warrants and Value Trust and Undervalued Assets Trust. No ambiguity here, either. It's value all the way.

This should come as no surprise to anyone acquainted with McLean's background. Before hanging out his own shingle he had studied under that legendary global investor, Sir John Templeton, and rose to become Managing Director of Templeton Europe. Prior to that, McLean cut his teeth on investment management under the auspices of James Pfaff at FS Assurance, an introduction to the profession which was as disciplined and quantitative as any around.

"I had studied economics and statistics at Glasgow University and from there became an actuarial student for a life office. I spent my first couple of years doing actuarial work. It was a time when actuarial students were used as calculators, pre the electronic era!"

Perhaps this early experience had a result which was not exactly the one intended. When you talk to Colin McLean about value, you quickly realise that here is no number crunching quant jock, but rather an investor who thinks deeply about all the elements of value and who eschews simply ratios for a more detailed and broadly based evaluation of his potential investments. What did rub off was the approach espoused by James Pfaff at FS which focused on strong company management, uniqueness of products and a *growth* trend.

"I differ from the traditional Graham & Dodd US approach, which was based, typically, on assets and on data which, I think in the UK, are a lot less reliable. There are a range of value investors going from people that purely bottom fish trying to buy things that are at discounts to assets – right up to people who just buy good companies they think are slightly undervalued. I am much more at the end where people are trying to establish whether something is a good company first of all. Most of the investments we make are in stocks which we think are inherently growing businesses, but which are valued no higher than the market averages. We are trying to buy growth at the right price, which is the way the Americans would supposedly classify it now, or buying good companies at a fair value rather than buying anything very cheaply.

> **We are trying to buy growth at the right price.**

"The way in which we do that is to pay less attention to earnings per share, because they can easily be distorted in terms of the trend. There's quite a variety of changes which can indicate an improving earnings per share, but don't necessarily indicate they're sustainable in terms of growth, or that a company's franchise is really growing. Things like interest costs or interest achieved on cash, or cost cutting, or margin expansion, or acquisitions. A growing franchise is something I would describe like British Airports Authority, where we know the physical number of passengers that are going through airports goes up by up to 7 per cent per annum."

His own marketing material states clearly how McLean goes about his business.

> Scottish Value Management's investment approach focuses on identifying 'undervalued' shares by analysing fundamental value – based on companies' long-term earnings power and dividend paying ability. It recognises that stock market movements are usually much greater and more rapid than the underlying 'real' value of companies themselves These exaggerated swings of sentiment mean that there will always be some discrepancies between market price and intrinsic value.
>
> SVM conducts detailed analysis of accounting data to assess underlying value – identifying companies' real growth trends, excluding any unsustainable sources of profit such as accounting treatment and excessive margin expansion. It focuses on free cash flow and reducing risk.

While McLean calls himself a value investor, the more you delve into his definition of value, the more you start to feel that this is not a definition which fits neatly with the first generation of value disciples. McLean incorporates variants on the traditional theme extending the calculation of value in ways which purists would not recognise. The preoccupation with the need for growth leads to a departure from 'value' orthodoxy. Therein lies the single most important factor which enables McLean to rise above the crowd. T. Rowe Price might, perhaps, have more justification to claim that McLean is in his camp though, in reality, an impartial observer would calculate that he falls somewhere in between these two schools on the investing continuum.

Value, as modified by McLean, has proved a rewarding experience for those who have backed him. Every single vehicle under his management has outperformed the FT All Share Index by an impressive *multiple*. Another astonishing aspect of his performance is that he has accomplished superior returns across so many categories of assets, global equities, investment trusts and warrants. A sample of Mclean's outstanding outperformance is shown in Table 9.1.

Table 9.1 Performance Records of Scottish Value Management (From date of launch – 31 December 1995)

	Multiple Relative to:	
	FT All Share	*FT Investment Trust Index*
Scottish Value Trust	NM	2.2
Warrants and Value Trust	NM	1.2
Undervalued Assets Trust	1.4	NM
SVM Superior Growth Fund	2.9	NM
Scottish Value UK Growth Fund	3.5	NM

Slice and dice McLean's funds into their appropriate peer group categories and the relative performance is even more impressive. SVM Superior Growth Fund's record looks good in isolation. Compared to other UK broker life funds it is outstanding. SVM was the top performer over the four years to November 1995 (since inception in November 1991) out of 391 funds, giving shareholders *twice* the total return of the *second* best fund in the sector over that period. The new Scottish Value Portfolio – European Growth Fund ranked top out of 82 for its first full year in 1994 as calculated by Offshore Fund Guide.

This sort of superior profile is a natural progression from his previous performance. At Templeton he was part of the team which launched Templeton Emerging Markets, without argument one of the greatest success stories in investment trust history. He ran Templeton Global Growth, which comfortably beat the Morgan Stanley Capital World Index, the relevant benchmark, during the 18 months under his management from late 1988 to early 1990.

This, in its turn, followed on from a period of superior performance during his tenure at FS Assurance. Between 1979 and 1984 the FS Segregated Fund beat the Willis Faber Managed Fund Index every year, and the Pensions Managed Fund, launched in February 1984, more than doubled by September 1985, when McLean moved on to other responsibilities, versus a rise of 40 per cent in the FT All Share Index during the period.

It hardly comes as a surprise, then, that McLean has a stack of awards to his credit. These include:

(i)   Scottish Investor of the Year from *Scottish Business Insider* in 1990;
(ii) *Money Observer* best overall UK Investment Trust in 1992;
(iii) Micropal 1993 top performer within the investment trust financial sector;
(iv) *Offshore Fund Guide* For Europe for 1994;
(v)   *Money Magazine* Unit Trust Manager of the Year in 1985;
(vi) *Mail on Sunday* 1995 best performing investment trust and unit trust PEP over three years.

No wonder *Scotland on Sunday* calls him 'Mr Midas'. The good news for the individual investor in the UK is that Scottish Value Trust qualifies for PEP accounts. According to the Allenbridge Group, it is the number one performing PEP fund in the UK over three years.

It is important to get to the guts of McLean's argument, because there is a compelling logic to the way he looks at a business, and this philosophy forms the base for every investment decision he makes.

REAL UNIT GROWTH IS GOLDEN

I try to get away from the the earnings per share way of assessing companies. I try to assess, at the top line, what the real franchise of a business is in terms of its turnover and its customers, and the sustainable level of that. I look at whether turnover is growing in real terms per share, and whether in physical terms on a per share basis after any acquisitions the real franchise and the real customer base have actually grown. If you look at British Airports Authority, you see improving turnover figures. Underneath you know they are physically shifting some 4 per cent more passengers each year. If you've got a real increase, you've got a growth business. Then it's simply a matter of trying to assess what sustainable margins are in that business."

To translate the generic into the specific, McLean cites several examples of what he means:

"I am much more inclined to think that risks are lower in companies where the margins are below average for the market and for the sector, and the risks are higher where they are much above average, so it's less risky to invest in something like Lucas and hope that its margins would rise from 7 per cent up towards 8 per cent than it is to invest in a BTR or Siebe and hope that margins would go up from 14 to 16 per cent. Margins will be different in different industries. It's a matter of looking at the industry averages. One can invest in the bus sector in companies like Stagecoach, where they are achieving margins of about 18 per cent, or there is FirstBus, which includes GRT, where they managed nearly 15 per cent and Badgerline, which was at 9.5 per cent. The third option is Go Ahead, where margins are only about 11 per cent. There you have the prospect of management improving margins with the Chairman's stated goal of 15 per cent, or of being taken over. I think that's a less risky investment."

> *I try to get away from the earnings per share way of assessing companies.*

FOLLOW THE CASH, STEER CLEAR OF THE DEBT

A variant on the value philosophy emerges again as McLean moves from assessing sustainable profit growth to scrutinising the balance sheet. If you think through the approach McLean is advocating, the basic premise would not earn him a passing grade in an exam entitled 'Value 101', but it is a souped-up version of an underlying approach much more in tune with the mix of business in the successful sectors of the economy, and so aligned most closely with what should prove to be the best performing publicly quoted companies of the 1990s.

"Another feature of what we do is to be less conservative about a particular capital structure. First try and assess whether this enterprise has a sound franchise, a good solid customer base, whether that's really growing, and then see what you can add or subtract for debt or net cash. A lot of analysts make a different calculation. Rather than adding in cash or subtracting debt as a lump sum, they tend to allow interest earnings or debt costs to be taken off earnings per share then apply a multiple to adjusted earnings per share. So they are really applying a multiple to the debt costs. You can end up with quite a different answer, particularly if a company is quite highly geared or if a company has a lot of cash. We found last year, for example, some of the fund management companies had quite substantial amounts of cash. When Jupiter Tyndall was taken over, about a quarter of its market capitalisation was in cash.

"Companies with large amounts of debt, Signet – the jewellery retailer – is an example which looks likely to be worth something. Certainly in any evaluation just now, you could say that the ordinary share was making losses and is going to carry on losing for the indefinite future but, if you stood aside from that capital structure and evaluated the total value of the stream of operating earnings it's making, you could actually see that the enterprise should have some value, in excess of the preference share value.

"Sometimes, when there is high gearing or very large amounts of cash, a company can end up being mis-assessed, if it's looked at purely on an earnings per share basis. And, of course, a corporate buyer would look at things much the same as we do. When they take something over, they are either going to strip out the cash or refinance the debt. They're much more interested in buying the operating earnings than they are in what the earnings per share was going to be before the merger. The way in which we look at things tends to be much more as another industrial or trade buyer rather than as a conventional investor would."

To sum up the above, gearing can be OK if the operations are sound, and value exists if the market capitalisation of a company, plus its debt or minus its cash, is modest.

Flick through the top holdings which recur across SVM portfolios and you can see the theory in practice. Large positions, as of December 1995, include:

Asda   –   A recovery story in the food retail sector.

Royal Bank of Scotland   –   A UK banking group with growing non-banking activities.

Cairn Energy	–	A small oil company with extensive reserves in the Far East.
Datrontech	–	A growing distributor of computer memory upgrades, growing rapidly in Europe.
Henlys	–	A manufacturer of buses and other public service vehicles.

When McLean starts to talk about his investments, he never tends to dwell that long on the numbers, even though his analysis is intensive to the nth degree. However hard one tries to focus on the analytical endeavours, he finds a way to get back to the topics which, to him, hold the key to whether an investor is going to make money. The approach is the same whether you are going long or short; only the diagnosis differs. This ability to appreciate the dynamics of the operations and the people running the operations gives McLean an edge over managers who remain more mired in a purely quantitative approach.

THE ULTIMATE TEST IS THE ABILITY AND THE INTEGRITY OF MANAGEMENT

"I like to be sure that, within companies, there are some internal controls. For companies of below £100 million capitalisation I like to be sure that, on the boards, there is at least one director who has experience of being a director at a public listed company of that capitalisation or more. That would probably give the person some experience of how to react to problems. All companies have problems at times, either leading to sacking a chief executive, or losing a large customer, or perhaps explaining a misunderstanding to investors. So I like to be sure there is someone there to blow the whistle if things go wrong, or to be accountable. To have a reputation to lose.

"And we will tend to stay away from companies where there are combined chief executives and chairmen, or where there is what we would classify as weak boards without anyone who would stand up and point out the problems if the chief executive chose to hide them."

... WHO PUT THEIR MONEY WHERE THEIR MOUTH IS

"For the smaller companies, I like to look at the executive behaviour, too, in terms of what's motivating them and whether they are drawing most of their reward from the company through its growth and through the share performance in the same way as we are. I would differ from those that just tend to look at whether directors are buying or selling, because I think you need to be more subtle about it than that. There are close periods where directors can't buy and sell; there are some directors who have more money than others, some that are older and some that are younger. I think that an important question is whether a chief executive has other interests outside the company, and whether he has a significant proportion of his own wealth tied up in the company.

> *An important question is whether a chief executive has a significant proportion of his own wealth tied up in the company.*

"Behaviour goes beyond simply saying whether there is an absolutely large sum. I can think of one very large company where a chairman has an investment valued at £3 million, but he is quite senior, and the sum invested is a lot less than his salary and bonuses drawn out over the last few years. The same man has a lot of other outside interests, so I would not regard £3 million as being particularly material in motivating him. It is interesting to recall that Gerald Ratner had relatively little of his own money invested in Ratner's. You can see this, sometimes, with long standing family management, and directors who may have very little personal wealth at risk in the businesses they run. That lack of financial involvement concerns me.

"Sometimes executives, particularly in smaller companies, will have quite a large stake that may have been achieved through floating something for which they actually put in very little cash, and their behaviour may not be of someone who actually has 20 per cent of a £50m company. It may still be the behaviour of someone who actually only spent £20,000 and mainly used debt, or other people's money, in developing the business. You might find by the time they have actually listed the company they have taken out more net than they have put in. The executive behaviour after that is not of someone who has got a large amount at risk.

"You have to include, as well, whether they have been buying or selling and what other things they are doing. There is a whole mosaic of information to collect. Take the compensation of executives. The average person in the street would be quite right to look askance at Cedric Brown type salaries. Sometimes these can cause real problems, either operationally, in terms of leadership of others paid less, or financially, in terms of hidden implications for pensions. I feel a lot more comfortable where senior people are drawing most of their long-term reward the same way as the shareholders."

And it's not just how the directors behave towards their own investment, but what they know about the business they are running on behalf of their shareholders, which leads McLean to make decisions on whether to invest or not. He has several tests which he has found useful in weeding out the good from the bad management.

"I've met a few who seem to know a lot about their share price, and are more concerned about that than they are about their product prices! Certainly there are company chairmen who sometimes struggle to give a price of their main products, but know what the price of the stock was that morning. On the other hand, it's very easy to be impressed by management who seem to know a lot, technically, about the business, and to be swayed by their apparent knowledge of technical detail within the industry. One company, which collapsed in 1993, had brought in a chap who gave a great presentation on what they were doing in their building division and how they were bucking the recession by putting up modular buildings in Moscow and things like that. I know very little about building and nothing about modular units, so there's no way I can verify what is going on in Moscow. The Russian profits turned out to be fiction at the end of the day but, during the meeting, they were unable to answer the accounting questions that I had, so I stayed out. In verifying what companies say – the main thing is to stand back and spend more time looking at the numbers. You have to let the accounts and the balance sheet speak for themselves and then do your own calculations as to whether the stock market has got the price correct."

Which is the perfect lead in to point out that basic analysis is the foundation stone for McLean. Here, too, he takes a somewhat different stance. He lays less emphasis on P/E ratios, ROE and EPS, indicators still at the forefront of the thinking of many fund managers. His antennae are more sensitive to the nuances to be gleaned from looking at *organic sales growth, operating margins*, and *return on capital employed (ROCE)*. McLean has become convinced, over 15 years of searching for the holy grail, that there are no easy ratios, no short cuts, not even a single complex formula that can lead you to investment nirvana. Instead, he concentrates on certain investment themes to find the investments which yield superior returns.

1. Temporary misrating of a business or sector

McLean is looking to find a fundamentally sound business where the price of the stock is depressed due to factors which will not last. In this category with true contrarian spirit McLean cites the Lloyds linked trusts. In CLM Insurance, which he owns, you can purchase assets linked to the market index at a discount and the good underwriting results for 1994 and 1995 are in for nothing.

He also highlights Utility Cable as a business with specialist contracting skills lowly rated because of excessive concerns that it will have no business left once cable systems cover all the UK. In reality they have other skills and are already establishing themselves in the utility industry as well as expanding onto the continent.

2. Alignment of shareholders and management

Are the interests of these two critical constituencies identical or potentially in conflict? What is more important to management – today's pay cheque or the share value long-term? It's fascinating to see how salaries start to rise more rapidly once managers cash in their share options.

"I can remember one occasion when Distillers' management came round and were trying to defend against the bid from Guinness. They talked about the potential for change in the company. I think we pointed out that the group of fairly young investment managers sitting round the table opposite together actually owned more Distillers' shares personally than the three directors facing us. The comparison was interesting."

3. Takeover candidates

Here we have one of those themes which everyone likes to talk about, but where few people actually understand how to make money, other than on an opportunistic basis. Rarely are predators simple. What really motivates acquirers or triggers a bid at a *particular time* is not often obvious.

McLean does not spend his time speculating on Tompkin's likely next target. Instead, he sets his mind to thinking through the logical consequences of change in an industry sector. In this respect, he is consistent in trying put himself in the position of an industrialist, just as he does when it comes time to value a particular property. Industries go through waves of consolidation. One of the earliest shares McLean ever bought was called Glass and Metal, which disappeared into another building materials company around 1977 at a time when a number of takeovers occurred in the sector. Finding the sector where there are economic imperatives is step one. Sifting

> *A leader in some particular niche which is relatively small but strategic is likely to disappear sooner or later.*

through likely buyers to identify those businesses that are likely to be snapped up requires different skills. Here McLean tried to find companies which have some unique capability which a bigger buyer needs and will pay up for. A leader in some particular niche which is relatively small but strategic is likely to disappear sooner or later. So McLean was a holder of Devenish, which was swallowed up by Greenalls in 1993 after a failed bid from Boddington. Devenish owned a well located group of pubs which were always going to be attractive to larger operators looking for suitable scale acquisitions in the turmoil of the restructuring between brewers and the pub industry in the UK.

The takeover theme was one which McLean latched onto while still at FS Assurance. Of the 24 holdings in the portfolio, as of 30 September 1984, three were taken over at higher prices by that year end. Others, like Imperial, the tobacco company, and Pleasurama, the casino group, were taken over subsequently.

4. Companies which are misunderstood

McLean is always on the look-out for a pattern of neglect by the institutions which can leave the field open to someone not so worried to make sure the right names crop up on the list of holdings at year end.

"We have, over the last year, in just over a year, almost doubled our money in Asda. People are waking up to the fact that it is one of the biggest food retailers. In fact, it was never that much smaller than the others, despite what people thought. They were stuck looking at a small market capitalisation and judging by what they saw on the stock market, rather than looking at its franchise as represented by its turnover and the potential for improving its margins.

"Distillers was a classic. You could walk round the West End and evaluate half a dozen separate head offices that the different brands had, complete with separate management teams and all that cash tied up in their property value. The board lacked focus, and didn't seem to have a good grasp of the business. You could ask them questions about why they didn't promote Lagavulin more because they didn't seem to be making very much of it, and make the suggestion that they might price such luxury malts a bit higher, or ask why they did not pursue opportunities in single malts or mixers with whiskey/gin etc. They didn't seem to have good answers."

GROWTH HAS VALUE

In December 1994 McLean gave a speech in Geneva to a conference of international investors which articulates so well the thrust of his approach:

It is necessary to take a broader view of value investing as a discipline – and I will explain what I mean by that. Value investors recognise it makes sense for investors to work out the underlying value of businesses – ignoring stock market perception – and then buy those that consensus opinion undervalues. At the root of this valuation is the assessment of each company as a business – ignoring, as far as possible, the impact of capital structure.

> *I am much more concerned with return on capital employed than on equity, and with real growth in turnover instead of earnings per share.*

All available information is brought into the analysis. I am much more concerned with return on capital employed than on equity, and with real growth in turnover instead of earnings per share. The key is real sales growth, stability of gross margin on that turnover, and consistency of rate of return on reinvested capital. Not surprisingly, heavy share issuers, those that grow by acquisition, and those without a genuine customer franchise do not emerge well from my analysis.

Throughout, the aim is to separate the transient – temporary tax savings, or unsustainable margin expansion – from recurring core earnings The latter represents the franchise that determines the fundamental value of the business. This value is then adjusted for net debt or surplus cash. It is interesting that, while there is no single measure of this fundamental value, there are much better indicators of value than the price earnings ratios with which Anglo Saxon stock markets are so preoccupied. In the UK, despite improvements in accounting standards, earnings per share can still be manipulated – particularly by acquisitive companies.

One of the reasons for McLean's success lies in the way he approaches risk management. Look at any SVM portfolio and a couple of things are likely to stand out. First, there will be an unusual concentration of assets. Second, the largest holdings often will have increased as a percentage of the portfolio over time. In both respects McLean is swimming against academic advice and, indeed, against portfolio practice across much of the investment industry. McLean has found conventional wisdom on diversification unhelpful. In his mind, the most probable outcome of reducing risk in such a manner is mediocre returns moving towards the mean. McLean has reversed this route and developed a different style which, while it may, on the surface, seem risky to his way of thinking, results in much less risky holdings.

A more concentrated portfolio you know better can be just as low risk.

"I'm not a believer in reducing risk just by diversification. A more concentrated portfolio you know better can be just as low risk. So, very often, I run profits on companies that I increasingly know well. Having the courage of your convictions is important where the stock market initially doesn't do what you want. Many of the companies that do well are ones which were neglected for a period. In the 1970s I bought companies like Eastern Midland Allied Press (now called EMAP), which, at that stage, was seen as a very small publisher, but was quite large within the magazine arena. A small stock like EMAP was 3 per cent of my portfolio initially, and it's been remarkably successful over a period of almost 20 years. But it didn't have the public profile of the large daily newspaper groups. Christies International was on a multiple about 5 – and an almost double figure yield, as was Saatchi and Saatchi at that stage. These were neglected, and we bought a lot of them."

One other vital hallmark of the SVM organisation is the flip side of the investment decision. McLean not only picks winners, he also excels at avoiding losers, and that can be even more important. If you can keep the duds out of a portfolio, then outperformance is assured. All you have to do is to be there and you will end up ahead. McLean emphasises this strength, to which he attributes much of SVM's success. In 1994, SVM stayed out of all ten of the worst new share issues. He also bought three of the ten best performers, but not buying the basket cases was more responsible for his stellar total relative return. McLean has identified a number of 'warning signals' that anyone can watch for and which can steer investors away from the wrong sort of investment temptation.

> *If you can keep the duds out of a portfolio, then outperformance is assured.*

"A willingness to dilute existing shareholders' interests gives a clear signal that executives prefer the business they are buying to the one they already run. Indeed, many of the high-profile, problem companies have tended to issue large numbers of shares. In contrast, nearly all the great personal fortunes in the UK have been built up in private companies, or those where the founders have kept a tight grip on their shares.

"The mistakes one can often make are to fail to see what drives earnings. There was an example in the newspaper industry not that long ago, when companies such as The Telegraph showed rising earnings through the recession and appeared recession proof, but growing margins were, in fact, largely made up of rising cover prices and declining physical sales. I would argue, at that time, that its principal newspaper, *The Daily Telegraph* was a declining franchise with an eroding competitive position. Physical volumes rarely change very rapidly, even in recessions. We tend, in most areas, to see only maybe a 3 per cent fall, so most of the rest is margin or destocking. But margin changes can be quite rapid, in terms of swing, as can pricing changes, when they come. A price war broke out almost overnight across the industry affecting both daily and Sunday newspapers and the share price fell by one third. The dangers can often be in areas where growth is not achieved in a sustainable way. I don't think you can carry on putting prices up for ever but, for short periods of time, it's possible."

What is clear from all of this is that you will not find much macro, big picture or top down asset allocation at SVM. What you will find is nuts and bolts superior, if slightly offbeat, analysis in search of bottoms up value one stock at a time. Some big hits stand out. As McLean describes one of his favourites, you can follow his thought process.

"One from the late 1970s, Photo Me International (the company that operates all the photo booths used for passport and ID photos), was a very good example for the 15 years I held it. It was one of the best performing stocks through the 1980s. But, during that period, it never issued any shares and the company grew organically with very strong cash generation. I never saw any research reports on it at all. It was in a niche entirely of its own. There was no competition. It didn't really have a high street presence, although people walked past booths every day. It was a remarkably successful company which grew more than 20 per cent compound over a very long period."

PUT YOUR TRUST IN TRUSTS

One relatively unusual element of the investment mix at SVM is a fund which invests only in investment trusts. This is an area shunned by the majority of investment managers, but with the proliferation of vehicles to the point where the number of listed entities comes close to exceeding the number of listed common stocks on the main market, there are great opportunities to exploit inefficiencies in the sector. The value that can be added by applying the same sort of skills and disciplines to the investment trust sector is evident from the exceptional performance achieved by Scottish Value Trust which is profiled in Chart 9.1. That a professional of McLean's standing should do so much better than the sector average is not surprising.

The extent of his outperformance, however, is impressive. Over only four and a half years an average investor who had chosen McLean's fund rather than attempting to select a personalised portfolio of trusts would now have £10,000 more to show for their selection for each £10,000 invested than the average IT investor.

Chart 9.1 SVT's Performance Relative to Investment Trust Sector. Total Return net Dividends Reinvested (% gain 18.7.91 – 31.1.96)

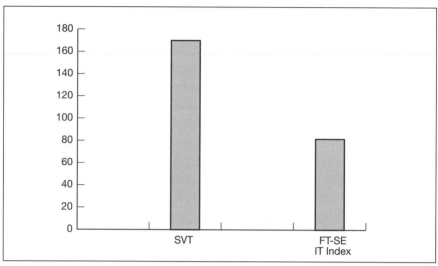

Source: Datastream

This involvement in the trust field has given McLean an extra dimension in which to exercise his eye for value. Here McLean has had enormous assistance from Duncan Duckett at SBC Warburg Securities. The net result has been a devastating combination which has worked to the benefit of McLean's shareholders.

"In 1991, Scottish Value Trust started buying into Ensign Trust which was, at that time, seen as an ailing fund with a lot of problems and potential liabilities. It was 80 per cent controlled by the Merchant Navy and Officers' Pension Fund. Ensign had been a star at one stage, but the price had fallen to about 20p from more than 60p. I had looked through the underlying portfolio. The sort of work we do, very often, is not just taking published information. We may go to Companies House and take out reports containing subsidiary information. You can see what shape the businesses were in before they were listed – how profitable they were, and whether there have been any accounting changes. So there's often a mosaic of information available just by poring over fiches we can get quite readily from Companies House.

"I did some work on the investments in Ensign and found that, certainly, some of them were almost worthless, but there were also some very valuable holdings such as in fund managers, Ivory & Sime and

222

Aberdeen Trust, and also an investment in Flemings. These were liquid and the price at which they were on the books reflected a conservative internal price. I satisfied myself that the real value of the company was in excess of 30p and that we could make an offer ourselves, in the order of something like 27p or so, to trigger some action if needed. Therefore, I didn't have to be too worried about the fact that we were a minority holder or that the Merchant Navy had 80 per cent.

"This occurred in the early days of Scottish Value Trust. The Ensign price kept on falling. It had gone down to 15p and, by that time, I had invested 15 per cent of my fund in Ensign, which represented quite a large bet. But one of the advantages with a closed-end fund is that you can actually see these strategies through. You're almost protecting clients from themselves or from their own nervousness. I know from the phone calls that I had at that time from some of the people who had just become shareholders that they thought I had blown the whole thing.

> *One of the advantages with a closed-end fund is that you can actually see these strategies through. You're almost protecting clients from themselves or from their own nervousness.*

"Within three months after that, in fact, the Merchant Navy suddenly announced that they were making an offer for the remaining stock. We got 43p for everything. So it was nice that it came right that we ended up having the resolve to see it through. There's a message in this tale. Value investors are often extracting a reward for illiquidity, buying when others need to sell."

There was an even earlier episode overseas with the restructuring of Pacific Property Investment Trust units into a purer play vehicle – Hong Kong Investment Trust. This share price has trebled since SVT's intervention.

Another theme which emerges is that McLean is not someone who will necessarily wait around for others to wake up and unlock the value he has found. If there is no other alternative, he will make the necessary moves himself.

"We try to be an active investor, but in a very discreet way. We write letters and make phone calls. We may meet management or directors to discuss our ideas. We should all have the same aims. Often that is the case and we are pushing against an open door."

Sometimes, yes. Sometimes, no. A foot in the door may be more like it, in many cases. Either way, no-one is arguing with the results. After Ensign came Drayton Consolidated and Worth. Institutions which have to reconcile multiple objectives, and who are less willing to rock the boat, are usually delighted to see McLean step in and go to work on shaking up poor performers. This may, in part, explain why several blue chip names show up on the roster of McLean's shareholders including Equitable, Legal and General, London & Manchester, Hermes, Royal Life, and even the Bank of England Pension Fund.

McLean attributes his superior returns to the same thorough nuts and bolts analysis of companies which makes his stock picking so successful, plus three other attributes:

1. Follow the discounts

The deeper discounts give greatest scope for above average returns. This is self-evident, but is only a starting point.

2. Identify a catalyst for change

Underperforming investment trusts need not necessarily be turned around by introducing new management, though that is always one possibility. In many cases, no such radical removal is required. Often a shift in investment style and focus can accomplish better results. A change in the capital structure can also unlock values. McLean carefully researches the likelihood that SVM can facilitate such change *before* making any investment.

3. Be prepared to become the catalyst

Since prudence is one prerequisite of purchasing a large – and usually less liquid – position, McLean must be confident that he can influence the existing management and/or is prepared to exert pressure where necessary to ensure that shareholders are treated fairly. SVM has been instrumental in converting trusts which were effectively cash shells into true operating companies as one more creative route to realising value. In 1994, Ballie Gifford Technology became Utility Cable at the prompting of McLean while, in 1995, he played a role in changing Worth Investment Trust into Caledonian Media Communications. This rather more radical solution to the discount problem adds that extra percentage point on to already superior returns for SVT.

In pursuit of this policy, SVT is willing to take unusually large positions in trusts, thus ensuring it has a seat at the table if necessary. McLean once owned as much as 29.9 per cent of Berry Starquest. In March 1996, SVT held four investments which represented over 15 per cent of the outstanding voting stock of the trusts in which he is a shareholder, and had several other holdings in the low teens. Table 9.2 lists these trusts.

Table 9.2 SVT Major Positions of Influence (as of 31 March 1996)

Trust	% held by SVT
ECU Trust	24.8
Northern Investors Company	18.9
Jupiter European Ord	18.0
Ivory & Sime Enterprise Cap	17.8

WARRANTS INTRODUCE ANOTHER VARIANT ON VALUE

In executing his business strategy of seeking out niche investment opportunities, McLean has homed in one other sub-segment in which the investor has been under-served. The warrant market causes ambivalence in the minds of most. Professionals tend to be one dimensional in their approach, following the Black/Scholes model for aggregating the time element and the intrinsic value. McLean has taken a somewhat solitary stance which has allowed him to exploit market inefficiencies. He approaches the warrant as if it is an extension of the underlying security. The value of the warrant becomes, if not exactly an afterthought, rather the residual calculation once he has done a thorough evaluation of the common stock. If the common stock can be characterised as undervalued, then the warrant offers a geared route to rich returns.

Following this train of thought, you can see why McLean would pick an area like the warrant market to ply his trade. The original placing document is quite explicit about his reasoning, and there is a consistency that converges on his search for areas of growth where market prices do not reflect the potential value of the underlying asset. The following extract from the WAVIT annual report gets right to the heart of the matter.

> Analysis of warrants is a relatively complex process. The Directors
> believe that many investors have traditionally been unable to justify an
> asset exposure to the investment trust warrant sector as the returns
> available can be disproportionately small in relation to the costs of
> analysing and monitoring all the warrants in the sector.

If that is not a sign of potential mispricing what is? No wonder McLean
likes the sector.

The example below, extracted from the report, illustrates, using
notional prices, how the premium and gearing factor of a warrant is calculated in the secondary market:

(a)	(b)	(c)	(d)	(e)	(f)
Fixed exercise price	Ordinary share market price	Warrant market price price per share	Effective subscription	Premium	Gearing
			$(a) + (c)$	$\dfrac{((d) - (b)) \times 100}{(b)}$	$\dfrac{(b)}{(c)}$
95p	120p	40p	135p	$12\frac{1}{2}\%$	3X

We believe that warrants are still a neglected and under-researched
sector of the stock market. Many investors tend to dispose of scrip
issues of warrants, often at prices that reflect short-term considerations
rather than long-term worth.

The nuts and bolts approach is as integral in warrant investing as elsewhere. Even in declining markets, big gains can be achieved if the right
strategy is followed. The focus is on exploiting discontinuities of value,
not just in the warrant price itself, but in the value of the company to
which the warrant is attached. During the down markets of 1994, when
many warrants fell by 50 per cent, McLean managed to find winners.

During the year, two of the larger portfolio investments – Indian
Tobacco Company and Bombril – benefited from tender offers for their
shares. In February, the fifth largest investment in the portfolio, West-
land Group, was sold following a takeover bid by GKN. The sum
realised represented a 133 per cent gain over cost. These show that
value can be identified by corporate bidders even when not fully recognised by the stock market.

The results suggest the strategy works with McLean able to deliver a
nice fillip to the normal returns an investor can expect from the underlying common stocks (see Chart 9.2).

Chart 9.2 WAVIT's Performance Relative to Investment Trust Sector (3.93 – 1.96)

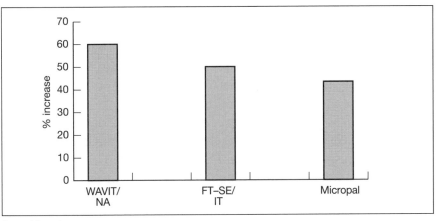

Source: Micropal

One common theme that has emerged in a number of conversations during the preparation of this book is a constant in McLean's investment philosophy as well. He has the stamina and inner fortitude to stick through situations which seem to be going against him, but where he is sure he has done his homework. Thus if, in the short term, a price is heading south instead of going up, as it should, provided nothing has changed, he can hang on, or even average down. This ability to stay the course proved essential in doubling his money at Ensign Trust and is a recurring theme at SVM.

> *McLean has the stamina and inner fortitude to stick through situations which seem to be going against him.*

"I don't have any bosses breathing down my neck; I don't have any external shareholders; I don't have outside bankers or borrowings and, if I want to make a decision that's contrarian, or even reverse a decision that I've got wrong, I can do those things without putting my job immediately on the line, which is the sort of thing that can easily happen in more political, or larger, organisations.

"Value investing is not just about different research, but it's about how you apply it and actually being structured to be able to see it through and react to events in a particular way. I don't think a risk of collapse is inherent in many companies. The risk is often about whether people would be panicked into selling at the wrong time at the wrong price. The same share can make money for one person and lose money for someone else. Equally, for something that you really run for a long time, for me something like Photo Me International, you can be up more than fifteen fold, eventually. For every person that's sat through that end game, they'll be 20 people who took a tenfold increase and probably a thousand who got out with double their money and twice as many that took a ten per cent profit the first month.

"The way in which people react to investments determines very much how successful they are. The stock market is more like backgammon in that respect. That perception of when your prospects have improved, and the right time to double up is quite important. Having the resolve to see an investment through, and not having your job on the line each month if you chose to make a mistake enables me to do that. Having closed-end funds is helpful here because, ultimately, I am answerable for performance, but only over the longer term."

Selling is always something that every great investor needs to do equally well alongside buying. Making the buying decision is somehow more glamorous, more intellectually inviting, and more interesting to talk about; but selling is when you book the profit. McLean has an approach which has evolved over his years in the profession that ensures he nails down profits when the right time comes to take them.

"If something is over-valued, we will sell it. We will sometimes even sell something which we still believe is cheap, if we really think there is something else that has a lot more potential. There has to be that inter-reaction, I think, between the things you buy and the things you sell.

"I suppose it's one of the things I've learnt from Sir John Templeton, that I usually have to be pragmatic about. There's no absolute buying or selling levels. There's what you think might be the right price for something but, as long as you're not finding anything better, why sell? I'm more like Buffett in that I prefer to run profits, particularly where I know a company quite well. I don't think you can add much value by trading a stock you want to hold long-term. The danger is that you're out at the wrong time. You may have merely replaced it with investments that you know less well. I feel a lot more confident about extracting the last penny of value out of something I know well and getting a lot closer to full valuation."

In appraising the investment climate of the 1990s, McLean sees a more challenging and more competitive environment, but one where more opportunities will be available to investors and where investment values will move much more quickly.

"Information flows far more quickly. There's still a lot more extraneous data floating around. There's still some systematic inefficiencies with people focusing very much on earnings per share, and projecting the future, not looking beyond 18 months and not trying to integrate that with the trend of the last five years."

Someone who follows accounting conventions too strongly can miss out on many of the best value opportunities.

"It was interesting, particularly in the 1970s, to see that most people were very anti service companies. In fact inflation was invisibly destroying the assets of the capital intensive companies. People were concerned about small companies but, in fact, it was big ones like Grand Metropolitan and Lyons that were in quite serious gearing trouble at that time. The quality of earnings of service businesses, like, say, Christies International, was actually much better than asset intensive ICI where the capital just couldn't be replaced with inflation at those levels. The systematic distortions were really very easy to spot. You just needed to do some current cost accounting and make adjustments to reported numbers.

"We went on to do a lot of the things that Terry Smith pointed out in his book, *Accounting for Growth*. I compare notes with him and agree that there are still some accounting distortions which are not picked up by the market, but there are fewer today. Against that, people are much quicker to spot anomalies. The gains tend to be smaller. There are far fewer things that double, which is why finding an Asda or Burton is particularly pleasing when it happens. On the plus side, that means you are much less likely to have to wait ten years for a full valuation on something you do find. It is much more likely that information will be disseminated, and that will move the price up towards full valuation. There may be smaller gains, but stock reratings happen more quickly now."

The types of businesses which will exhibit the sort of growth that can turn in exceptional profits are also likely to change. McLean is not into sector rotation as such, but has homed in on one area he intends to avoid in the 1990s. He is wary of the consumer sector but, in particular, of food companies and branded household products which were all the rage in the 1980s. He pointed out, in a recent interview, the danger of brands which are expensive to build and often even more expensive to maintain. Even cola is not immune from price wars, as has been very evident with own label taking share on supermarket shelves from Coke and Pepsi. Against that, it is those businesses with intangible values, often based on information and relationships, that are likely to feature strongly in the wealth creation of the future, and that, unfortunately, is not good news for the average individual investor.

"I do think it's going to be increasingly difficult for investors to get into the most rapidly growing businesses at the fast stages of growth. One theme is going to be an increasing amount of intellectual capital in businesses, and very often intellectual capital won't meet up with financial capital. Only one will appear on the balance sheet. I think what we're going to find is that venture capitalists may gain from backing some of these start-ups but, in other cases, because they're knowledge based businesses, very often individuals will start them up without very much capital backing.

"The stock exchange really revolves around capital, and that's where people will make their money in equities. In future, it may be harder to be part of that. The result may be that companies like MAID or Datrontech, when they come to the market, may already be valued pretty highly with the entrepreneur charging quite a lot for other investors to come in alongside. We're seeing that problem more and more, with Sony paying £10 million to youngsters who have developed new software.

"It even applies to businesses like mine, which started off with a limited amount of capital. I don't view SVM as a business that would list, but it's clearly in a growing area of activity as, indeed, many financial businesses are. For many investors, the only ways to get into young growing businesses will be to back venture capital companies, going in at the front end, or to pay higher price. If more and more of our growth over the longer-term is going to be in these knowledge based businesses, they may be under-represented in the stock market at the fastest stage of their growth."

Looking forward, McLean can see a couple of trends which should prove helpful for investors, provided they make sure the companies they invest in either fit the profile of a positive attitude to shareholders, or are positioned to be gobbled up in a more competitive market.

"One of the things that are helpful now is that companies are much more active about buying in shares. More companies are focused on making more efficient use of capital, so that's a way of releasing value which you didn't often see before.

"There is this increasing globalisation of companies which actually means that some quite sizeable UK companies, if there're trying to be competitive in a global market on a £500 million capitalisation, are really mere minnows. You just know that that can't last indefinitely. There has to be a pattern, as markets evolve and get more concentrated, that means a lot more corporate activity and many more take-overs."

That apart, McLean remains sceptical of the ability of any investor to use macroeconomic factors to lead to superior investment decisions.

"I tend to think that, in the long term, politicians can't affect things a great deal, particularly as we have got an open economy and a float-ing exchange, and we trade internationally. Even in the past I can remember when the Tory government in the 1970s tried to control the price of bread and almost everything else that they thought was affect-ing measured RPI inflation, and they failed. I tend to operate on the basis that there's very little in terms of political intervention that seems to matter. I don't look for political decisions to make or destroy value within the portfolio. I try and look beyond that. A lot of people pay too much concern to elections and political parties and have too narrow a view of what's politically sensitive. You have to look at them in a gen-eral, social context. The political persuasion of the Government doesn't matter much."

Economic factors, however, can affect how McLean looks at certain sectors and will cause him to favour one type of business over another.

"There are sometimes patterns which I can apply in investment. The impact of disinflation in the early 1990s was quite interesting. A lot of businesses which relied on asset inflation for the returns had their eco-nomics turned on their head. They ranged from businesses like Queens Moat Hotels, where people in hotel property business were getting quite low revenue returns from that business at around 5 per cent, but were expecting inflation of 5–10 per cent to add on and make a realistic real return. Sometimes the actual return on capital was quite low, but the way in which they were trying to convert that into an acceptable return on equity was just to gear up. That was the pattern at Tiphook, as well. These were all, in their own way, asset based businesses where the actual cash return on capital was low and the return on equity was flattered by leveraging up. There's still a lot of house builders where, if you strip out the impact of rights issues and take out selling the land on through slightly higher pricing into the house, it's not too difficult to show that these businesses aren't really growing. Trafalgar House was one where, in the late 1980s, if you stripped out property trading, the underlying business wasn't making much money.

"There was a quite a large number of companies which had been helped by inflation and the learning process for the UK stock market has been quite a gradual one through the 1990s. We are still having surprises.

"I see a lot of people in intermediate goods being squeezed, such as food manufacturers supplying Sainsbury's. We've seen BTR, as well, affected by that. Companies that lack final pricing power with the consumer worry me at the moment because I can see them being squeezed between slightly rising raw material costs and consumer resistance or sometimes very strong countervailing power from retailers themselves. That's been a theme that I've applied in recent years."

In one extremely important respect, I can be supremely confident that McLean is unique even among the investment manager grand masters in Britain today. His business partner is his wife. Margaret Lawson has a formidable track record in her own right, if of somewhat shorter duration than that of her husband's. Together they are a tough team.

Not only has McLean left all indices in the dust, but he has achieved this without incurring excess risk.

"In terms of having a business partner you can really have no better partner than your wife. The process of setting up in business requires an awful lot of other things to be done. To have that combined resolve to tackle all those things is a great advantage. Also our approach to investment is complementary. She brings in different skills.

"Henlys, the coachbuilder and bus manufacturer, is one of her picks, which has done extraordinarily well. Colleagues, the direct marketing services group, which is one of our larger investments, is hers. Something which I would spend a long time working through the numbers to recognise, she has the remarkable ability to spot immediately in a meeting with management."

A husband and wife team is not the only thing which is unusual at SVM. The performance for shareholders is unusual as well. Not only has McLean left all indices in the dust, disproving yet again the academic adage about the perfect market, but he has achieved this without incurring excess risk. Analysis by Smith New Court has shown that the volatility in McLean's funds is no greater than that of the market as a whole, which has to be of great comfort to his investors. As comforting as the name of his firm. How could someone ever go wrong operating under the banner 'Scottish Value'?

* Concern for the downside is a key feature of his investment strategy

* A great fan of Convertibles and Preferreds

* Outperforms around the world on a risk adjusted basis

PEREGRINE
MONCREIFFE

One Eye on
Return, the Other
on Risk

Peregrine Moncreiffe does not like talking about himself, or his career but, get him on the subject of an esoteric warrant with the call price linked to spot lead issued by a South Korean company primarily traded in Hong Kong, and you will enjoy torrents of enthusiasm. Anyone who confines their investments to blue chip UK stocks and gilts can skip this chapter, but readers who are looking for unlikely ways to spice up their own portfolios will find Moncreiffe's insights richly rewarding.

Context is important because, without an understanding of Moncreiffe's mindset, it is difficult to understand why his approach works so well. Buchanan Partners is unlike any of the other firms featured in this book, and rather a rare bird, even today, in London's increasingly diverse financial community. A word of explanation will help to get to grips with what it is he is doing.

"We started with three partners: myself, Kevin Rowe and Sharanbir Brijnath. We were all proprietary traders at Credit Suisse First Boston at one time or another, which means we traded using the company's capital and did not service external clients. When we went out on our own, our goal was to produce an investment product that was remarkably different from other things on offer. There were always a lot of funds run by great speculators around using a macro approach. We developed a product which used hedged strategies to produce returns independent of market direction – and, by that, I mean stock markets, bond markets and currency markets, which is where most people try to make money speculatively.

"Generally managers are paid to outperform the standard benchmarks and, therefore, we must look at any means of doing so. In our case cash and bond rates were our original clients' benchmarks and so we have focused on arbitrage and long/short strategies. We have now ended up also in the more traditional business of managing long equity money."

The genesis of the style at Buchanan Partners stems directly from the evolution of the trading environment in which the principals had operated prior to striking out on their own. Each of the principal directors who have subsequently joined, Jason Hathorn, Mark Pearson and Richard Webb, have added their own backgrounds in quantitative investment and trading. Moncreiffe himself has been around the markets for some 24 years, a period during which enormous changes have occurred. Most obvious inefficiencies, especially in mature markets, have been priced out. To stay ahead of the crowd requires a new level of imagination, and a continuing commitment to research and development.

"There used to be considerable discrepancies between the yield curve created by real demand and supply of money on the one hand, and what was likely to happen in the future. Once futures came in, you suddenly started competing with a million or so doctors and dentists in the Mid West of the US, some of whom are pretty smart. The fixed interest market is now much better at discounting the likely future course of events.

"At the beginning of Buchanan's development we were looking for areas of the market where anomalous pricing of securities meant we could construct hedged positions which would make money independent of the market's direction. This led us to warrant and convertible arbitrage, particularly in the Japanese market, and to arbitraging discounts on closed-end funds."

It's difficult to get the exact details of the prior performance history of the principals at Buchanan Partners in their former incarnations due to the confidential nature of the account records at their previous employers. What we are able to share is that CSFB's *proprietary* trading group was one of its most profitable areas for many years and that was impressive within a firm which was noted for making money in trading. Peregrine Moncreiffe was the youngest Executive Director in his day at CSFB and following that had been the youngest Partner of Lehman Brothers when he ran their US Treasury Bond Department. So it is not stretching things to say he was acknowledged as a star by two of the toughest peer groups in the investment industry. The record continues now he is out on his own. In the third year of operations which Moncreiffe admits was an extraordinary year, their accounts show that Buchanan Partners Limited earned over 100 per cent on capital before incentive compensation and tax.

If that is not enough, and it seems pretty extraordinary performance by any conventional yardstick, then suffice it to say that the name Buchanan Partners, and Peregrine Moncreiffe in particular, elicits the sort of respect around the City which is usually reserved for someone who has retired rather than someone who remains an all too active rival.

Let's look at each of the main themes which, together, make up the Buchanan investment philosophy.

Closed-end Fund Arbitrage

The game here can be boiled down to two essential elements. Find cheap bundles of assets and squeeze them hard until they perform properly.

"We buy closed-end funds at a discount, hedging if possible. If the actual expected return is high enough relative to the expected volatility of the underlying assets, we would not necessarily hedge our position.

"When you are able to buy at a 40 per cent discount, as we were doing in 1992 and 1993, that is an expected return of over 65 per cent, if you can create an exit at net asset value. To identify these opportunities, you must have good screening and monitoring ability, as well as an understanding of the shareholder base and legal considerations.

"There has been a lot of academic work done on why so many closed-end funds trade at discounts. One of the reasons which is perfectly understandable, is that expenses and costs combined with underperformance, can eat up the advantage. Another is that they are usually marketed and sold when the theme of the fund is very popular. Take Asian Telecommunications. When they are strong, everyone wants to invest and a fund is sold by salespeople who are financially motivated to do so. In order to prevent these funds falling to large discounts, you have to have almost the same amount of selling effort; but the maximum sales effort is at the time of launch, and all the most likely buyers are called at that time. In addition you often start off by paying £1 and getting 95p in assets, because of the issue costs and commissions, and the immediate drop in net asset value after the issue date discourages further purchases.

"Subsequently, the theme goes out of favour and people want liquidity. At the margin, all the basic buyers have been taken out and there is no positive motivation to the salespeople through commission, or negative motivation through job risk. So it drifts down.

"It also appears that investors put far too high a premium on liquidity. That is a source of opportunity in the closed-end fund market and most markets in general. In particular most investors are prepared to sell assets at a price which is not truly representative of underlying value, because they have a belief that they will be able to make extraordinary returns by redeploying the money elsewhere into a better idea. The liquidity preference is usually too high relative to its true value. Providing liquidity to people when they are desperate for it is a very good way to make money. Equally, selling closed-end funds when they are at premiums or a very small discount is usually a sensible strategy, because that is usually when both liquidity premium and equity risk premium are low."

The outline of the operation is relatively straightforward, though carrying out the strategy is rather more complicated. Investors should never lose sight of the full range of opportunistic plays which can arise in the closed-end arena. Moncreiffe has spotted several variants on this core theme.

> *Providing liquidity to people when they are desperate for it is a very good way to make money.*

"You can also find situations where markets in which funds are invested shoot up and the funds are left behind. It sometimes takes a sustained and broad market rally with international investor interest to close the discounts which have opened up.

"When that occurs, you can get a period of over-extension. At the beginning of 1994, I was told that Jardine Fleming had to stop taking money into some of its Asian mutual funds. When something goes bid only with no offer after a sustained upward movement, it's usually a sign you are near the top of that particular mania. That wall of money was one of the arguments being used for the continuing price rise but, actually, it was the final bell. Discounts on funds became very, very narrow, which was another clue. When you see discounts out of line with normal trading, or even premiums appearing, and if that's not purely the result of a collapse in the local market not yet reflected in the quote of the fund, then it's usually a sign of the end of a bull run. It tells me that investors' liquidity preference has declined dramatically and there's a negative return to buyers and a positive return to someone supplying the securities. A good asset allocation model should include data on whether closed-end vehicles are trading anomalistically as a signal."

The big danger, with closed-end funds, is that you find a value which is real enough, but then nothing happens. Moncreiffe is well aware of this problem, but he has a series of solutions to solve it.

"You can buy at a 40 per cent discount and find that it's still there in four years' time, and you haven't made any excess return. Also many managers underperform the market, so you have explicit costs, but also implicit costs, which is having the money managed by someone who is likely to be doing worse than the market.

"Every fund tends to have its own quirks about voting and management agreements and every fund has a different group of shareholders. We have to take a view on how easy it will be to get our money back at nearer to net asset value. That may require a mandatory winding up or we may be able to persuade the managers to create value by realising some investments. On the whole, we would rather work with existing managers to restructure a fund. Where the board have tended to ignore the share price performance, we have been willing, with the support of other shareholders, to replace the board. This is sometimes unpopular, but is helpful to shareholders."

Seeing this strategy at work allows one to follow Moncreiffe's thought process. He is concerned not only to secure superior returns by exploiting inefficiencies, but also tries to do so in a way which keeps the risk to a minimum.

"Govett Atlantic was a fund mainly in the US market. We acquired a stake at a discount of more than 25 per cent which, for a fund invested in liquid securities, is rare, and we were able to hedge the market risk quite efficiently, by borrowing the underlying stocks and shorting them in combination with a short position in S&P futures.

"One other shareholder and ourselves had over 10 per cent of the fund, so we told management we were prepared to requisition an EGM unless they came up with a better idea for eroding the discount. There, the board did put forward a restructuring proposal. The bulk of the portfolio was liquidated and a stub of less liquid investments was distributed *in specie* in a different vehicle. So investors got close to 97 per cent of net asset value over about six months [a return of more than 60 per cent annualised]."

When push comes to shove, Moncreiffe is the wrong man to push. If all else fails, he is prepared to take a more aggressive stance. Malaysia Smaller Companies' Fund had a rather recalcitrant board who were not receptive to the suggestions. Buchanan requisitioned an EGM, a vote was held, the board replaced and the Fund put into liquidation.

"We will always have holdings in closed-end funds as long as there are discounts in the market, especially in our closed-end emerging markets fund, where we have about 50 per cent in other closed-end funds."

This Buchanan Fund has outperformed its MSCI Emerging Benchmark by around 10 per cent in the last 6 months alone.

Offbeat Securities

Moncreiffe is a man who likes things that are out of the ordinary. There is a certain perverse pleasure in a strategy which spurns basic bonds and common stocks and plumps for hybrid instruments; but that's also where an investor who is not stuck in a rut can find the best bargains. Moncreiffe is open to buying into situations which more traditional minds cannot, or will not, take the time to understand. This lack of interest allows him to add another element which contributes to his superior track record.

"We will always have a sprinkling of interesting securities such as preference shares, convertibles and warrants. There are areas of inefficiencies in these instruments which give us a leg up in getting a better return than in the underlying market. To do well, you have to be able to assess both the potential and future volatility of the underlying stock, and return advantage you can get from buying a derivative.

> *There are areas of inefficiencies in preference shares, convertibles and warrants which give us a leg up in getting a better return than in the underlying market.*

"One example of this is Samsung preferred shares, which we have been able to buy at a 45 per cent discount to the ordinary shares. These are not true preferreds. They are similar to ordinary shares in all respects apart from the lack of voting rights, but pay a slightly higher dividend and have almost double the yield of the ordinaries. We consider that the value of the votes is relatively small for a foreign shareholder. Often these companies are controlled through cross shareholdings by other industrial or family groups, and there is very little hostile takeover activity where votes might have a value."

There are some drawbacks to delving into the backwaters and byways of the unusual security. Sometimes you hit a dead end. The instruments are usually somewhat illiquid. They can be hard to get into, and harder to get out of. Failing a forced conversion, an investor can be stuck: stuck with a great bargain, in theory, but unable to realise true value in practice. Time is probably the greatest risk of all, and Moncreiffe accepts that some of his holdings will be bogged down. It's a price he has to pay. With a diversified portfolio, the price is reasonable, but following this strategy mandates either broad diversification or a very clear exit route.

There an Option, Here an Option, Everywhere an Option

Options can come in many shapes and sizes. Warrants can add a kicker to an equity. Market options can be used to infuse a short element into a portfolio. Then there's hybrid securities. Moncreiffe has warm words for convertible instruments. This is particularly true at times like March 1996, when many developed country markets are at, or close to, all time highs.

"Convertible bonds give you some kind of a floor. Then, if you're wrong about the market, you've at least preserved a substantial portion of your capital. It's worth paying something for that sort of insurance."

You have to be aware that as markets fall, the risk of bond default probably grows, and so Moncreiffe warns that convertible bond floors can become unstable when markets are in distress.

"Put options are probably worth more after a big market run up. If you assume price distributions are log normal, theoretically they should not be worth much more but, where people do feel exposed, it's a good idea to pay for a bit of insurance. The implied volatility on S&P options is currently quite high, particularly on the out of the money puts. In a sense, there's an intuitive understanding on the part of the market operators that insurance is worth paying for at this stage in the market."

Temporary Imbalances in Markets

While the focus of Moncreiffe's work is to find securities which are structurally misunderstood, and therefore mispriced, he is not averse to short-term trading when conditions for arbitrage are created.

"Bid situations provide opportunities to take a position in the market. At the extremes, where you find a company which is extraordinarily cheap on a cash flow multiple basis and, when something is really out of favour, these stocks often become attractive to predators, even if they do not appear to have a great future. We found that our value analysis pushed us into companies such as William Low (a chain of supermarkets in Scotland) before it was bid for by Tesco's and Sainsbury's. Even though the earnings downgrades were pushing us away from the stock, value became predominant and we maintained a substantial position.

"As long as the company was not going out of business, it is hard to lose if you buy based on a very low cash flow multiple. If the perceived prospects don't improve, it's likely they will become subject to bid speculation. This is why it's also useful to look at price to sales ratios. If it's cheap on price to sales, even if the prospects for growth are not good, someone else can probably make those assets work better."

> *As long as the company was not going out of business, it is hard to lose if you buy based on a very low cash flow multiple.*

There are also arbitrage situations which can arise temporarily. This can be seen where two variants of the same share trade on separate exchanges and where there are two classes of stock, as is common in some emerging markets where foreign ownership is restricted.

"Telebras ordinary in Brazil is voting stock and the ADR in New York is non-voting. We monitor the discount on a real time basis. What's interesting is that the non-voting usually trades more expensively than the voting, because a lot of people are not set up to buy domestic Brazilian stocks. We trade the discount range.

"Sometimes international demand will cause departures from the normal range of a relationship between domestic and foreign prices. Popular companies, such as San Miguel in the Philippines, or Bangkok Bank in Thailand, can see premiums on the foreign eligible shares going over 50 per cent. When that happens, we won't hold that asset, but we will find an alternative either in the closed-end fund market or finding other access to domestic stock. It is important for international investors to ensure that they are not exposed to situations which are dramatically overpriced for reasons of convenience."

Managing Risk to the Minimum

All of this sounds somewhat speculative and a lot more risky than sticking with the better known names but Moncreiffe is, in fact, rather risk reverse. Overlaying the whole investment philosophy is a paranoia to protect his shareholders from too much exposure to market risk. He starts out with the view that he has a duty to protect the downside – so far, not unusual – but then he goes the next leg and sees how, in reducing risk in his portfolio, new opportunities to make money open up. He likes to buy securities which he believes are protected on the downside either by a high yield as in the case of preferreds, or by a high earnings yield. If they go down, they are almost certainly too cheap. Stocks on high PE's in contrast have a long way to fall if they go out of fashion.

"When you lose money quickly you have to try and make it back slowly."

Some examples:

"In order to get that extra return, we might buy a convertible and short the underlying security. In June 1994 we maintained a short position in Sega, then trading at ¥7,700 and bought the convertible at 100. A month or so later we sold the convertible at prices between 102 and 104 and bought back our short in the ordinary shorts at prices between ¥7,240 and ¥7,678.

> *In order to get that extra return, we might buy a convertible and short the underlying security.*

"Or we might buy a cheap convertible and short a security in the same sector which we liked less. In 1993, Toa Steel convertible looked cheap, so we bought that, but shorted Tokyo Steel shares. The Toa common subsequently declined 20 per cent as did Tokyo Steel, but the Toa convertible hung in, declining by only 5 per cent, because it had a relatively high yield. This trade was only on for about three months, and so the annualised return was around 50 per cent plus.

"We might find a way to get into the underlying security more cheaply than buying it direct. To get into Mitsubishi Petrochemical we bought Mitsubishi Kasei warrants. In May 1994 Mitsubishi Petrochemical had announced merger terms with Mitsubishi Kasei, which was trading around 3 per cent below the merger ratio equivalent level. We shorted Mitsubishi Petrochemical at ¥716 and bought Mitsubishi Kasei warrants which were cheap relative to the underlying shares. The warrants were bought at $16.25 and sold at prices between $18.50 and $23.50 in October, when we repurchased our short in Petrochemical at 702. The existence of attractively priced warrants gave us the ability to make a substantial profit on both sides of an otherwise good but ordinary risk arbitrage transaction."

Long/Short Strategies

At the heart of the portfolio is a series of linked positions which represents the core investment theory practised *chez* Buchanan Partners. This is employed over about 65 per cent of the total money under management. It all stems from a constant desire to control risk and, where risk results from buying a position in a company, be it the equity, or a bond, or something in between, then the first question that comes up is how to reduce that company specific risk. Moncreiffe is never satisfied until he has lighted on a way to stay hedged, at least in part. Hang on here, because what follows is not for the faint of mind. This is where you have to put down your glass of wine and concentrate. It's not too complicated and it's worth the effort.

"Long/short strategies can be created on the basis of a number of different qualitative or quantitative criteria. We are able to do this particularly in equities in Japan, the UK and France which are large liquid markets. To a large extent, these are process trades which result from our analysis of all the actively traded companies in those markets. We have developed our own assessment of what causes a company to underperform or outperform and, based on back tests and our experience, we came up with a series of quantifiable ratios which allow us to rank all securities from least attractive to most attractive.

"In terms of criteria used, the underlying theme is value, though we do make adjustments for growth and changes in earnings. We get earnings forecasts on 12,000 companies around the world, which adds a forward looking aspect to our models.

"We also look at residual reversal in some markets. Here we are tracking the process by which some stocks, which have outperformed for a period of time in certain markets tend to revert towards a more mean level of return, and stocks which have underperformed tend to revert also to a more normal performance and, therefore, do better. You can break down what causes the relative performance of a stock in terms of a number of factors, including its sector, leverage, balance sheet and earnings characteristics. We can explain how that relates to the market overall, but there will also be part of a stock's performance which cannot be explained. Some of that unexplained move is likely to be reversed.

"One other thing we do which most quantitative managers don't do is to adjust book values for listed investments and bond holdings. This is particularly important, still, in Japan. If you looked at Fuji Photo in June 1995, you were able to buy the shares net of its cash and securities holdings at around $3\frac{1}{2}$ times gross operating cash flow. On that basis it was cheaper than Eastman Kodak."

The private investor cannot begin to attempt to do this sort of analysis on a systematic basis, but there is no reason not to factor in this line of thinking for any single stock which might be under consideration.

"Another reason why we have to have a large number of positions is that it can be difficult to find enough borrowable stock. You don't want to have too concentrated a short position, or be too big in any one stock."

Imperfect Pairs

Start out by trying to forget everything you thought you ever knew about how to construct a theoretically well matched portfolio of longs and shorts, and you might be getting close to how Moncreiffe looks at his long/short portfolio construction.

"We don't usually look at our trades in terms of pairs – at least, not explicitly – but, implicitly, you can eyeball relationships between longs and shorts in our portfolios. We aim for optimisation of the total portfolio of all our longs and all our shorts. This gives us much more flexibility than a classic pairs trader. A classic pairs trader is really constrained because, if there are two chemical companies, say Dow Chemical versus Dupont, then you'll find those companies have different leverage, and differences in many other things such as the amount of export earnings, and they are not really similar in many ways that matter. We have been successful in 'pairs' arbitrage between company's securities which trade in different guises such as Royal Dutch versus Shell.

"We usually have some sectoral risk, because value may be concentrated in certain industries and because some of the return from earnings forecast revisions comes from sector mismatch, but even that's relatively small. We like to find the cheapest and most expensive company in a sector and trade those to reduce risk by eliminating the sector mismatch."

Moncreiffe provided illustrations of how the theoretical underpinnings translate into specific long/short pairings. Some will be similar companies within the same sector, but a match is not made solely on the basis of industry. Another characteristic which can lead to a pair is the result of cross-shareholding structures.

"An example of a pair in the same sector was our purchase of Calsonic early in 1994 at ¥492 versus a short position in Suzuki at ¥1437. Calsonic was then one of the cheapest stocks in the auto sector. In September 1994 we covered Suzuki at ¥1230 and sold Calsonic at ¥682."

There are pitfalls in a shorting strategy, even one which is designed to reduce risk. The problem is more one of market structure and procedure than of good or bad investment decisions. Anyone who sees the merit in Moncreiffe's approach needs to proceed with caution and an awareness of how a well laid plan can come adrift. Realistically, for the individual outside of the US market, shorting of any sort is fraught with administrative hurdles, and this is more one for the professional or full-time investor. To a large extent, individuals still have put options as the hedge of first and last resort, though, for anyone interested, it should be possible to short specific stocks if you run an account active enough to have clout with a broker.

"We don't like to talk about short positions which we have on. The amount of borrowable stock is limited and, therefore, particularly in non-US markets, where the free float can be quite small relative to the market cap – the Japanese banking sector is an example of that – people really can squeeze you. This was a mistake some very smart American investors made in the summer of 1992. They talked about their shorts and some specific banks. They were heavily squeezed. IBJ (Industrial Bank of Japan) went up around 105 per cent between the end of June and the beginning of September that year while the Nikkei only rose 17 per cent. There's another lesson here. When you see other investment managers specifying shorts, you should gang warily."

> *When you see other investment managers specifying shorts, you should gang warily.*

Still, even with all the possible problems, this is a strategy which has a lot of intrinsic appeal for any investor who can execute the trades. Effectively, you got the double whammy of having two ways to make money for the same level of net cash exposure while significantly decreasing the systematic market risk. "We have been able to produce outperformance on our longs and underperformance on our shorts. It has been fairly evenly split." Has Moncreiffe found investor nirvana?

It's not just the companies themselves which count. The characteristics of the companies can influence Moncreiffe's portfolio construction. You do not want imperfect pairs with four left feet.

"Another factor we are concerned about is the relative leverage on either side of the portfolio. You can reduce the exposure by balancing that across sectors. In engineering, you might be short a highly lever-aged company and long one with low leverage. Over in the retail sector, you can be long a company with a lot of leverage and short one which is under-leveraged."

For those who have a yen to get really fancy, you can progress into three-dimensional risk trade-off. The added layer of complexity comes when you extend this analysis across different geographic markets.

"We have found there are correlations between companies in the same sector across different markets. The more developed the markets, the better the correlation; but managing the risk is more difficult. It is easier to look at shares within each market and then separately choose the markets which have the best return expectations."

This line of thinking can also embrace strata of stock within a market.

"You sometimes tend to be long slightly smaller cap companies than the ones which you want to short. There is a frequent tendency for larg-er cap stocks to be more fully valued and, in the mid-cap area, there's often less efficient pricing. So you have to control any bias there."

And segment again, based on cer-tain other yardsticks which lead to the best balance of over-versus under-valu-ation for the total portfolio.

> *You have to be careful in case what you think is a measure of value may be just a measure of bankruptcy risk.*

"You have to be careful in case what you think is a measure of value may be just a measure of bankruptcy risk. I am told that if you had bought all the cheapest companies in the US market on a price to book basis in 1928 and went short the more expensive ones with high price to book ratios, you would have lost money between 1928 and 1933. Some of the 'cheapest' went out of business."

Something of a Quant Jock

There's a touch of the professorial about Peregrine Moncreiffe, though his activity is anything but academic, and his entire effort is harnessed to enhancing actual profits in a real portfolio. Top proprietary traders, including his former employer, went through a phase of hiring eminent theoreticians from the tallest ivory towers to test their concepts, which came from years of back testing. The more esoteric and complex the black box, the better, though Moncreiffe emphasises that the computer is just a tool not the master. The growing presence of computers, which became integral to trading floors in the early 1980s, meant nothing new lasted for long, but it did place a premium on efficient utilisation of computing power. Moncreiffe is quite at home with such a regime, but has adapted it to the real world constraints of data availability and actual market conditions.

"We have a highly systematic, bottom up stock selection model. This approach works most effectively in relatively less efficient, but relatively liquid, markets where there is not too much inside information and you are competing on a reasonably level playing field. Leaving aside the US, it has been successful in Japan, the UK and France. We have found that it has also proved successful in selecting long positions in less developed markets such as Mexico, Malaysia and Brazil."

Specifically, Buchanan focuses on a small, select band of core ratios and quantifiable criteria. In most markets they are variants of the following themes:

- Earnings yield (the P/E reciprocal)
- Price to book
- Price to sales
- Earnings revisions

"You must look at the enterprise value which, in part, is derived from its sales. A company whose margins have been squeezed can sometimes be an attractive takeover candidate."

Once the process is complete, there is a top to bottom ranking available. This ranking is not used blindly, but it is the starting point for building up the long/short portfolio.

"We look at the companies at the top and bottom in detail. We try to make sure our longs and shorts are correlated in terms of risk. We try to control the risk of divergence, which we call tracking error. We tend to construct portfolios in the UK and Japan with tracking error of around 3 to 4 per cent. That means that there is a 17 per cent chance of losing more than that in any year just because of the risk inherent in the portfolios.

"In Japan we may have as many as 300 positions, 180 long and 120 short out of our universe of 1,500 stocks. When you are trying to capture extra returns, you can have difficulty trading in size without moving the price adversely. The market won't always let you focus your positions at extremes in very large size."

It's rather relieving to hear that there is still room for human intervention somewhere, though more as a common sense check than as a determinant factor.

"To a large extent, the process is forced upon us by the system which we have created. If we're not happy with what the computer is saying, it means we have to justify changes to the program. If you put too much human reaction against a system which is properly tested, it's usually a mistake, because you are missing the element of objectivity which the system is there to provide.

"In the early days of our UK strategy VSEL looked very cheap, but we said, 'This company has no future. Who's going to be buying submarines?' So we didn't buy when it was £4, even though the system was telling us to buy; and it has been a stomping success. We soon learnt that the system was right and bought it at just under £9 and finally sold at £15¼.

"Our process highlights the orphans and steers us into sectors which are cheap. We were buying banks in 1992 and more recently tobacco related stocks like Molins and BAT. Wellcome got relatively very cheap two years ago because of people's concern about the patent position on their top selling drug, Zovirax, and we were long but at the same time we were short Glaxo. We will do things which go against the grain. The trade worked well when Glaxo bid for Wellcome, but we have found that we do tend to be on the right side of takeover bids – short buyers, and long the acquired companies.

"When asked, I say that in general 80 per cent is the system and 20 per cent is people, but that will vary from market to market. And don't forget, people build and update the system. Of course, the smaller cap you go, the more the specific risk, and we look more closely at the numbers in order to make our own adjustments. It's an expert system using statistics, not a statistical system, and all the weightings reflect the experience of the experts who manage the portfolios.

"One good thing about our rigorous process is that you tend to follow the adage, 'Bulls and bears make money and pigs don't.'

"We have been short so called favoured stocks which had gone ex growth, like Spring Ram, the kitchen cabinet company, and fashion favourite Laura Ashley. We've found that you often have to wait a long time for these sorts of shorts to work. When they do, often after a profits warning, you get a big leg down, sometimes followed by another leg down, so you don't want to take your profit too soon. Conversely, people should be careful about buying disaster stories before they have a second, or even third, move down. Systematic evaluation enables us to make a rapid assessment of the relative attractiveness of the stock at each price level."

To give you a flavour for how Moncreiffe keeps tabs on his positions, Chart 10.1 on the following page, contains an extract from the summary sheet which is used to track the various characteristics of the investment portfolio. It illustrates how this quantitative bent drives weighting. Institutional investors will feel at home. Others may prefer a less challenging chart.

Macro/Micro – Shake it all About

Moncreiffe's model has a combination of active and passive ingredients. He eschews a lot of traditional economic variables in favour of a back to basics earnings driven approach; but his focus is not on absolute levels so much as the significance of change. If something moves, that is sending a message. If something stays static, that inactivity is telling you something, as well.

"Many people will tend to look at GNP growth and inflation and interest rates and lots of data derived from macro economic assumptions. These models may work over the longer term, but they have a lot of difficulty in timing and, as a consequence, are not easily tradable.

"We feel that movements in stock markets are partly explained by the movement in interest rates relative to earnings yields, and also by the relative change in earnings forecasts for the aggregate of all companies in a market which is a reflection of sentiment. So, in a country where analysts are becoming more bullish about earnings, that market will tend to outperform a country where earnings are being downgraded. There is also a tendency for momentum in forecast changes to continue. Where there are mostly upgrades, you tend to get more earnings upgrades in the future, until the trend is broken.

"Analysts tend to be conservative and work in a discontinuous process. They may look at a company every six months when, actually,

Chart 10.1 Portfolio Extract as of 1 April 1996

Company Name	BRDG	Price	Sector	Ind	Company Alpha	Earnings Revision	Revision Chg	Last Change	Res. Rev.	TOTAL ALPHA ecl.res	Grad bp/w	Sxs
U.K. EQUITY MODEL				Avg	0.0%	0.0%	0.0%		0.02%	-0/2%	-2	
				Mod	0.2%	0.2%	0.0%		0.00%	0.1%	-1	Long Sht.
			Index	Stdev	5.0%	2.3%	1.2%		0.49%	5.7%	28	Net
EXISTING POSITIONS			1 = FTSE	Max	14.6%	6.8%	6.0%	26 Mar	1.50%	17.9%	65	Agg.
01-Apr 96			2 = 250	Min	-16.6%	-7.5%	-6.3%		-1.50%	-21.6%	-82	
18:56			3 = Other Allshr						(+ve = has outperformed)			
			4 = Other NMS		Portfolio exposure 1.86%	0.70%			0.03%	5.69%	12	0.63
Company Name	BRDG	Price	Sector	Ind	Company Alpha	Earning Revision	Revision Chg	Last Change	Res Rev	TOTAL ALPHA excl res	Grad Top/w	Sxs
Lloyds Chemists	LYC	477	STORES	2	1.2%	1.1%	0.0%	29-Feb	0.00%	17.2%	37	2.97
Standard Chartered	SIAN	609	BANKS	1	-1.4%	3.2%	-2.0%	22-Mar	0.29%	16.4%	30	2.97
British Aerospace	BA	859	ENGAER	1	0.2%	4.5%	-3.0%	27-Mar	0.32%	14.1%	61	1.81
Mirror Group News.	MGN	218	MEDIA	2	5.9%	0.4%	-0.4%	19-Mar	0.02%	13.8%	27	1.52
Misys	MSY	726	ELTRNX	2	-5.9%	5.1%	-1.3%	05-Mar	0.22%	13.8%	36	2.97
Dixons Group	DXNS	447	STORES	2	-4.4%	3.5%	0.3%	22-Mar	0.36%	12.8%	56	2.67
Molins	MLN	909	ENGGRL	3	1.9%	0.3%	-0.2%	19-Mar	0.25%	12.2%	13	2.05
Hogg Robinson	HRB	230	B SERV	3	6.6%	0.0%	0.0%	05-Feb	0.20%	12.1%	13	1.15
T & S Stores	TSS	204	STORES	3	8.0%	1.2%	0.0%	28-Mar	0.05%	11.9%	30	0.52
Bet	BET	203	B SERV	2	-0.1%	0.2%	0.0%	14-Mar	0.35%	10.9%	5	2.23
Amstrad	ATD	188	ELTRNX	3	9.3%	1.5%	-0.2%	08-Mar	0.83%	9.8%	65	-0.35
Unichem	UNC	243	HEALTH	2	11.6%	0.8%	0.5%	14-Mar	0.01%	8.9%	21	-0.72
Cowie T	COWE	346	MOTORS	2	3.4%	3.7%	3.1%	19-Mar	0.16%	8.8%	24	0.38
Lex Services	LEX	317	MOTORS	2	13.7%	-1.4%	0.0%	19-Mar	0.00%	8.7%	11	-0.74

changes are happening much more quickly than that. One thing an analyst will take into account is what he or she has said before, because of the need for subsequent justification. He will also take into account what other people are saying. So he may try to come close to the average, avoid extremes and try not to make as much of a change from the previous estimate as might be justified by his calculations.

> *The aggregate of all earnings forecasts in a country is most interesting as a measure of sentiment for the corporate sector.*

"So it's significant when someone moves away from the mean; and it's particularly significant where you see the high or low forecasts moving away from the mean. The patterns of earnings forecast changes are important to monitor.

"The aggregate of all earnings forecasts in a country is most interesting as a measure of sentiment for the corporate sector. There should be much more validity to scores of analysts doing work on hundreds of companies and their prospects than the economic expectations for the country, derived from a few economists' macro-models."

Dealing with a Lot of Data has Drawbacks

The old saying, garbage in, garbage out, is as applicable in investment decisions as elsewhere. The up-front data entry step becomes critical and managing the inputs is where Moncreiffe and his team add a lot of value.

"Sometimes there are problems with the data. You have to adjust for extraordinary items. You have to look at accounting policies. For example, in the UK, acquisition accounting is an area of concern. Is the depreciation sensible? Is the amortisation sensible?

"If you test everything, you will find relationships which appear to work when you back-test, but it's a fluke and, in fact, they have no bearing on the outcome. Data mining can be dangerous. If you work hard enough, you'll find apparently sensible weightings and figure out how to get the best return based on what happened, and it can still be meaningless for the future."

Don't Get Side-tracked by Momentum

Inevitably, there are touches of the trader rather than the investor in Moncreiffe's make-up. These assert themselves every so often and, for the most part, in a positive and constructive manner. It takes one to know one, which means Moncreiffe can increase his investment performance by being a smart trader. That can add a crucial point or two each year. His trading background manifests itself in a few simple guidelines investors should learn by rote.

"Many investors find it very hard to keep their hands off securities which are moving higher in price, or stay away from securities which are heading down."

Sell when you See the Money Heading in your Direction

"When there is too much money flowing into the market, our process involves selling positions because of probable overvaluation. We try and use liquidity when it comes in to sell, because that's the best time to realise less liquid securities. The discount on a closed-end fund is, to some extent, a function of the equity risk premium demanded by investors so, when it diminishes we will provide the market with stock to meet the demand."

> *We try and use liquidity to sell because that's the best time.*

WHAT NEXT FOR 1996 AND 1997?

Understanding the past is helpful and important, but there is a limit to what an investor can do with historical insight. Being able to tap into the thinking of a grand master of the markets and see where he believes the best opportunities will be in the future can open up more avenues for profitable application.

"My perception is probably a bit too much in line with other people's, which is that emerging markets are at least now [April 1996] somewhat undervalued, relative to some of the developed markets; and that the Continental European equity markets still offer opportunity because they are under-owned by domestic institutions.

"Equity investors in those countries are not competing, to the same extent, with pension funds and insurance companies, which are trying to buy a growing annuity stream to hedge their future liabilities. You don't want to compete with people who are prepared to pay an insurance premium, because people nearly always pay too much for insurance. Though the US stock market as a whole may be overvalued, you can still find individual companies which are under-followed, under-owned and, therefore, undervalued. From time to time, you get exceptional values in small to medium small caps, even when the market is highly rated.

"In the UK and the US, many of the best opportunities now are in the smallest listed companies and in the unquoted sectors, though it's hard to find solid growth companies in the smaller cap sector in the UK, which limits the opportunities here. That's why I think North Atlantic Smaller Companies Investment Trust is so interesting. It is far better not to be exposed in what is popular, especially after a large run up such as we've seen recently. It's tempting to put money into things which have performed well, and that strategy can work when momentum is with you, but leaves you very exposed when the market turns."

So much for those safe, familiar shares. No more IBM or ICI or good old gilts for the investors of 1997, at least, not those investors who are serious about positioning their portfolios in the path of profit.

> **The greatest money making opportunity is in emerging markets, which are out of favour.**

"The greatest money making opportunity is in emerging markets, which are out of favour."

The question of the hour is what does that mean when we look forward into 1997? Moncreiffe did not hesitate to describe where he felt the best investment ideas were. His reasoning has a longevity, while individual recommendations inevitably alter with the passage of time.

"From a UK point of view, the area where investors should be looking to make a lot of money is Eastern Europe. It's the growth region in our backyard.

"Our number one pick, right now, would be Russia. It may still go lower. The largest Blue Chip, Lukoil, is trading around $4.00 today. The privatisation voucher auction came at around $3.00, so it hasn't quite hit rock bottom, but it hit $9.00 in September 1994 and I'd expect it to be quite a bit higher than today's price a year from now. There are, needless to say, better opportunities in other counters.

"One of these in Russia is in preference or 'privileged' shares. Take Lukoil. The preference shares trade at $1.30, and the ords are at $4.00. Lukoil's prefs have the same, or better, cash distribution rights than the common, but trade at less than one third, and it's just about that simple. So we're long the prefs and short the ords.

"The prefs don't have votes, except if someone wants to change their rights, but that doesn't really matter in Russia unless you are a strategic investor. In most emerging markets, it's not worth valuing votes highly. You have to accept you're going to be at someone else's mercy. You do have to pay attention to other peoples' votes to know if a dominant individual or group will act to the detriment of the portfolio investors.

"Another example is Norilsk Nickel, which has about a quarter of the world's nickel market. 25 per cent of the shares are in prefs, which get 10 per cent of the net profits in dividends, but the ords aren't getting any dividends. The ords trade around $4.40 and the prefs at $3.20. If the government makes any further sales of Norilsk shares, according to the Company charter the prefs should become convertible into ords, and that's quite likely. Most of their revenues are dollar referenced, which reduces some of the rouble risk.

"There are pitfalls. They may delay paying until the rouble collapses, or they may not pay out in full. There is a large health warning attached to all transactions in Russia, as in addition to the registration risk, there is the risk that companies will use various devices to avoid making payments in situations when declared profits look decidedly larger than cash flow. Most of the prefs are owned by workers and management so at least you are in the right camp."

Of course, most of these positions, though extremely interesting, cannot be emulated by the vast majority of investors. So whither Sid?

"Flemings has a Russian fund. Brunswick is the investment advisor locally in Russia. They're good. You could also look at Templeton's Russian Fund. If you're going to invest in Russia, there are ways to do it. You'll find the composition of these funds is fairly similar. Also, you can buy companies in the power sector on one times earnings, such as

Mosenergo at 22 cents, which has level 3 ADRs but will probably go to level 1. Lukoil has level 1 ADRs trading in New York."

Moncreiffe sees Russia as a market which is flat on its back and, therefore, a clear contrarian play, and believes that it will bottom out before the election, as Brazil did two years ago. [He was right!] Next on the list for investors whose measurement is sterling total return comes Pakistan. This is not your everyday choice, either, but Moncreiffe manages to make it sound appealing. Pakistan is at least more accessible than Russia, and most major brokers can deal, or have a counter party who can deal, in that market.

"Part of the reason for Pakistan's market weakness was bad cotton crops which adversely affected the textile industry in 1994 and 1995. Last year's harvest has dramatically turned around prospects in a market which is still very dependent on the agricultural sector. The market has suffered from difficult fundamentals and bad technicals, the latter exacerbated by the overvaluation of the international placement of PTC, the national telecoms company. As a result valuations on the whole are much lower than in India, but you have a similar dynamic in terms of a fast growing motivated population and rapid economic development.

"We particularly like a company called Telecard, which is a pre-paid pay phone operator. The shares are around 75 rupees. It should break even this year and, for 1997 we are looking for 20–50 rupees a share. There's a tremendous uncertainty in the earnings numbers because the potential is so great. There's incredible exponential growth in this business, because there's very low penetration of telephones in Pakistan. Its valuation has been affected by the recent situation which has led to their Karachi network being switched off. We feel that this state of affairs will not last much longer and represents a buying opportunity.

"What people forget, when they buy the big telecoms in these countries, is that one thing they have for sure is a mass of employees and a huge infrastructure to support. Radiotelephony has revolutionised the industry in emerging markets. Telecard can install a telephone in minutes, once they have the base station infrastructure in place, and can roll out phones very quickly.

"There is a fund in the US run by Morgan Stanley, which is another way in."

We asked for his top three, and the third choice proved a bit more conventional, if no closer to home. Moncreiffe has found that the

Japanese market has thrown up a lot of valuation inefficiencies in the past, and this continues to be the case in 1996.

"You have to be careful, because you could lose on the yen, but there has been a big adjustment since the middle of 1995.

"It's difficult to see the case for Japan on a pure earnings basis, so you also have to look at the underlying assets to give yourself some protection.

"In Japan, you can buy what I call net/nets [stocks selling at less than net current asset value per share], and that is a reasonably safe way to play it. It won't give you the same upside as, say, Russia, but there's a lot less risk."

Note that Moncreiffe has adapted Graham's original calculation to the particular circumstances of the Japanese corporate system. He includes certain items which would not qualify for Graham's definition, in particular liquid investments held for the long term, and certain real estate which is readily realisable. Table 10.1 contains a few which meet his criteria as of May 1996. They are listed alphabetically and readers must assume that valuations will have changed. This list is not an investment recommendation.

Table 10.1 Selected Net/Nets Among Japanese Public Companies (as of May 1996)

Name	Main Business
Daidoh Limited	Maker of mainly woollen apparel for men and women.
Kurabo Industries	Vertically integrated textile manufacturer – mainly natural fibres.
Nisshinbo Industries	Originally cotton spinner. Now diversified into industrial and consumer textile products.
Nittetsu Mining	Producer of limestone, gravel and other mining products with some manufacturing.
Gunze	Maker of socks and underwear.
Oak	Non-store retailer.

Other markets Moncreiffe likes are France, where property is trading at distress levels, but his concern there is what you make on the index you could lose on the currency. Looking both further ahead and further afield, there is always Mongolia, which might be one for 1999. Vietnam could soon present a lot of attractive opportunities when they actually start trading shares. He also likes commodities, and feels that investors should have some allocation to the sector, perhaps through a fund such as the BZW commodity tracker. No recommendation comes without the customary wealth warning and concern to be clear that investment risks lie just around every corner. There is even a cautionary note about his favoured emerging markets.

"On a one to two year view, I think there's a lot of money to be made, but I'd be quite wary about a five year view. Longer term, you have to consider currency convertibility, the concern over political risk, and the possibility of major crises as certain Asian countries' changing economic importance becomes reflected in political instability."

AN ACTIVE INVESTOR

Throughout this chapter, it is apparent that Moncreiffe is more than just an investor. He operates somewhere close to the middle of that spectrum that extends from tick by tick trader all the way to investors who leave stock certificates at the bottom of the sock drawer and hold assets for decades. Once he's found value, he wants that outed so he can book the profit and move on to the next. It is not surprising, therefore, that Moncreiffe is willing to press pretty hard if progress is slow. No more surprisingly, he believes the investment climate needs someone to stir it up every so often.

"It's healthy to have investors who are able to take reasonably aggressive actions. It is good that there are investment management concerns which are independent and prepared even to go hostile and reconstruct a company. Otherwise, the investment business becomes too cosy, shareholders' rights are not upheld, and relationships between executive and non-executive directors become too close. Where some of the larger investment management groups themselves manage close-end vehicles, they are often loath to be aggressive with other people in the same business. Where they are connected with a large bank or, worse, a corporate finance house, they have understandable difficulty being aggressive with a company for fear of upsetting fee-paying corporate clients.

"Unless you have people who are prepared to rock the boat, markets will not be as clean as they otherwise would be. Too many brokers on emerging stock exchanges spend their time protecting their own interests before their clients. Perhaps London, before Big Bang, was too cosy and vestiges still linger."

To prove the point, Moncreiffe has even been prepared to litigate what he saw as an obvious abuse of minority shareholders by a corporation, and he has not shirked his responsibility to remind directors of public companies of their fiduciary duties. When Moncreiffe moves in, everyone bene-

> *Unless you have people who are prepared to rock the boat, markets will not be as clean as they otherwise would be.*

fits, so, in a way, he fulfils his own role model as an advocate and a shareholder activist willing to take on entrenched interests. In this respect, he has much in common with Christopher Mills of J O Hambro, who was profiled in *The Financial Times Global Guide to Investing*, page 681. Interestingly enough, Moncreiffe is a director of North Atlantic Smaller Companies Investment Trust, one of the JOH stable.

When that fund fell to a deep discount, Mills did not wait to be prodded. He went to the board and proposed a restructuring off his own bat which was supported by the directors, Moncreiffe included. The shares of NASCIT were split into convertible and ordinaries which, combined with a redemption programme, cut the market discount from over 30 per cent to less than 10 per cent. Everyone was a hero and all the shareholders made more money. Moncreiffe practises what he preaches.

Just as he does not seem to enjoy talking about his own abilities, Moncreiffe is strangely reticent about his outstanding performance record. He emphasises the rigorous systematic approach developed by the team at Buchanan, and sees himself as the facilitator who helps oil the wheels. If anyone is in doubt as to whether these strategies pay off, a look at the results should put all doubts to rest. As of December 1995, Buchanan Partners had dazzled its investors with some stunning numbers (which are displayed in Chart 10.2 overleaf).

The special Emerging Markets Fund which was relaunched under Buchanan's management at the end of September 1995 is off to a spanking start. It was up just under 17 per cent through April 1996 compared

Chart 10.2 Buchanan Performance versus Relevant Sector Benchmarks (From Inception to 12.95)

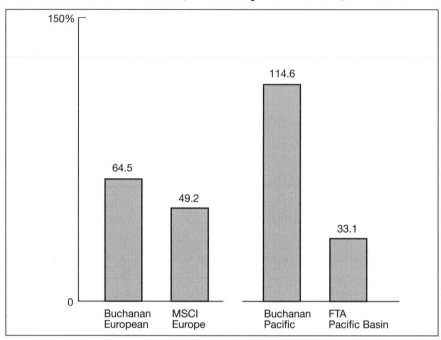

Chart 10.3 Risk/Return Characteristics Compared. Global Equity Markets versus Buchanan Strategies (January 1991–December 1995)

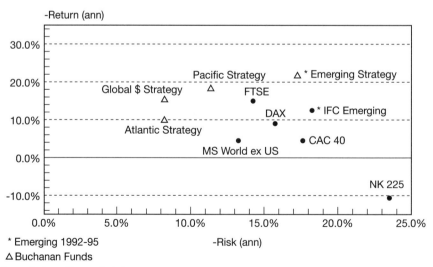

* Emerging 1992-95

△ Buchanan Funds

Source: Buchanan Partners Limited

to a rise of only just over 6 per cent in the MSCI Emerging Market Index during the same period. Through May 1996 the Buchanan family of funds has outperformed their relevant benchmarks by a factor of 2.5x since inception – a truly staggering success.

Consistent with an approach which always has Moncreiffe looking over his shoulder to see what level of risk is coming up behind, Buchanan assesses its own performance on a risk adjusted basis as laid out in Chart 10.3. You can see that all their family of funds are in the right position on this chart relative to their relevant index. Buchanan delivers not only superior performance, but also achieves this while limiting risk.

Every Buchanan strategy gave shareholders a higher return than the relevant benchmark with less risk than the overall market. What more could an investor want?

✳ Believes the ideal portfolio should be well spread:
"goes against everything that all fund managers are taught"

✳ Holds good shares for long periods: "the long distance guy
who manages for consistency will stay the course"

✳ Ranked No. 1 for total return over ten years among
international general trusts in each of the last seven years!

MICHAEL MOULE

Broadly Diversified, Low in Risk

To manage an investment trust which turns up in the top 15, ranked by performance, over both five and ten year periods would be an exceptional accomplishment by any standard. To be responsible for two such successes is truly remarkable. Placed in the context of all major financial markets around the world today, such an achievement may well be unique. Michael Moule, of The Bankers Investment Trust plc and the Law and  Debenture Corporation plc, stands alone as the individual who can be credited with such an achievement.

After 29 years in the relaxed 'boutique' atmosphere of Touche Remnant, Moule has had to adapt to the tightly run, closely monitored environment of Henderson Administration.

There is cadre of strong managers at Henderson, such as John Alexander, Brian Ashford-Russell, Stephen Peak, Richard Smith, Michael Watt and recent arrival Tim Woolley. These managers run a number of investment vehicles all of which have done extremely well; though no-one inside or, indeed, outside of Henderson can match Moule's long term record.

Moule has been at Bankers' for the best part of 20 years. To be precise, he was appointed manager in July 1977. His involvement with Law Debenture goes back even longer, but his era of influence is more limited. Moule has been the predominant force on the investment direction of that fund since May 1987. Along the way, he also managed TR City with some distinction between 1982 and 1991.

It is useful to take a close look at Bankers Investment Trust, which is the main Moule fund. Bankers is a venerable institution, now in its 108th year, and one of the oldest public investments trusts still in existence. The objectives of the fund have an important influence on the way in which the management must operate. As stated at the 106th AGM on 18th February 1994, and replicated in that year's annual report, these are:

- to maximise shareholders' total return by means of a broadly diversified international portfolio;
- to achieve long-term asset growth in excess of the FT Actuaries All Share Index;
- to achieve regular dividend growth in excess of the increase in the Retail Price Index.

Bankers has delivered on all these objectives. Listening to Moule describing his investment philosophy is to understand how these objectives translate in practice. Certain key words recur constantly in the conversation: 'broadly diversified', 'long-term asset growth', 'regular dividend or yield'. We will pick up on all of these themes which are at the heart of the Moule approach later in the chapter.

Moule's record at Bankers' was built upon a somewhat rocky foundation because that trust had been a below average performer in the period prior to his arrival. The task was complicated by the yield. Bankers was the eighth highest yielding trust in the UK, just beneath River Plate, with an 8.2 per cent yield. That required a transition period while the portfolio was rejigged to achieve more capital growth, while retaining some level of income and negotiating around statutory dividend

Table 11.1 Top Performing Investment Trusts

Over 5 years from 28.9.90			Over 10 years from 30.9.85		
Fund			Fund		
First Philippine	4232.27	1	Candover	8923.52	1
TR Pacific	4123.91	2	**Law Debenture Corporation**	6979.52	2
New Zealand	4019.52	3	North Atlantic Smaller Companies	6956.52	3
Templeton Emerging Markets	4001.66	4	Capital Gearing	6914.85	4
Pacific Assets	3936.99	5	Pacific Assets	6776.26	5
American Opportunity	3913.04	6	English National Def	6049.92	6
Scottish Asian	3491.27	7	**Bankers**	6020.99	7
North Atlantic Smaller Companies	3298.97	8	Second Market	5973.08	8
Law Debenture Corporation	3289.99	9	Govett Oriental	5689.46	9
TR Far East Income	3255.54	10	Foreign & Colonial	5650.67	10
Personal Assets	3138.19	11	Foreign & Colonial Pacific	5625.24	11
Gartmore Emerging Pacific*	3131.71	12	TR City of London	5439.54	12
Pantheon International Participations	3091.78	13	Murray Smaller Markets	5394.67	13
Bankers	3080.70	14	Martin Currie Pacific	5296.95	14
Henderson Strata	3039.02	15	Mercury Keystone	5214.17	15

Source: HSW. £1,000 invested, close to close, NIRP
*Reproduced by permission of *Investors Chronicle*

restraint. By 1981, the portfolio was 'Mouleised' and the external environment in which investment trusts operated was more 'normalised' following Thatcher's first budgets. This is, perhaps, the proper period from which to measure his impact.

Documenting Moule's performance is not difficult. The only problem is picking which set of numbers to show. They all tell the same tale – Moule's shareholders have been very well rewarded for deciding to buy either Bankers or Law Debenture. Let's start with the 13th October 1995 edition of *Investors Chronicle* (Table 11.1 on page 268).

Fortunately, records go back even further and show an unbroken history of outperformance of all relevant benchmarks. Moule has come close to doing a double compared to the FTSE All Share over fifteen years, comprehensively and consistently beating the market overall. Chart 11.1 captures this fine record.

The story does not stop there. Share price is alone an incomplete measure of how well Moule has done. Since taking over, he has been acutely conscious of the need to deliver dividends as well; and he has managed to do that without detracting from the growth in capital gains. He

Chart 11.1 Growth in Share Price of Bankers versus FTSE A All Share (Fifteen Years from 30.9.80 – 30.9.95)

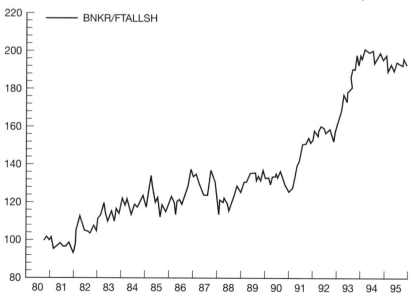

Source: Datastream

Chart 11.2 Growth in Dividend (31.12.85 – 30.9.95)

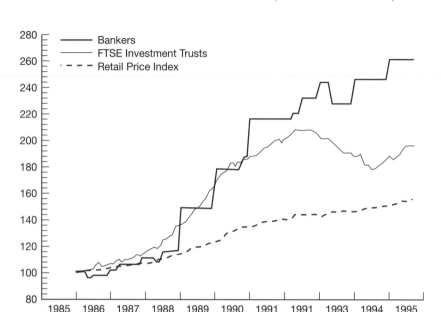

Source: Datastream

has outperformed the Investment Trust Index with growth in dividend more than 50 per cent greater than the average during the last ten years, and achieved a very *real* return compared to the RPI Index. Chart 11.2 reflects the superior income Moule has delivered to shareholders.

After a few minutes of conversation, you quickly understand one reason why he has been so successful. The conversation rapidly escalates into a monologue as Moule bubbles over with enthusiasm for the market and how he operates his funds. No-one could mistake his love for the investment business or his knowledge about markets, as well as his encyclopaedic memory for specific stocks, which is absolutely awesome. Yet there were no obvious indicators of such a talent in his early years.

Talking to Moule about influences which may have contributed to his move into the investment world, you notice that a trading bent and a love of numbers manifested themselves among interests while he was still in his formative years. Notably, Moule did not spend a lot of time on sport nor did he exhibit any particular application to the academic side of school; which left plenty of opportunity to indulge in other extra curricular activities.

"I always enjoyed bartering, whether it was cigarette cards, or football cards which came in packs of chewing gum. I loved anything involving numbers. I collected stamps and was lucky to be a train spotter when steam engines were predominant. I also enjoyed board games (Monopoly etc.) and my father taught me a whole variety of card games, which is good training for remembering things.

"In the investment world, it's very useful to be able to remember facts, figures etc. Dredging the old memory banks can be a vital source for staying out of trouble, as well as spotting an opportunity.

"My elder brother had worked for Barclays, which he found stultifyingly boring. Then he went into Lloyds of London, which he found only marginally more interesting. So when it came to thinking about a career, I didn't fancy either banking or insurance, but I had always liked the stock market. I was sure it was more exciting than either banking or insurance. People seemed to wear smarter clothes and move a bit faster.

"I was looking for a sort of job where, without any qualifications, I could rise reasonably quickly, which wasn't a dead man's shoes . . . where any aptitude would be rewarded fast. Low basic, but big bonuses. I worked out that some sort of broking would get me a reasonable standard of living and allow me to move up.

"My godmother's neighbour was a stockbroker, and was willing to take me on. I started at the bottom in 1964 as a messenger at Blount & Co, and then worked in the back office doing transfers and then became a blue button, which is an unauthorised clerk, which got me to the sharp end of the market. You obtained information for clients but were not allowed to deal. After a while, that became a bit boring, and I found myself asking the dealers a lot of questions about the companies and why people were buying, but they were mostly interested in how to get the best price and make a turn."

Moule's first experience in the investment industry came in 1967 when he joined the Standard Trust as an analyst. Moule describes ST as 'very Victorian'. At that time, everyone was a generalist and most trusts were a sort of throwback to the Empire, where tramways or tea estates had been nationalised but there were a few genuine trusts. There he graduated to 'chief cook and bottle washer'.

This was his first introduction to international markets, since ST had a far flung portfolio. Moule refers to this era with affection as 'ex pat' investing.

"We had something everywhere they spoke English, but nothing in Japan and only one or two investments in Europe."

Moule was part of a small team, so he was involved in all aspects of the trust and, within a year, was meeting brokers and performing basic analysis. He also started to make actual investment decisions, though his initial efforts were noticeably devoid of the successes which were to become routine later in his career.

"I bought a share called Cope Allman, run by a persuasive rogue called Leonard Matcham, who seemed to spend most of his time in the Channel Islands. I invested £50, which promptly went down to £30. In the end, I sold for £25.

"It taught me quite a bit. It is actually probably best if you lose money on your first investment. I realised I had allowed myself to be talked into it. I had paid a premium for Mr Matcham's financial engineering skills, but it went down because they disappointed on profits, which also called into question the quality of the earnings. This highlighted a problem with conglomerates which lose their mystique – like Hanson today. In those days, I wasn't really an investor. I used to stag new issues and that sort of thing, and still had some fast track stockbroking in my blood looking for quick profits."

This was just one of a series of educational experiences which started to shape Moule's thinking.

When asked to describe his portfolio theory, the element which comes across most strongly is the importance Moule places on diversification and his emphasis on stock selection among larger companies.

> *The element which comes across most strongly is the importance Moule places on diversification.*

"It can look pretty staid. You need a pretty solid base of blue chips. I do pay lip service to weightings of the largest twenty companies in each market. The top ten companies in the UK account for 36 per cent of the All Share Index (as of November 1995). You have to have a serious view on each of the top 20 shares, because they are such a large part of the market. You can't funk this issue. You have to make the choice to put some in and leave others out. That gives a very good solid, broad spread of sound companies. My ideal portfolio is particularly well spread. It is not concentrated.

This is probably the furthest you will get from centralised management and goes against everything that all fund managers are taught – which is that you must back your selections with a lot of money, and have a very concentrated list."

If you look at the spread for the year end of Bankers Investment Trust for 30 September 1995, you can see that Moule does, indeed, manage a portfolio which is very broadly spread. The top 40 investments represented only 30.1 per cent of his holdings. Moule also has an unusually large number of holdings, no fewer than 180 separate securities as of December 1995.

Contrast that composition with our other leading managers, most of whom have that much in as few as 10 top holdings, and also invest in a much smaller total number of companies. 1995 is not an aberration. Look back and you will find this characteristic prevails in portfolios of the past. In 1988, the top 40 accounted for 38.6 per cent of the total, and in 1983 they made up even less, at 35.2 per cent. Moule's reaction:

"I have found I am better at timing than stock selection. This diversification also lends itself to a much smoother performance."

Moule is careful to construct a portfolio which suits his temperament and will make the directors and shareholders feel comfortable. He will have a much heavier percentage in blue chips than most other top performing managers, though his list is carefully culled.

"I'm never going to shoot the lights out in either of these trusts. I don't set out to be number one, but aim to stay just behind the leaders and try to make less mistakes. It's sort of the fast tortoise approach. I'm always there, but going steadily in the middle lane. In bull markets some managers may streak by tanked up with five winners, but then they may blow up several miles further on. It's the stamina, the long distance guy who manages for consistency who will stay the course. The shareholders at Bankers and Law Debenture are not looking for excitement, they want a consistent above average performance with all risks kept to a minimum.

"There's a terrific equilibrium in my style of management. There is no sacred cow at Bankers or Law Debenture. If you are very concentrated on a few stocks, the manager starts to like something too much. A favourite holding becomes part of the furniture. You get loaded up with one or two stocks and ride them up and up and never get out, which is what killed Ivory and Sime. They were the most successful investment trust group in the 1970s. Their concentration was amazing. They selected some brilliant shares, but couldn't sell them. They fell in love with them."

Look at the actual portfolio and many big names are present, exactly as you would expect – at least, in the UK. In 1983 you find positions in BTR, British Petroleum and ICI. Fast forward to 1992 and you find British Petroleum, BTR, Glaxo and Hanson. The US selection is a touch more eclectic. 1983 highlights IBM, but also Yankee Oil and Gas and Cincinnati Financial while, in 1992, the largest US holding was Pep Boys, but then came McDonald's. Over at Law Debenture the story is similar. The largest holding in 1994 was Shell Transport. Among the runners up were BAT Industries and Nestlé.

When Moule ventures further afield, his holdings also tend to be among the bluest of chips, such as Fuji Photo and Hitachi in Japan, BHP in Australia, Swire Pacific in Hong Kong, Unilever in The Netherlands and Bayer in Germany. This spread of individual investments across the portfolio is also reflected in a spread of sectors. Almost every area of economic activity finds a place somewhere, be it ever so small. The 1983 Bankers annual report lists no fewer than 36 separate industry classifications, the largest of which is 6.95 per cent and the smallest only 0.2 per cent.

That does not mean Moule won't spice up the portfolio when he spots a stock which seems to have unusual appreciation potential. What he won't do is go overboard. He will buy a relatively modest stake.

"My approach is highly disciplined. If the company is smaller and riskier, I will have less money in it. I put less on the 30–1 shot but, when you do get a five bagger, it's still worth having."

The only time Moule broke this rule was with the purchase for Bankers of a small computer bureau called Electronic Data Processing. The company was based in Sheffield and was run by a resourceful entrepreneur under the eye of a very conservative chairman. The company was debt free, occupied its own freehold and had a well spread base of blue chip clients. The valuation looked far too cheap; a PER of 7, yield of 5 per cent and a discount to book value of 20 per cent. Between 1984 and 1990 Moule acquired 18.1 per cent of the company at a book cost of £1.4 million, a large commitment in those days. In 1991 the potential of the company was recognised by other investors and the stock rose 400 per cent. The company was significantly rerated and between 1992 and 1995 Moule sold 70 per cent of the holding to realise proceeds of

£5.1 million. Bankers still retains 5.4 per cent of the company with the investment now valued at £1.3 million against a book cost of £425,000.

"The UK it is still the ultimate 'value' market. You are paid a lot more money while you wait than, say, in the US, which offers much less in dividends. If you've chosen the assets correctly, sooner or later, and normally sooner – because in a small country, no set of quality *assets* is allowed to be undermanaged for too long – you usually get rewarded. In Bankers and TR City, we used to catch about seven out of ten take-overs because of the style and breadth of the portfolio. The danger in a concentrated portfolio is that you have to ignore the weightings, and can be cut off from values as they change."

Some people deliberately set out to target take-over candidates as part of their investment strategy. Moule sees it as one factor which has contributed to the growth in the asset value of the trusts, but this has arisen as a result of the portfolio selection approach rather than influencing how he selected his portfolio.

"Corporate activity has played quite a large part in these portfolios. If I'm buying in distress, you have to ask yourself, 'What is the exit? Is this company undervalued because the business they are in is literally dying, or is there a set of assets which cannot easily be replicated, but are unpopular and aren't making much return?' It could be a paper mill, a chocolate factory or a savings bank.

Moule does not focus on any one year. His concern is how well he did over ten years.

"Of course, there are periods when value investors will be left behind. The second half of 1995 was like that, with growth investors powering past, but value will out one way or another."

There has to be an acceptance in investing that even the most successful of styles will not win out to the top in each and every twelve month period. Investors must be willing to look longer term to maximise capital appreciation.

The relative performance ranking makes the case clearly. Moule does not focus on how Bankers does in any one year. His concern is how well he did over ten years. Within its category, Bankers only ranked first once in the last ten years for one year performance, but it ranked first in seven of the last ten years for the more important ten year record. Table 11.2 bears testimony to this spectacular consistency.

Table 11.2 Bankers Performance Ranking Among International General Trusts (NAV Total Return on £100)

	1 Year	5 Years	10 Years	No of Trusts
31.10.95	6	2	1	15
31.10.94	10	1	1	15
31.12.93	2	1	1	17
31.10.93	1	1	1	17
31.10.92	5	2	1	13
31.10.91	2	1	1	15
31.10.90	7	4	1	15
31.10.89	13	7	3	16
31.10.88	3	3	3	17
31.10.87	12	8	7	17

Source: AITC

Only a truly confident and secure manager can afford the long-term focus. Fortunately for shareholders at Bankers, Moule is strong on both counts.

"TOP DOWN DECISIONS MAKE THE DIFFERENCE"

This one sentence does more to characterise the Moule approach than any other. You have to break up the statement into several separate constituent parts to see how such a simple phrase disguises a complex set of decisions. Moule is constantly weighing and measuring his portfolio like a parent rocking a cradle striving for perfect balance to make sure the baby sleeps through the storm. In seeking this perfect balance, he considers:

(a) market timing and the market cycle;
(b) the economic cycle;
(c) interest rate movements;
(d) relative currency rates.

When he has taken a view on all three macro economic and global market factors, then he can fine tune his relative country positions and the industry holdings or sector weights. Only then can he give proper consideration to whether he should buy more BP and sell some Chevron, or add Elf Aquitaine in France. Of course it doesn't quite work like that. As with many budget processes, there are some bottom up elements, but the predominant force in how Moule operates is top down.

By market timing, Moule does not mean so much when to be in equities and when to be out. He is more focused on when certain sorts of equities will do better than others.

"There's so much more documentation, now, on the economic cycle and the stock market cycle, and on different styles of investment and when you should adopt them. I've tried to modify my value style when there's a growth phase.

"You have to start by asking yourself, 'Are we in a bull or bear market?' If you feel that we're in a late stage bull market but getting reasonably over-bought, you have to reef in the sail and not pile on the spinnaker. You have to let the other guys go by and end up with a bit more cash than anyone else.

If you feel that we're in a late stage bull market you have to reef in the sail and not pile on the spinnaker.

"If the market feels expensive and there's nothing to buy, you listen to that. You should go through the portfolio and sell some of your wackiest, highest beta things. That is a way the manager adds value. Taking money out of the markets at the really high moments when everything is a bit overcooked is very important."

A quick look at the records shows that Moule was a net seller in December 1993 and January 1994, and the UK market topped in February of that year. Going back to the infamous year of 1987 when underwritings were coming thick and fast – starting in July, as the market hovered at what was then an all time high, Moule stepped back and declined all offerings. He was not caught long of any new issues from that period which included more than its share of bombs.

A big part of the secret of making money over a period of time is not losing money. Here Moule is in his element. Market timing is one aspect of reducing risk. There are others.

"I've learnt a lot about avoiding risk. I'm continually analysing the risk side of the equation rather than the return. You must learn from your mistakes. It's very painful to analyse the losers, but everyone knows the winners. It's important to keep remembering where and why you've lost money. Was it timing? Was it poor analysis, or creative accounting at the company? I've been able to avoid most of the really big disasters, like Polly Peck, although I was caught with a small amount of British & Commonwealth Convertible in TR City. In part, that's because I don't want to take on excessive risk. Normally, very large companies are rescued at the end, so there's more risk when smaller businesses run into trouble."

One vital part of his portfolio selection is an industry screen. He starts out by deciding which industries are good and which he should stay away from. In the UK over the last 20 years, there have been several sectors which have delivered a slow, painful death to long-suffering shareholders. Moule has rarely invested in machine tools, shipbuilding, construction or textiles. Keeping away from dog businesses has contributed to his total returns.

"I do have a feel for what we're not good at in the UK so I can relate to dying industries. Obviously, you can get down to a situation where the last guy who has a garage, however awful the business, will make a lot of money. There are times when you know it's a rotten industry but, like British Steel, now there's only one left it's making serious money."

Few people have the resources or, to be frank, the ability to use a top down investment approach with any hope of beating the market but, within this philosophy, there are many practical messages which investors can employ to improve their own investment returns.

Let's have a look at the thoughts of Michael Moule.

Avoid a Mismatch of Assets and Liabilities

"1974–5 was a very difficult time. Law Debenture was heading for the rocks. It had big Swiss franc borrowings invested in America, which was a recipe for disaster; and the Swiss franc kept going up and the investments kept going down, and the dollar was falling, so the American investments were going down at a geared rate.

"To this day, I won't have a speculative liability position. I'll only borrow Swiss francs if I have Swiss franc assets. Law Debenture didn't. We just thought 2 per cent looked awfully cheap and we found out why."

Gearing is the Fund Manager's Friend

Moule accepts that he has a fiduciary responsibility to be more or less fully invested at all times, given the nature of the trust. That said, the market is going up about 70 per cent of the time and that is good odds which argues for being in the market with leverage most of the time. Over the last 20 years, the range has been from 97 to 120 per cent fully invested.

> *Where you should get shot is if you go liquid at the bottom of a bear market.*

"We're fairly long-term bulls of equities. It pays to be geared most of the time. We don't have the gall to radically second guess the market, but where you should get shot is if you go liquid at the bottom of a bear market. So you won't find us with even 20 per cent cash. If our competition is invested 90–105 per cent, then over time, we should do better."

Look Behind the Balance Sheet

"Sometimes, old industries that have been great in the past have large amounts of fully depreciated assets and fabulous chunks of land sitting there, and even the odd art treasure. One of the oldest businesses in this country is brewing and you would be surprised at what has turned up on the walls of some board rooms. You could also find property on the books at 1948 values and wildly below actual market – that sort of thing.

"In the US in the early 1980s, everyone was talking about the sun belt, but no-one was talking about the winter belt, which had 100 years of manufacturing excellence but had become heavily unionised. Most of the richest pickings for BTR and Hanson have been in old centres such as Pittsburgh, Cincinnati, Cleveland or New England. Siebe buying Foxboro is another example. These grand old companies like Carborundum had assets some of which were written down to zero, and yet the value of those assets was going up in that inflationary period.

"There aren't many gems left now. Dobson Park has been picked off by Harnischfeger and Portals went to De la Rue. Forte was a treasure trove of undermanaged assets, and the replacement value of Pilkington's glass plants and Blue Circle's land assets is considerable."

There is Such a Thing as a Free Lunch

"We had this corny old approach which was common among stockbrokers: 'Why don't we get our money back?' If you sold enough to get the cost out, the rest was free. Back at Standard Trust in 1967 we did this with our investment in Lesney. Lesney was the manufacturer of match box toys, which had an overnight success making a replica of the coronation coach and went on to satisfy children's' addictions for collectibles. It was the first to manufacture these types of toy in moulded plastics. We wiped our face on the initial share price and then ran the balance making eight times over four years on part of our investment.

"You always feel better doing this. Going back to the racecourse. If you're lucky enough to win on the first race, the rest of your racing is free for the day. On the few occasions when I don't do this I usually wish I had."

Be in Front of the Crowd

"Many investment managers believe a degree on crowd psychology would be most appropriate for the job. However, it pays to 'go with the flow' 70 per cent of the time. If you can spot anything early on you may see a trend in the USA, which will travel to Europe and can investigate the potential. Of course, the ultimate case study here is buying new issues. The new issue market continues to provide opportunities for profit, particularly in the USA but, in many cases, the ability of the average investor to participate is restricted. Institutions tend to snaffle the lion's share of anything desirable and the costs discourage many companies from soliciting the small shareholder; but there are other elements to this dictum which make it meaningful to all investors."

If you Can't Get Ahead, then Go against the Crowd

"Believe me, it's quite lonely. If interest rates are falling and everyone is getting more and more excited, it's not as easy as it sounds to go against the market. Everyone has stars in their eyes. You don't want to be the Jonah, the guy who spoils the party, but my attitude when things are in full swing is to back off towards the door and leave a bit early. When in Pamplona you are running with the bulls, but why not let the other guy run the last leg? Why stay to the end? So, when the market's going up, we tend to ease out of the sexiest least marketable stocks.

"On the other side, do you buy the dips? Looking back, I think I've bought every dip. When the market is low and every fundamental is wrong – and there has to be a lot of doom about to get the market down – then most people are raising cash but only a minority has the bottle to reinvest near the bottom. My approach is to put in a little bit more cash systematically on every down spike (basic pound cost averaging).

> *My attitude when things are in full swing is to back off towards the door and leave a bit early.*

"An example of this was when I was a trainee in New York during 1972. It was the peak of the nifty fifty boom which encompassed the philosophy of the one decision stock; you bought and never sold. Two incredibly powerful banks, Morgan Guaranty and Manufacturers Hanover, had collared a big chunk of the pension fund industry. They had happened upon the best quality stocks and said, 'Why do we need to buy anything else? They aren't going to let us down.' But, by concentrating the money, they drove their multiples up to 2.5 times the market, and some of these stocks were on 50 times earnings, but the earnings of some of these companies were growing at only 10–15 per cent per annum. It's very dangerous to pay a significant multiple above the earnings growth rate unless the growth is accelerating."

> *It's very dangerous to pay a significant multiple above the earnings growth rate unless the growth is accelerating.*

Things Always Get Overdone

"With very few exceptions, optimism causes prices to go too high and also, on the other side, of course, they can get too low. Normally, at the top, people are excited. They are piling more money in, and that gives someone like me the chance to get out. When profits are falling and dividends are being cut, that's the exact time to be investing.

"It's mainly about psychology, and fear and greed. People hold on to their winners but, eventually, the winners get over-cooked. There is an advantage to being a generalist. You're not too caught up with one thing. I'm at 50,000 feet looking down on all this; and I can see where the specialists are metaphorically sitting on a window ledge. When they are just about to jump, you know that area is cheap. When they are totally demoralised and do not wish to discuss their speciality, it's an area worth investigating.

"If you accept that 80 per cent of the stock market is fairly valued, then I try to discipline myself to look at the 20 per cent which is well above, or well below, trend level. Most valuation extremes are justified, because the fundamentals have changed, but it is rewarding to study new highs and lows. When there's extreme pain, you have shaken just about every weak holder out on the way down, and when you have extreme good fortune, everyone's in. There's a crowd mentality at both ends. Everyone wants to be in or out, and that's an area of opportunity."

Bad News Brings the Best Time to Buy

"On most of the big crises, we tend to gear up. In September 1992, at the start of the Gulf War, we went in and when there was the attempted coup in Russia with Gorbachov, we were buyers and geared up. We can be quite punchy. When the tanks rolled in to Tiananmen Square, we invested money in Hong Kong and that proved to be the lowest level for that market, as stocks there were in free fall."

A recent example of this philosophy at work, and working well, was the electric utility market in the UK.

"We had Littlechild Wednesday while many fund managers and brokers were down at Cheltenham [race meeting] when the regulator decided to rewrite the rules; and the whole of the REC (regional electric companies) sector went down 25 per cent. It was blood red on the screen. I did feel the market had overdone it, and that day was a day to do something. There was not the usual luxury of picking off lots of little layers on falling prices. I was underweight and I went back to weight in just a few days, going big into Eastern (subsequently acquired by Hanson only six months later)."

Remain Detached at All Times

"Every urge within you is to fall in love with the thing that's doing best. If you have a favourite share you find it hard to sell. I have stated that every share in the portfolio is for sale. There's nothing I wouldn't part with – at a price. You have to be detached and dispassionate. That can be pretty hard, but you must do it."

When All the Good News is in the Price – Sell

"We had the Chairman of a US technology company in the other day. His shares had gone up six times – three times in 1995 alone. His company is now very well recognised. Every analyst and his wife is following it. The multiple of earnings had expanded from 8 times to 28 times. but the business was cyclical. You can't afford to trip up at 28 times. At 8 times you can afford all sorts of rubbish coming out.

"I started chipping away early in the year. You get a feeling this thing could go to the moon but, of course, it can't, and you have to be heartless and start to sell out."

Spot the Cyclicals

"In the early 1970s I was given three UK sectors to look at – shipping – God rest its soul – composite insurance, and overseas traders. They linked up quite well, with cargoes going round the world needing insurance and being geared to world trade.

"They were remarkably cyclical sectors. The insurance cycle was separate. The big companies in traders were Harrisons and Crossfield, Guthrie and Inchcape. Shipping also had its own cycle. Analysing them was very interesting, because you could see the volatility over time and how badly things could go wrong. As business picked up, you could see how competition came in."

Only Bet What You Can Afford to Lose

This general dictum applies to all aspects of life, but is particularly apposite when making investment decisions, particularly if you are partial to speculative investments.

"If you go back to the first horse race I attended – a point to point – my father said to me, 'Only take with you what you can afford to lose. If you want to have an enjoyable day, if you can afford to lose £5, fine – just bet £1 a race and you will have had a good day, even if you're cleaned out!' Those sorts of things stick, so I have always had an innate level of caution which has carried over into the way I invest."

It's Never a Profit Until You Take it

"1968 to 1969 was the hairiest phase of my career though fortunately I was not managing any money at the time. It was the era of the Australian mining boom which threw up Norman Shierlaw who seemed to create a new company once a week. This was the environment of the wonder stock personified in Poseidon Gold and a get rich quick mentality. Enormous amounts of money were made but also lost when buying dried up. I was not too heavily caught up, and learnt that it's always smart to take a profit when one is available.

Follow the old Rothschild adage of 'buy early and sell early.'

"This also taught me the advantages of being early. This was a market where you needed to follow the old Rothschild adage of 'buy early and sell early'.

"Witnessing something which, literally, was a bubble was an eye opener. We had one other bubble stock in the portfolio at Standard Trust. We made a lot of money which grew to be a huge holding. Lesney, which manufactured match box toys, became one of the most highly rated shares on the stock market. It was by far the outstanding small growth company and nothing else at the time was growing in the UK at the same pace. We took modest profits on the way up but we were left with most of our holding all of the way down when it went 'ex growth'. People began to collect other things and there came a point when Lesney was close to bankruptcy. So we made some money but not nearly as much as we could have if we had sold smarter."

Buy and Hold

"Tony Arnaud, a great doyen of the investment trust industry, had developed several buy and hold techniques. He didn't disturb shares unless there was a reason and was a great exponent of low turnover.

"Of course, the initial investments had to be chosen particularly well . . . and you need lots of patience."

Looking back through the portfolios of both Law Debenture and Bankers, you can find perennial favourites that Moule has held for years, even though the *level* of investment can fluctuate, and even though the overall rate of turnover is quite high. Take Bankers in 1994. The top 20 list contains no fewer than six of the same companies as it did a whole decade earlier.

Extend the analysis a little more broadly, and stability is even more apparent. Every UK holding in the top 40 in 1994 which was a public company back in 1984 was in the 1984 portfolio. Reverse the analysis: out of 43 UK listed companies named in the 1984 report which were still public as of year end 1994, no fewer than 25 appear on the 1994 list. Interestingly, there is much more contrast and turnover outside the UK. There are only two survivors out of 20 in the corresponding Japanese representation over the same period.

PORTFOLIO ALLOCATION

When Moule focuses on the individual elements of his portfolio, he is at his closest to a value fundamentalist in selecting stocks. He makes a few concessions to the technical crew, but assets other than equities and convertibles find little favour. His first major move, on inheriting Bankers, was to get rid of a chunk of poorly performing preference shares bought for stability and income in 1974 but long past their sell by date once equities were on the move again in the 1975–1978 period.

"By and large, funds should be invested in equities. If you're borrowing money, you could buy a gilt and then you'd be matching one fixed interest security with another. If you put money into fixed interest over time, the trust would suffer a lack of performance."

THE CONTRIBUTION OF CHARTS

"I can see history repeating itself. I'm not a fully fledged, paid up disciple, but I enjoy charts, because it's so easy to look back. If enough people believe you can get some self fulfilling prophecies; and there have been occasions when you get good patterns. There are reasons for trend lines, but very few trends continue for ever. It's very interesting to see when the relative strength breaks.

"I am 90 per cent fundamentalist, but I have to leave 10 per cent to look at the charts, because it's a humbling business. If the technicians are against you, and if you are dealing with absolute weakness, relative weaknesses and no chart support, you have to be that much more careful."

So whither Bankers? Moule is forever sifting through sectors and juggling industries to decide which will be his favourites looking forward.

"There are about four natural growth industries I can see in the developed world. They are driven by demographics.

"The first is health care and death care. No matter what people say about Hillary Clinton reducing drug prices, the demographics are fabulous for medical stocks. Your cheapest way of treating any medical problem is prescribing a pill. Hospital stays are still mind bogglingly expensive so anything reducing the stay such as mobile services, home rehabilitation, or non-invasive surgery will continue to be in great demand. Everything from nursing services to hip joints. OK, Smith & Nephew is pretty staid, but it's going to keep on growing. There are no quoted funeral companies left in the UK. The US funeral companies are going very strong but have high ratings now (June 1996).

"Second comes leisure travel and sport, everything the affluent young and mobile elderly do. They fly around a lot and take a lot of trips. There's a natural growth in many leisure areas, theme parks, sport, museums, and eating away from home. The cruising business caters to this crowd. Airports and air transportation is a unit growth business. Airlines are notoriously difficult, but owning airports is another way to play that. The airline business itself is very cyclical, so you might look for a company in the service business or just invest in the airport.

"You hear much about air freight numbers. That's in a growth phase. Most products are getting lighter, and the lighter things get, the more can travel by air.

"The third group is electronics, telecommunications and technology – no longer the preserve of a young minority of programmers and systems analysts. Technology is becoming more accessible and the new generation will be completely at ease in a digital world. Companies which provide an essential service in exchange for long term licensing fees are less exciting but a more comfortable investment than manufacturers of mobile phones, semiconductors, and personal computers.

286

"My fourth favourite is centred around out-sourcing which is a trend that's here to stay. Governments, Local Authorities, banks and very large corporations are all seeking to cut costs and focus on the end product and the ultimate consumer. Peripheral activities such as catering, security, prison management, transport, cleaning etc. are increasingly being outsourced."

The demographic argument extends much further than picking sectors within an existing economy. Historically, the focus for Moule has been the UK, with strong representation in the US, and occasional weightings of importance in Japan, Hong Kong and Europe. Recently, he has recognised this is not the wave of the future and, in the early 1990s, started to invest in a broader spectrum of geographic markets.

"You cannot fight the demographics. You have to make an effort in young underdeveloped countries ... (emerging markets!) ... but the sector and stock selection techniques can be different. Steel and cement are often the fastest growing businesses."

Currently, Bankers has only around 4 per cent in 'emerging' markets, but Moule has made some moves which he feels are a foretaste of things to come. In August 1995, Bankers bought into Taiwan after that market came back 45 per cent. His first, tested the emerging market waters with the purchase in 1986 of the largest cement Thai company.

"At Bankers and Law Debenture we're winning on consistency rather than on spectacular performance. Everyone has to sleep at night, including the manager."

That appears to be the perfect note on which to end, for both Moule and his fortunate shareholders.

* Over 30,000 new businesses launched

* Overall portfolio rate of return exceeds 25% compounded annually

* Focus is on putting people before profits and providing active support

CHAPTER

12

THE PRINCE OF WALES

Investing in People

Name the top investment minds in Britain in 1996 and few people would include The Prince of Wales on such a list. That would be a grave mistake. A garden blooming with investment opportunities for fund managers and individuals alike requires someone to plant the seeds and bulbs. Evaluation of investments in established businesses, while complex and challenging, benefits from the availability of information and a structured  context in which to take a decision. Someone who sets out to back new businesses based on nothing more than faith in one or two people and a plan on paper is an investor in the purist sense of the word.

No-one has done more to invest in the emerging end of the market in Britain over the last decade than The Prince of Wales. Through The Prince's Trust, he has developed a business start up scheme administered by The Prince's Youth Business Trust. His success is so extraordinary that it is a mystery how it has gone largely unnoticed. Consider a few statistics. This scheme set up in 1986, is, only ten years on, already the largest non-Government new business agency in Britain, and the only national organisation at the start up end of the investment spectrum. The Trust has to its credit:

- over 30,000 new businesses launched;
- of which over 60 per cent are still active after three years based on the performance of the current portfolio;
- over 60,000 people in productive employment;
- £12 million in outstanding investments as of 1996 by way of loans and grants.

Far from slowing down they expect fiscal 1997 to be the busiest and most successful year ever with over £9 million to be invested and an expected 4,000 new businesses to be launched. Add this on to a compound annual growth of capital formation in excess of 40 per cent pa. What other investment group can come close to such a track record?

No-one has ever sat down and tried to tabulate the full financial profile of every enterprise in which the Trust has invested. In reviewing their progress and financial performance with senior management, we tried to put a few parameters around all the existing businesses as of

January 1996 treating the Trust as one widely diversified conglomerate and The Prince of Wales as its Managing Director and Chief Investment Officer. What you end up with is aggregate annual turnover of the order of magnitude of £800 million and an investment portfolio of businesses which could show an equity value of over £200 million.

This is no mean feat. Unlike professional venture capitalists, who sift through hundreds of business plans prepared by sophisticated and experienced executives, discarding 19 out of 20, and doing detailed due diligence before dispensing any money, the Trust deliberately looks for the most unpromising material, usually people out of work, who have no other source of finance – young to start with (18–29), inexperienced, and often disadvantaged in some way – and tries to unlock talent which is latent at best. The stationery used by the organisation makes this mission explicit. 'Among young people, the Trust is particularly concerned to help those from ethnic minorities, disabled applicants and ex-offenders.'

The origins of the enterprise were not rooted in a desire to make money, but stem from a strong sense of social responsibility which is evident every time The Prince of Wales talks about the Trust.

"In the early 1980s, there was a series of riots in Toxteth and one or two other places. I rang up the Director of The Prince's Trust and said we ought to see how we could make a contribution to prevent such things happening again, by dealing with some of the root causes. It was a time of growing unemployment. I felt strongly we should do something to tackle this.

"We came up with this idea of enabling people to start up their own businesses as a means of trying to counteract the growing levels of unemployment and the difficulties associated with that. We wanted to enable people who were in disadvantaged or deprived circumstances and, inevitably, found it incredibly hard to achieve their own particular ambitions because of lack of financial resources and good advice, by providing them, in a small way, with what they lacked to begin their own enterprises. That was the genesis of the Youth Business Trust."

It is important to understand how the Trust operates. There is a core team of just under 300 full-time employees, of whom only 120 are paid by the Trust. Companies, local authorities and other bodies second and/or fund around 150 people on a full and part-time basis who contribute to the organisation. On top of that are some 5,500 business advisers, experienced executives for the most part, who agree to devote a minimum of four hours a month in support of one of the Trust businesses. This structure is presided over by 38 regional boards made up of local business people who volunteer their time. The boards scrutinise all applications for assistance, each aided by dedicated area managers who are full-time Trust employees.

There are overall objectives and some limited central policy, but a great deal of decentralisation to ensure the Trust is sensitive to local considerations. The investment programme of the Trust offers help to new businesses which consist of cash and support in kind.

(a) Cash assistance: Start up loans up to £5,000 with 'soft' terms.
Expansion loans of up to £5,000.
Grants up to £1,500.
Test marketing grants up to £250.

(b) Support: Each new business is given its own business adviser available for four hours a month in theory but in practice often for much more, to troubleshoot and act as mentor. The adviser is officially designated for a three year period but often remains attached for much longer.

Cash and counsel are the twin components of the programme and each is essential. There are a slew of success stories and everyone has their favourite. The Prince of Wales was hard put to select one that stood out from so many where he felt strongly about the people and their progress, but he did highlight a couple which he feels have done particularly well.

> *Cash and counsel are the twin components of the programme and each is essential.*

"Julie Dedman is a great example. She was a classic example of someone who had been made redundant – from a dairy, I think. Instead of sitting around doing nothing, she decided she would start her own business and it's been an incredible story. Last time I saw her, she modestly stated that her turnover was in excess of £1 million. She now employs a number of people including her husband.

"Isis is another. David Brown does English courses for foreign students and he has come a long way in a short time.

"There are so many now. There is Uwe up in Newcastle, which makes very lovely washed cotton garments. They are brilliant."

The best way of conveying the impact The Prince of Wales has had through these investments is to look at a selection of the businesses which, backed by his capital and the services of the Trust, have blossomed into flourishing enterprises.

1. West Riding Laboratories

West Riding was started in 1985 as a specialised testing business for farmers needing to know the basic butter fat and plate counts in their milk. Julie Dedman, who had a background in agriculture from college, had been made redundant from her job with an animal feed company when milk quotas came in. While calling on customers at their farms, she spotted the need for such a service and her first thought was not to find other employment but to set up in business for herself.

A £1,000 grant proved sufficient to acquire the very minimum equipment. Dedman rented a corner of an old dairy and by the end of 1985 had won over some 20 clients who provided total revenues of £18,000.

Fast forward to 1996 and the picture is totally different. West Riding has 2,000 customers today, not only farmers but many corporate clients, including Müller (the yoghurt company), Robert Weisman and the Milk Group. The company conducts over 4,000 tests on samples sent in each week.

The range of activity has also been upgraded to a significant degree. Dedman was not content with her initial offering as she could see a cluster of related services which were needed by her customers. Positioning West Riding as a more responsive alternative to the Milk Marketing Board her motto was 'large enough to cope; small enough to care'. One demonstration of how well she is attuned to her customers' needs was the way she organised a fleet of refrigerated vans to collect samples directly from their premises. This innovation ensured sample quality and, therefore, gave higher confidence to the test results. In addition to milk, West Riding now also tests a full family of milk related products including butter and cheese.

Dedman has come so far that her most recent purchase was a £250,000 Combifoss 4000, which analyses milk for fat, protein, lactose, urea and somatic cells. Unlike her first acquisitions this was a brand new piece of equipment and will further upgrade and extend the Company's capabilities.

Mrs Dedman is forthright in her appreciation for the role of the PYBT.

"Without their initial help and contribution of £1,000 I can say without reservation that we would not be here today."

2. Isis

With only five years of history, Isis has already broken the £3 million turnover barrier. Formed by David Brown and Robert Darrell with a £5,000 loan, the company has two main activities:

(a) Educational tours for students: Some 15,000 will take their tours during the 1995/96 academic year. Most are for UK students going overseas but, since 1994, the company also caters for foreign students coming to the UK. The service is comprehensive, designed to meet student budgets (university residences, guest houses, host families etc.) and interests (museums, opera). The tours are varied, ranging from Shakespeare's Country to the Great British Pub Tour.

(b) Summer language courses for foreign students: Isis rents 14 educational premises around the UK and provides a mix of English instruction and sports/social activities for students from over 20 countries ranging from France to Japan and Russia.

Now employing 14 full-time, and up to 300 temporary staff, Isis expanded rapidly, building on its expertise in how to provide the student market with travel and education related services. Selling is the name of the game. Isis has already made its first acquisition – a year round language school in Greenwich offering a broader range of courses, including business English and computing. Isis has also set up a second travel company starting to segment its market by price to offer cheaper programmes under a separate name.

Like Mrs Dedman, David Brown credits the Trust for setting him on this path.

"I don't think we would have ever got off the ground without the Trust. Not only did they provide financial help after we had tried all the banks, but they helped us get the ABTA bond."

Interestingly, Brown stresses "invaluable help from our two Trust advisers" as even more important to their initial success than the finance. Both Brown and his partner, Robert Darrell have made the time to become advisers in their turn, because they believe so strongly in that aspect of the Trust package.

3. Dockspeed

Dockspeed is a carrier of sensitive, short shelf-life temperature controlled products from the UK to the Continent.

The company was one of the earliest Trust businesses. It began life in 1986 after Andy Ingleston, whose grandfather had been a lorry driver, spotted a niche collecting trailers at Dover resulting from the costly delay in custom clearance for foreign transportation firms. The Prince's Trust, along with the Kent Foundation, provided the £3,400 deposit needed for the HP finance on Ingleston's first vehicle. His parents provided an office in their house. 1986 turnover was £9,127. 1987 moved up a gear with a second vehicle, deposit also provided by the Trust, and turnover rising to £105,840.

In his third year in business Ingleston started to provide a chilled transport service to France for a UK distribution company. As ports became more efficient around the UK the rationale for the original business began to fade; but by then Ingleston had identified a more serious problem. How can UK suppliers make frequent deliveries of small quantities of perishable product to the continental retailer?

The solution – use Dockspeed. Business that had been going begging could now be filled economically through a shared service. With clients including Northern Foods, Sainsbury, Zeneca and Geest, Dockspeed has grown to 51 employees and a turnover of £6 million. They were runners up in 1995 in the International Operator section of the Motor Transport Industry Awards For Excellence.

Due to the fact that all these companies are privately held the individuals concerned are reluctant to publish details of their financial performance but information provided on a sample of the more established concerns shows that the Trust has scored some truly extraordinary investment gains. An analysis by this author of the value created across a range of more mature businesses started with the backing of the Trust suggests an overall average multiple on capital invested of 200×. When that is broken down to allow for the period of investment the internal rate of return comes in at approximately 150 per cent. That is a truly extraordinary rate of compound annual growth in capital formation.

> **The Trust has scored some truly extraordinary investment gains.**

Some naysayers may be tempted to scoff and say these sort of stunning returns are easy to achieve when you start with such a small investment. It is true that we are talking about lump sums of £1,000 to £5,000 in most cases; but do the maths. £2,000 compounded at, say, 100 per cent reaches £1 million by year 10. If making that sort of money this way was so easy everyone would be doing it; but the Trust stands alone. In practice venture investing is very tough and most people lose money. The rule of thumb says that 1 in 10 works well, 3 will do OK and 5 will fail. The Trust not only has a track record of picking winners, but over 6 in 10 of its businesses do OK, and the top tier achieve performance which puts them at the pinnacle of investment returns. The Prince of Wales has no peer when it comes to his investment record. There is not a venture capital trust around today which can top his results over the last ten years.

Of course, the Trust is not about investing to make money in the traditional sense. It is an altruistic organisation designed to give underprivileged people a chance to build a better life. Dockspeed, Isis and West Riding may be exceptional examples, but it is worth remembering that all these entrepreneurs had been turned down by traditional sources of finance before they got their start with the Trust. How the worm has turned! These days banks frequently look to lend alongside, providing matching funds to Trust businesses. Even in a sector of the financial community traditionally sceptical of the small company loan market there is a recognition that The Prince of Wales has found something special and that Trust investments usually make sound credits and seldom go sour.

So how is it that the Trust can achieve such phenomenal dividends on its investment when more traditional investment firms, some with over 100 years of experience, are scared even to stray onto the same start up patch? There appear to be four main elements in the equation which underpin the extraordinarily high success rate at the Trust.

1. Putting people before profits

The first step for an investor is to set suitable investment objectives. The Trust eschews quantitative goals, since start ups are, in any case, so much pie in the sky. It's all about backing people. If you pick the right people, the

If you pick the right people, the profits will follow.

profits will follow. The definition of right, in this context, is primarily enthusiasm of the applicant(s) who should also possess some marketable skill on which a business can be built.

Richard Street, Chief Executive at The Prince's Youth Business Trust, underscores this point.

"The business plan is important. There has to be a real business, but it's not the business plan, however beautiful, that tells us if someone can succeed. We are looking for skills in an individual which can be used in the business and we look for enthusiasm for the particular business. You also have to look at the personality, because, in a start up, you need the ability to persevere."

2. Provide active support

The very essence of the Trust is its network of advisers. This group includes people capable of giving advice across a broad range of issues, and who could be expected to help an entrepreneur solve almost any problem likely to arise. Many of these business executives or professionals, such as lawyers and accountants, are effectively providing £1,000 of free assistance per month and all are at the other end of a phone available for consultation to their sponsee company at any time. There is no debate about the immense value of the role these people play, which can range from helping set up a payroll system, to essential encouragement when times get tough and the entrepreneur feels alone and in need of a sympathetic ear.

There is great emphasis on training at all levels, both formal and informal. Every entrepreneur needs to acquire a broader range of skills to survive, let alone flourish. Inherent in the selection of adviser is a screen which identifies the key ability the entrepreneur lacks and the system pairs him or her with an adviser whose strength balances their weaknesses. So, if a super salesman has no numerical ability, he is likely to be mentored by an accountant. The adviser's role is taken very seriously. There are regular meetings, and progress reports compiled by the advisers are submitted monthly. Cash flow statements are a key monitoring device. Even at the Trust, they recognise that 'cash is king'.

Talk to almost every entrepreneur who was started in business by the Trust, and they will credit their advisers as having been critical to their success. The Prince of Wales himself is the first to home in on the element he believes has been so essential to ensuring that Trust hatchlings learn how to use their wings.

"The really critical part of the whole exercise is having this network of voluntary advisers. They do make the difference and we could not succeed without them.

"I've often said that anyone could hand out money to people who can't get it from the banks and say, 'go on, start up your own business'; but a lot of those people would collapse by the wayside very quickly. The secret of our success has been this hand holding operation, which does make a stupendous difference."

The really critical part of the whole exercise is having this network of advisers.

In addition to personal advisers, each Trust entrepreneur gets access to a range of special services at the local and national level. There is a hotline for Trust businesses with questions about matters of law run by Hambro Legal Protection, a tax advisory system sponsored by Arthur Andersen, and the RAC provides free memberships.

Then there are the Trust cross selling opportunities. The Trust actively encourages and facilitates Trust businesses to purchase from/market to other Trust businesses. The quarterly magazine, bulletin boards, regional shows and a referral network, including regional directories, are all part of this added service.

There is central marketing help including an exhibition programme. For every £ the Trust spends it gets £8 of help from exhibition organisers and partners. Marketing venues include the NEC, and local events such as the Stockport County Show, where the Trust participates and arranges free stands for selected Trust companies. Like all large organisations, the Trust also uses its clout to obtain special discounts for its members. So advertisers in Thomson Directories can get 25 per cent off the normal rate card.

Recently, the Trust launched a brand name, which perhaps not surprisingly derives from the name of the organisation – Trust. This will operate in retail outlets for all Trust businesses manufacturing fashion, jewellery and homewares and will play an integral part as a group identity umbrella.

People who see special favours for the privileged are wrong. There is nothing arranged here which any large business would not seek to achieve for its smaller subsidiaries. The difference is that the Trust acts as a buying co-op for a large number of separate, often very small businesses, giving each one of them the critical mass to have purchasing power.

At the same time, there is another subtext at work which is 'help but don't hinder': give what is needed, but no more. Even though advisers are appointed, they are not there to suffocate a business – rather the reverse. Richard Street makes the point.

"Some of the businesses want a few contacts and that's it. In other cases, it's not the technical expertise so much as just having someone to talk to. Our view is they should stand on their feet where they can, but you have someone outside family and friends to turn to when you have a problem. In some cases, the biggest problem is isolation, and the adviser's role is purely emotional. If you think about start-ups which don't have this sort of support, you begin to understand why so many fail. It's not one of the issues a bank thinks about."

3. Low cost companies are more competitive

There is no doubt that the average Trust start up is low cost, and this is by design. The capital invested is minimal. The entrepreneur skimps and strives to find a way to stretch every pound. There is a culture which emphasises the bare essentials. Once the business is stable, the next phase of expansion is structured to minimise financial and operating risk – little external finance, taking on part-time people when first ready to start hiring extra employees. The growth model is caution. Survival is put before size. The budget and business plan emphasises the need to cut the cloth to fit the circumstance. It works. Trust businesses keep costs very much under control, and so emerge able to produce products and deliver services competitively. This also seems to help explain the very high return on investment achieved.

4. Loans not grants

The Trust started out as almost entirely 100 per cent grant, but has evolved to 80 per cent loan, 20 per cent grant and believes strongly that this approach works better. Richard Street explains the reasoning behind the mix.

"It's the psychology of starting up a business and committing yourself to it. You give people self confidence by backing them with a loan and all the support. Their self esteem goes rocketing because, in many cases, they are used to failure and being turned down. It's all part of the enthusiasm and perseverance. A loan strengthens both those things and it increases self esteem more than a grant can. With most people, a certain stubbornness comes in. You have a loan. It should be repaid. It's a powerful driver."

THE INVESTMENT DECISION

The criterion for who qualifies is clear. How investments get made is somewhat more idiosyncratic depending, to a large degree, on semi-autonomous area managers and boards which have enormous discretion. That said, the process has proved remarkably successful in weeding out unsuitable candidates. The Prince of Wales puts great emphasis on the need for a solid business plan.

> *The Prince of Wales puts great emphasis on the need for a solid business plan.*

"We do look carefully at their applications and their business plans. I think we are getting better at helping people start up, seeing from trial and error what will work and what won't.

"It's terribly important to remain as true as possible to the business plan and not get led off into thinking you can sell everything to everyone.

"There was a period when we had a lot of T shirt business applications and you could see that some just weren't going to survive. I said, 'We have to be very careful that we build up the quality of the businesses and that quality doesn't get forgotten about,' as they have to be competitive."

Here is a list of criteria commonly used by professional investors backing private companies which play *no* part in the deliberations of Trust investment committees:

- higher level education;
- prior experience: managerial and in the relevant industry;
- other sources of funding (in fact, applicants have to be able to show they have *failed* to obtain funding from other sources);
- financial return to outside investors;
- good contacts.

What you are left with are four key requirements:

1. a viable business idea;
2. personal commitment;
3. demonstrated initiative of an individual;
4. a recognisable skill.

Fortunately the Trust is able to call on people skilled in shepherding applicants along who are able to sift out entrepreneurs who truly meet those tests. This is investing in people at its purest. Richard Street describes the process as more of an interactive screening than anything which a traditional investment manager would recognise.

"If you have a continuum of unemployment to long-term employment, we get the people in the bottom end of the spectrum. They come to us with a business plan: at which point, we say, 'Is it good, or isn't it? Are we going to back them or not?'

"Once we decide it's yes, we appoint the advisers. Instead of arriving with a cheque, we often get the advisers to go for a chat first and tell them, 'It's a difficult thing you're about to do. Are you sure you want to do it? This is the attitude of mind you're going to need. This is what you need for the business plan.' So we're giving quite a lot of careful counselling to sift out the serious enquiries. Then we send them off to the local library to improve the plan, perhaps arrange some training, and are available for guidance before they start. We may give them a test marketing grant to see how it goes. There are about 35,000 enquiries each year and only about 5,000 actually progress to formal applications. We grant about three in four once they get this far.

"This last stage is extremely subjective, and relies on the skills of the boards, because they are made up of a very experienced group of people – solicitors, accountants, editors, bank managers, company directors, and usually someone from the TEC, education, and often a minority community leader or an established Trust business executive – who can make sound decisions. It is one of our strengths that we have no formal guidelines. The local boards have great discretion and are very flexible. Rural Devon will be totally different from inner city Birmingham."

Start up investing is high risk. Most venture firms won't do it, and the average reader should not be fooled into thinking this is easy, nor that what works for an unique organisation like the Trust can be translated into a personal investment portfolio with similar financial results; but, with care, parts of the approach can. This is particularly true for someone working part-time or who has taken early retirement and who can afford to use a small slice of personal capital in an unorthodox manner. The key is to use your own experience and expertise in tandem with the enthusiasm and energy of someone in their early stage of a career who shares an interest, if not a passion, in a similar area. A specific example should help. A manager of a garden centre willing to put up £5,000 and spend one day a week working could help a young person who likes an outdoor life and has some affinity with plants to start a landscaping service.

Street stresses the benefit of harnessing this dynamic to the investment decision.

"The important thing is to back motivated people who really want to start this business. We have the advisers who can train and help them. These advisers are selected for skills they can bring, but also they must get on and be sympathetic. They are going to be with a business for three years and they have to be able to get back to basics, as they will be flung a huge range of problems in a micro environment. They will go from doing the cash balance through to how to hire employees as the business expands."

Advisers on the roster of the Trust run the gamut of industry from the managing director of Hermes (UK), to the ex Sales Director of Raleigh, the bicycle company, and a senior manager from Kodak.

Advisers normally work one on one, but there can be teams bringing multiple skills to a group of businesses, and there are clinics for businesses which experience problems. Advisers report monthly to area managers, which ties all this activity together and means each business does get the level of monitoring it needs.

RETURNS ON INVESTMENT COME IN MANY FORMS

Investment returns are not computed in the same way at the Trust as at other organisations but The Prince of Wales has clear goals.

"There is the question of trying to ensure someone will pay the loan back, which is useful for the organisation. What I want to see above all is someone being able to achieve their potential and, very often, having their life transformed."

There are no politics involved at the Trust, but you have to wonder why Tony Blair went to Singapore to announce his 'stakeholder' concept when The Prince of Wales has mastered the practice of social capitalism right here in Great Britain.

> *What I want to see is someone being able to achieve their potential and having their life transformed.*

The range of businesses started by the Trust spans almost every area of economic activity from fashion to computer sales. There is a preponderance in the sectors of personal services, such as hairdressers, plumbers and teaching, and in crafts such as ceramics, jewellery and stained glass but, taken as a whole, there are over 225 separate business classifications. To provide a bit of flavour and demonstrate the diversity, a few more examples are worth cataloguing.

- Sean Denton set up the Bonsai Garden in Gower Swansea, and now sells bonsai plants to nurseries and flower shops.
- Jean Watt started with a Caribbean take-away and is now diversifying into contract catering.
- Trans-Europe Recoveries collects car wrecks from the continent.
- William Turnstiles manufactures, services and refurbishes turnstiles.
- Freewheelers provides a national car sharing agency.
- Northern Sole, run by Mark Beaby, makes historic styled boots and belts for re-enactment groups and films.

Some Trust offspring are truly innovative companies which have carved out new niche markets and attracted the attention of demanding blue chip customers including Rolls Royce, Harrods, the Oval Cricket Ground and Madam Tussauds, as well as celebrities such as the Rolling Stones and Bob Geldof. Some of these businesses produce products of a calibre to compete anywhere in the world. Rachel Skinner who makes hats is an example of a Trust entrepreneur now achieving top flight recognition.

Critics will carp that The Prince of Wales does not personally deserve the credit for the success of his organisation. Certainly, it is true that so much could not have been achieved without the efforts of many others. That is missing the point. None of these people would be there today if The Prince had not had the vision to start up the Trust and then put considerable energy and his personal prestige behind its expansion. To prove the point here are a couple of extracts from just a few of the letters received by The Prince of Wales in November 1995.

> "I have the greatest admiration for your work and am grateful for the chance your organisation gave me." City Gent Salons.

> "I owe you and your Trust a very great deal. Your money helped me get started when all other possible sources of finance has turned me down". The Design Advantage.

His involvement is the cornerstone of the edifice, and he remains active in every aspect of the activities of the Trust that carries his name. This is not limited to the more obvious elements of support, such as meeting with his top management team to plan strategy, sponsoring fund raisers and corralling top people in industry to participate. His role encompasses all that, but also goes much deeper. A few examples should suffice to show just how multifaceted The Prince's involvement is.

1. Fund raising

No investment group can function without capital. There are more of these events than is generally realised. The 1995 première of *Goldeneye*, the latest in a long line of James Bond movies, was a benefit for The Prince's Trust. The Prince of Wales is the first to recognise the importance of this activity, which occupied a good deal of his time in the first few years, though is more self perpetuating in 1996.

"I've done endless dinners. I've attended film premières, variety shows organised by David Frost, and pop concerts. You're constantly thinking of new ways to raise money.

"The real build up was at the time of my fortieth birthday. The Trust said to me they wanted to raise £40 million. We managed to persuade Lord Young, who was at the DTI at the time, to match what we raised. I suppose he thought we'd raise a million or two. When we did raise nearly £40 million it didn't go down all that well at the Treasury."

2. Recruiting

Not many people say no to The Prince of Wales when asked to get involved in the Trust. It's a little bit of a parade of the great and the good, but the emphasis is on the word good. Among those he has personally signed up are Khalid Aziz, Lord Forte, Eddie George, Sir Angus Ogilvy, and Lord Sheppard of Didgemere.

"In the early years, I spent an awful lot of time begging people to become advisers. I used to go to the Institute of Marketing one day and British Nuclear Fuels the next, trying to persuade them to help. As a result of talking to these people, writing to them, thanking, pleading and cajoling, we built up over 5,500 advisers.

"Recently I wrote to all the advisers asking them if they could recruit another adviser and the numbers went up by almost one third."

These people, in turn, have a fair bit of personal pull, so you get a knock on benefit as well as an entrée into almost any serious business throughout Britain. What other venture capital organisation can call upon companies as diverse as Barclays Bank, British Airways, British Telecom, Esso, ICI, Kiss FM, Readers' Digest, and Yorkshire Electricity to lend a helping hand? Spread the net wider. Who, other than The Prince of Wales, could enlist people as diverse as Diane Abbott, MP, Jasper Conran, Sir John Harvey-Jones, Kevin Keegan, Trevor MacDonald and Lord Weatherill?

3. Marketing and sales

The Prince of Wales supports the Trust business in several areas of market development:

- He was personally the impetus behind arranging an annual exhibition exposing Trust products to trade buyers. By 1995, this had evolved into a fully fledged trade fair and was in the NEC in Birmingham showcasing 195 exhibitors and attracting 45,000 visitors.
  "The first one was in an old hanger at Manchester Airport in 1986."
- He had the original idea which lead to the opening of a shop located, as it happens, in King's Walk, off the King's Road in London, to act as a flagship for the Trust companies where store buyers can visit, at their convenience, to see a selection of consumer products suitable for a wider retail market. Principles are providing the space and Saatchi's among others are supporting the shop with advertising and design assistance.
- Direct intervention and personal contact. The Prince of Wales calls on his personal connections to pitch in. He gave one example of how this can help.

"There is a girl called Fiona Ray who does these marvellous enamel cufflinks. Through my people, she was put in touch with one of the buying staff at Aspreys, and now she supplies them. They are very happy with her work. There's a lot of wheels within wheels helping in this way and passing people along."

4. Purchasing

The Prince of Wales is a customer of a large number of Trust businesses. Every year he buys many Christmas presents at the Trust Trade Fair or, more recently, through the Trust shop. His selection includes shawls from Ulrike Textiles and clothes from Uwe Raw Cotton. Overseas visits, state ceremonies and VIP presentations often feature products originating from

Trust firms. On the 25th anniversary of The Prince's investiture at Caernarfon Castle, the plates to mark the occasion were made by JD Ceramics. Artisan Crystal in Belfast has supplied suitable sculptures for a number of royal occasions.

5. Training

Nothing comes higher on The Prince of Wales' list of priorities for the Trust than the need to train the people who are starting businesses. He cites the role of the shop as a recent extension of this dimension.

Nothing comes higher on The Prince of Wales' list of priorities for the Trust than the need to train people.

"We have to help them become more efficient in their marketing and more effective in their packaging and presentation, which is not something a lot of young businesses starting out realise is important."

The feedback from trade buyers is passed, through shop staff, to the businesses. The Prince personally takes an active interest as a Trust customer, relaying comments back about purchases so they can make improvements. There are other ideas for training, which are bubbling up at Trust.

"I'm looking to start a sort of apprenticeship scheme for people who have good ideas but don't quite have the training, the experience, or the practice, to pull off what they want to do.

"They need to learn from someone else. There's an idea that we will pay apprenticeship fees for someone to go and work at one of our businesses, or where they only need a part-time person. This is a sort of marrying up of two separate needs."

6. Publicity

The Prince of Wales can use his personal pull and access to the press to get free publicity for some of the Trust stable. Word of mouth also has rather more than the usual impact when it's a royal mouth. Cameras and reporters follow him everywhere, so The Prince can, on occasion, outdo the Pied Piper and bring the press to call.

7. Demonstrating his own personal commitment

Reviewing the troops is as important in the Trust as when you are colonel of a regiment or CEO of a major company. It is precisely because he cares so much that The Prince of Wales can convey some of his own passion to everyone involved in Trust businesses; and this enthusiasm can work wonders in getting extra effort out of entrepreneurs and advisers alike. Enthusiasm is an attribute he brings to all his activities and the value of enthusiasm and motivation is too often underrated in an investment context. A little encouragement can add a lot of value.

The Prince of Wales is a great motivator, whether it is dropping in to catch up on progress at Dorians Restorations, a Trust business, or in a related activity – Business in the Community – presenting the 1996 Ambassador Award for outstanding personal commitment to a most deserving recipient, Frank Nicholson, Managing Director of Vaux Breweries.

Readers tempted to downplay The Prince of Wales' personal contribution would be wrong. If the previous pages have not been convincing, then a few testimonials should put the proposition over the top. Let's start with Richard Street, who is in the best position to know.

"A remarkable amount of what we do is The Prince's invention. He's very aware of what's going on. He meets with advisers, and there's a terrific motivation if it's known he gets involved. He visits businesses. On away days, he will always try to tuck in a visit. He will go and meet companies who are major corporate sponsors. He has held events at Highgrove as 'thankyous' for donors."

Interestingly, when you ask The Prince of Wales why the Trust has been so successful, he is willing to give credit to practically every other aspect of the activity except his own contribution, which he downplays; but there can be no doubt who is really the driving force.

"I think I annoy [the executives of the Trust] intensely. I write notes and memos all the time saying, 'Why don't you think of this, and don't you think we should do that, and what about this idea?'"

It is important to emphasise the point made elsewhere in this book by Michael Hart, and others, that no organisation, investment or otherwise, can be a success solely based on one person. In addition to the advisers, The Prince of Wales wanted to give particular credit to Sir Alcan Copisario, who helped start the Trust. "An extremely effective man who worked wonders."

It is hard to calculate the total real return on investments made by the Trust, because they do not keep records that way; but the return on capital employed is off the charts, and puts the professionals to shame. In any event, how do you put a quantum on 60,000+ people who are now able to support themselves? If the aggregate value of Trust backed businesses is about £200 million, as of 1996, that value has been created through a total investment of £60 million since inception, which is a total return of well over 300 per cent. Given the pattern of investment outlay, heavily skewed to the most recent five years that translates to a *compound annual* rate of return of over 25 per cent across the entire portfolio.

If the past can already boast of spectacular successes, the future holds even more promise. The Prince of Wales has a clear vision of where he wants to see the Trust.

"Twenty years down the road, with any luck we might have a very substantial number of people with very substantial businesses who will never forget what was done for them at the start, and who will want to put something back into this country. It's already happening. Those who have done well have already started to give money to someone else to start a business.

"All I've ever wanted to do is put the Great back into Britain, and I feel these investments are one small way of making a contribution towards that, which is going to get bigger over time. It is a true investment, because it is an investment in people's lives, and a regeneration of their communities. When a town which is so dependent on a particular industry for jobs loses that backbone to their lives, it can be devastating. That is one of the reasons why I was so keen to invest in starting new businesses which can, perhaps, provide partial replacements."

> *All I've ever wanted to do is put the Great back into Britain, and I feel these investments are one small way of making a contribution.*

Proving that he is not parochial, the second long-term goal of The Prince of Wales is to see Trust activities spread around the globe.

"I was hoping that, before long, other people in other parts of the worlds would notice what we were trying to do. There is a Trust now in India. I'm going to Canada in April to launch one there. There's been interest expressed in our ideas in Japan. The other day, I sat next to the French Prime Minister at lunch after President Mitterand's service, and we got on to the subject of youth unemployment. I started talking about the Trust and he got quite interested in it, so we've sent him the bumph.

"You can have derivations in other countries which are specifically suited to the environment and their particular way of doing things."

This is, of course, a two way street. The strategy of improving your domestic investment record by watching developments in overseas markets, so well expounded by Nils Taube in the next chapter, has also been taken on board by The Prince of Wales.

"I get lots of ideas from going to other countries and picking up things they do. I picked up this idea called Second Harvest, on a visit to Canada, which is recycling surplus goods. We have extended the concept to office equipment, furniture, you name it, things which companies are frequently getting rid of but which these young firms can't afford. I want to have a proper database to enable people to pass on useful things."

Looking at what has been accomplished here, it is remarkable how little realisation there is among the general public of The Prince of Wales' prowess as an investor and a builder of wealth. He has seeded so many businesses in Britain. There is no other investment organisation like the Trust and the speed of its growth and the level of its success, against all the investment odds, is astonishing.

It is remarkable how little realisation there is among the general public of The Prince of Wales' prowess as an investor and a builder of wealth.

The Prince of Wales identified a couple of long standing basic truths about investment and stuck with them. Identify motivated people with a realistic business plan and give them the financial wherewithal and the support of experienced business people and the probability is high that even unlikely entrepreneurs can succeed. The Prince may not have added to his personal wealth through the Trust, but there are a growing number of Trust millionaires who are living proof his concept works and more than 22,000 successful businesses which can testify to the power of his investment acumen.

The team at St James's Place: From Left to Right John Hudson, Cato Stonex,
Nils Taube

* Global diversification is a key theme: "The exciting thing is to look for something where you are Columbus"

* £1 invested in December 1969 had grown to £54 by the end of 1995!

* "Has earned an unparalleled reputation for money making" *Money Observer*

NILS TAUBE

Use your Eyes and Plagiarise

Some people make reputations and others make money. Nils Taube is not a name which appears in the papers with any great frequency, nor does he spend any time cultivating personal recognition – rather the reverse. He is self-effacing and retiring, preferring to let his track record do the talking, which it does – most eloquently. In fact, Taube is on record as saying that he regards it as unlucky to have his picture published, which means that one of Britain's truly great money managers is almost anonymous outside a small circle of investing cognoscenti.

These are also some of the reasons why few people realise that Nils Taube is the longest serving manager in London continuously running a unit trust. He has been in position at St James's Place Greater European Progressive for 26 years, and at the International unit trust for 24 years. Contrast that with the industry norm. According to research in the *UK Fund Industry Review and Directory*, published in 1995, over 40 per cent of all managers had only been in place since 1993. There is a lot to be said for longevity and continuity, at least when the helmsman is someone of the calibre of Taube.

Taube has played many roles throughout a long, distinguished and varied career in the investment community, but his first love has always been stock picking. So much so that, in 1994, Taube resigned as an executive director of St James's Place Capital plc, the holding company for the fund management activities, in order to concentrate on his role as Principal Investment Advisor to the Group. It is a role in which he excels.

Taube has been picking up awards and accolades with the sort of frequency others in the profession can only envy. The list is long, but a suitably edited excerpt will demonstrate this author's contention that Taube has been consistently among the winners and that all, or any, of his funds have been a safe haven of satisfied investors for many years.

In 1987, a year most managers mention with a grimace, as if biting on a bad gherkin, Taube triumphed. His Bishopsgate Progressive ranked as the top investment trust in its sector over ten, and five year periods. This kind of leadership continued into the 1990s.

In 1994 the Group received the Micropal Award for the Best Unit Trust Group (smaller category) over the prior ten year period. Also in 1995 the Group won again this time for both five and ten year periods.

315

In 1995, data from Micropal showed that the St James's Place UK and General Progressive unit trust had outperformed all the other 488 PEP qualifying unit trusts for the preceding five year period, with a gain that was more than *triple* the average in the sector. The list is so long that, rather than go on and on, it's easier to reprint, as Chart 13.1, an extract from the promotional flyer put out by the parent company in 1995, which more or less says it all.

Awards are one thing, but the proof of the pudding is in the loyalty and admiration of his clients. Taube makes a point of managing these relationships with the same sort of care he lavishes on the stocks in his fund. He knows many of the older clients personally. It shows. When Taube moved over to J. Rothschild, clients moved with him en masse. Many are still there 14 years later.

At the end of the day, results matter most, and here Taube scores best of all. One pound invested in December 1969 in his Greater European

**Chart 13.1 J. Rothschild Assurance Marketing Group
Advertisement (1995)**

ONCE AGAIN, HEAD AND SHOULDERS ABOVE THE REST.

1ST

BEST UNIT TRUST GROUP
(SMALLER CATEGORY)
OVER 10 YEARS
1992

1ST

BEST UNIT TRUST GROUP
(SMALLER CATEGORY)
OVER 10 YEARS
1993

1ST

BEST UNIT TRUST GROUP
(SMALLER CATEGORY)
OVER 10 YEARS
1994

For the third consecutive year, the lion has walked away with the Micropal 10-year Best Unit Trust Group awards (smaller group category).

It is a unique record of consistent investment success.

But it is by no means the end of the story. In the same category in this year's awards, we took first place over five years, and third place over one year. And our individual funds took an equally remarkable share of the spoils, with other awards including:

- North American sector: 1st over ten years.
- European Equity sector: 1st over ten years.
- International Equity sector: 1st over ten years.
- UK Equity Growth sector: 1st over five years.

With nine awards in all, the 1994 Micropal awards make it plain once again that when it comes to consistently outstanding investment performance, the lion reigns supreme.

**J. ROTHSCHILD
ASSURANCE
MARKETING GROUP**

**ST. JAMES'S PLACE
UNIT TRUST GROUP**

171-1 (2/95)

Progressive Unit Trust is worth over £54 in 1995. Why work for a living when, for very little money, you can have Taube working for you? This, by the way, is my attempt to plagiarise one of his own best themes, of which more later in this chapter.

Taube is unique in that he has managed to cram two careers into one working lifetime. While always within the financial community, broadly defined, his initial contribution was at Kitcat and Aitken, starting as an office boy in 1948 and ending up as Senior Partner in 1975. The broking business held his attention for 34 years. Most men would be quite content with that sort of success. Not Taube. In 1969, he formalised the first steps of a transition into investment management, where he has spent the subsequent 26 years. This transition was completed in 1982 when together with Gilbert de Botton he joined Jacob Rothschild to devote himself entirely to the investing side of the envelope. GAM was set up initially to be the vehicle for a number of private clients previously served by Kitcat & Aitken on an individual basis.

"I didn't like the idea of operating stock broking as a principal. I felt strongly, and still do, that you should be an agent for your clients rather than dealing with them on the other side."

Of course, the distinction is not so precise that his career divides into two separate halves. The brokerage business contained within it many elements of investment management activities, and shareholders in funds can, on occasion, require as much hand holding as private clients.

One early departure from the remit of a run of the mill broker, which presaged much of what was to follow, was Taube's voracious appetite for fundamental analysis. This led him to co-found the Society of Investment Analysts in 1955. Taube did not see himself in the traditional broker role, even when he was in the mainstream of that activity. Rather he would call himself an investment analyst. This distinction is fundamental to understanding how Taube looks at the financial world – which is with extreme care and scrutiny, all the while searching for value discrepancies. This philosophy has been at the core of his investment thinking since he first started in the business in 1948.

"In those days, investment analysis was a kind of journey of discovery. The first piece of serious analysis I did was in 1950, when I discovered that Americans published estimates of cigarette sales for each brand in a journal called *Printer's Ink*. BAT owned Brown and Williamson and their sales were printed in this publication. I put their sales against the average profits of all the other cigarette companies which were quoted and worked out that something like 60 per cent of the profits of BAT came from America, information which was not published. At the time, people were paying a 36 per cent dollar premium to buy American shares and here we could buy a share at a very, very low multiple of earnings, which effectively was an American company, and for much less than the other comparable companies in America. I wrote a circular on the subject which got us millions of orders and changed the price. This set me off on the analyst route.

"Then there was H J Heinz, which had exactly the opposite situation. It had an English subsidiary. By digging in Companies House, I found out how big that was and how successful, and we bought 15 per cent of Heinz for our clients. Back then, it was all about digging for unusual values rather than themes, and looking for situations, transatlantic primarily, where people missed what was in another location. Hoover was another American company which had an English subsidiary which was vastly more successful than its American parent. You did an international arbitrage of values.

"BP was as good as the American oil companies and perhaps more successful on the exploration side. After losing Abadan to the machinations of Dr Mossadeq it had built a refinery at Aden, which sounds mad now but, in 1954/5, was quite clever because there was a shortage of refining capacity in the Middle and Far East and they saved themselves £2 plus a barrel in shipping costs. We raised the price of the whole company by 20 per cent in a week by highlighting that advantage. It was something of an analytical coup."

You can see that, from the start, Taube had mastered the skill of lateral thinking. He was always on the lookout for assets or earnings which were mis-priced because investors in one country could not see, or were not aware of, the value of operations in another; or where valuation in a domestic financial market failed to take into account the international diversity of a business; or where a business had made a fundamental shift in its structure which had not been understood by investors. As an analyst, Taube was not only ahead of his time, but also he did not stay on any one recognised path. He continually searched for new ways to assess value.

"I went on looking for the migration of ideas, new ways of looking at things. One example of this was in the life insurance industry. I had got

318

to know a man called Shelby Cullom Davis, who was a doyen of insurance analysts in America. In the 1940s, he had an insight into how life insurance companies should be valued. Up until that point, a life company wrote its business, debited the expense of writing its business against the P&L account, and then let the business unwind, with the result that, if the business grew fast, they produced dreadful earnings and virtually went broke. He amortised the cost of writing business over the life of the policies. It was the forerunner of GAAP accounting, but it became understood in America. Instead of selling on a 4–5 per cent yield basis, the true values were recognised.

"He taught me how to do this and I applied it in the English market to companies like Legal and General, Equity and Law Life, Eagle Star and, to some extent, Prudential. Subsequently this was applied to German companies with even more interesting results. One company, Victoria, went up nearly 100 times in ten years, including the appreciation of the Deutsche Mark.

"This is really no more than trying to plagiarise and use your eyes, if you remember the Tom Lehrer song."

While Taube was thinking about this type of cross border value migration, some companies were doing his work for him by applying new approaches to their businesses. Taube was able to spot, in advance, the likely benefits of such moves and the probable implications for the share price when the improvements were more widely recognised.

"In the very early 1950s, some English grocery companies started copying the American self-service system: Tesco and Victor Value in particular. Victor Value was less well managed, but Tesco got it right. Tesco was a small operation and could be bought for pennies. It grew from there, and was a great long-term play.

"When xerography was invented, John Davies, the head of Rank, managed to persuade Xerox to do a 50/50 deal, on the grounds he had a precision instrument and optical company. He put half his holdings into Rank and half into Rank Precision Instruments, which was 40 per cent owned by A Kershaw. By buying Kershaw and its effective ownership in the joint venture you could buy 10 per cent of the Rank Xerox business, in the early 1960s, for £1 million, because the market did not trust it, or did not understand it. So you had a valuation of the whole of Rank Xerox for £10 million at a time when Xerox in America, was valued at between $1 and 2 billion."

319

There are two particular aspects of Taube's investment philosophy which bear detailed discussion. These are the need for a broad *geographical* balance in the portfolio, and the importance of *comparative shopping* for value across markets. The two go hand in hand, but need to be evaluated separately to appreciate their relative importance.

COMPARATIVE SHOPPING

An obvious extension of Taube's global approach is to look for trends or values in one country which have not been recognised in another, and invest accordingly. If this sounds simple, it is only because the theory is a lot easier to articulate than the practice is to implement. Comparative shopping is, however, one aspect of valuation arbitrage which everyone can look out for. Taking a holiday or business trip abroad offers the possibility to see what others may have missed.

> *Look for trends or values in one country which have not been recognised in another, and invest accordingly.*

Taube is a master at applying the strategy. In an interview given to *Money Observer* in January 1995, he states the case succinctly and serves up a classic example of how rewarding the right cross border analysis can prove.

> A long time ago, maybe 30 or 40 years ago, I discovered there was such a thing as international plagiarism in investment. Buying supermarket shares such as Tesco, I argued simply that they already existed in America, where they had been successful, and that they were likely to repeat that success in Britain. Now we can apply that whole approach once again in eastern Europe through buying supermarket shares over there. . .
>
> It was very odd how slowly some of these developments travelled. Now they travel much more quickly. But really the whole process was like saying: 'We have seen the future and it works.'

One of Taube's current big positions is in Banque Nationale de Paris, the French bank which is valued at just 2 per cent of its deposits, compared with perhaps 6 to 8 per cent for the big clearing banks in the UK. That potential remains unlocked as of early 1996. The French banks have not been as aggressive as the American banks were five years ago but Citicorp rose more than eightfold in the last few years by ruthless write-offs and subsequent recovery.

"We always take a global view of stock markets, and on this basis we prefer to be in shares where the values are cheaper. . . Our investment some four years ago in Italian telephone companies was typical of the way we operate."

Taube felt that Italians did not need to be told by the likes of Bob Hoskins that it is good to talk.

"I felt that Italians would chatter to each other more than most other nations. I was sure the demand was there and that a one times cash flow was a very reasonable valuation. We noted that the Mexican telephone company was selling at about 10 times cash flow. We were also aware that there were 50 million Italians, about half of whom had telephones and there were about 100 million Mexicans, about 5 per cent of whom had telephones. We put a lot of money in and the shares went up sixfold."

There are literally no limits to comparisons Taube will draw across markets in his search to exploit inefficiencies. Lack of knowledge, or bias, or plain parochialism, allows a global thinker to spot valuation anomalies locals often miss by applying a universal logic across Australia, Mexico, USA, Japan and, indeed, all around the world. This, then, is the cornerstone of the Taube philosophy and, if there is one thing to point to which explains, in some measure, his extraordinary success, you would have to choose his skill in seizing upon cross border discrepancies. One critical caveat: The measure of relative value is not always obvious. Earnings multiples is only one of many options.

Even in a world of global markets and more rapid communication of information throughout the financial community, these inefficiencies persist. The good news for investors of Taube's ilk is that the rest of the market now takes less time to catch up, and so he does not have to hold an investment so long before it receives the recognition and uplift in value that such an undervalued stock deserves.

GEOGRAPHIC SPREAD

Given the vision inherent in Taube's global style and his ability to think globally, the outcome is that he deploys the portfolio around the world wherever he sees that as advantageous. Taube looks at the relative position of the major economies and makes allocation decisions based on both spotting value in individual securities, and also by assessing how the market, as a whole, is likely to perform going forward. Such analysis drove a specific shift in his mix between 1974 and 1975. The following is extracted from the 1975 annual report to shareholders.

> Your managers believe that the economic recovery in the United States and Japan will continue for some considerable time, albeit at a slower pace than has been indicated by other commentators, but remain uneasy about the prospects for UK industry . . .

During that 12 month period, the percentage of overseas stocks in the portfolio rose from 30.3 per cent to 51.6 per cent, with large increases in US and Japanese exposure. This ensured that Progressive was well positioned for what followed. Table 13.1 illustrates some pretty radical period to period shifts, in fact *understates* the volatility of the geographic mix. Japan, in 1989, was up over 23 per cent of the portfolio from nothing at all a couple of years back and below 8 per cent again by year end 1990 – a remarkable round trip.

The shift has been so pronounced that the fund has even changed its name to St. James's Place Greater European. It is hard to find anyone who is able to make these sorts of significant repositioning across countries work well, but Taube can. Geographic timing and rotation are a very vital key to understanding the success he has had relative to more pedestrian managers who have preferred to keep their feet firmly on the ground in the UK, or who have been restricted to a single market or region.

Table 13.1 Geographic Split of Bishopsgate Progressive Securities 1974–1995 (selected year ends: % Total)

Market	1975	1980	1985	1990	1995
UK	47.9	68.6	28.0	14.9	19.2
North America	38.4	25.9	37.1	20.5	0.3
Canada		5.4	5.6	3.3	0.1
Continental Europe	0.1	0.1	26.7	45.5	71.2
Japan	5.2	–	–	7.9	
Australia	8.4	–	–	1.8	3.9
South Africa	–	–	2.6	6.1	

Not only does a portfolio which is diversified geographically increase the scope for selecting winners, but backing certain countries can provide an additional uplift relative to a UK or world index. For example, in 1985, Taube went into Sweden strongly with holdings in Astra (a drug company) and L M Ericsson (an electronics business which has emerged as a leading supplier of telecommunications components in the 1990s), which made up nearly 10 per cent of total securities at a time when Sweden hardly featured, even with so called leading edge global asset allocators.

Taube also went into Switzerland in a relatively large way. The 1990 portfolio contains holdings in Motor Columbus (a power company), Nestlé (the consumer products/food company) and Roche (the pharmaceuticals concern) which, in aggregate, represented over 9 per cent versus a nominal weighting in world indices.

By 1994, eastern Europe was well established among his holdings, with Poland, Hungary and the Czech Republic adding up to over 7 per cent, at a time when most money managers were still trying to decide whether to nibble at these markets.

Taube refuses to be distracted in his search for value. The flight of US institutions in the late 1980s from South Africa presented a buying opportunity for those willing to look longer-term. Taube took positions in the leading blue chips there, Anglo American (mining based conglomerate), Barlow Rand (financial services and investment) and De Beers (diamonds), taking that country up to nearly 6 per cent of his holdings.

Geographic diversity and the ability to move between the markets of different countries is one of Taube's greatest strengths.

Geographic diversity and the ability to move between the markets of different countries is one of Taube's greatest advantages and greatest strengths. He is almost always weighted well away from the Morgan Stanley Capital Index. He is also unusual in the degree to which he will cover a large number of markets. That comes through clearly in the 1990 portfolio which contains securities from a total of 57 companies but spread over 12 different countries.

Using those two main planks of his platform, it is interesting to peer underneath and spot several sub strands which bridge the gap between theory and execution. First and foremost, Taube subscribes to the catechism which says:

"IT'S THE INDIVIDUAL STOCK STUPID . . ."

Taube focuses on individual companies and their management, and the valuation of individual shares. "People always ask me what I think of the market," he says. "But I argue it does not matter much what I think. It does not go up or down because of my views. In all the years I have been investing, I reckon there have probably been only five or six occasions when the overall performance of the market really mattered." That, he says, was the case in 1974, 1987 and also for a short time in 1990, but the overall state of the market is usually not important. (*Money Observer*, January 1995)

BUY THE BEST OF BRITAIN . . .

One specific, and particularly positive, aspect of Taube's focus on comparative shopping is his ability to see what is Best in Britain. The UK still remains the largest single country in most portfolios, but it earns its place. Taube focuses on answering the question: 'What does Britain do well today?' He comes up with some surprisingly strong answers about the comparative advantages of a select group of British companies even as against global competitors. His analysis has to be an encouraging indicator for certain sectors of the economy.

> "If you think of the big international companies Britain is rich in some of the best ones. Take Guinness – nobody else in the world can make whisky in the quantity and quality that it can." In the UK & General unit trust two general strategic themes have emerged: "We don't want anything very much to do with the consumer," he says. "We think the story is about exports and companies which make things well in this country."

He cites Rolls Royce as an example . . .

> "Britain has essentially lost its motor industry as far as names are concerned, but not when it comes to the manufacturing plants. Car manufacturing here is very successful and management under Nissan, BMW, Honda, Ford, Toyota and General Motors is palpably better than British managements ever were. But British companies like Lucas and GKN continue to make the clever components, so we are happy to invest in those sorts of companies." (*Money Observer*, January 1995)

LET SOMEONE ELSE SWEAT

In terms of spotting specific stocks, Taube has some concrete advice for other investors which derives from another favourite old ruse of his: getting talented people with the right motivation to work hard on his behalf. (See commentary in *The Financial Times Global Guide to Investing* by this author, page 304 and following.)

"If you find a business which is run by people who have a lot of their own money in the business and who are dedicated, you should stick with it. A very good example is Sainsbury's, when they first went public. Following individuals who run successful businesses is the most useful thing you can do.

> *Following individuals who run successful businesses is the most useful thing you can do.*

"The people who started National Car Parks have had fantastic success creating wealth. In his formative years, Lord Hanson was one to follow. Now it's too big and you'd have to be a magician to go on at the same rate."

Taube is more cautious about making specific recommendations when it comes to his own profession.

"As an individual, it's very difficult to do well on one's own for any long period. I have had dry periods in my life when I haven't had anyone sitting opposite me who said, 'Look, don't do this or don't do that.' You need a mirror.

"I had a very good time with Nick Roditi and a very good colleague in Gordon Grender, and I now have very good colleagues in John Hodson and Cato Stonex. You need to have an alter ego. You can be *primus inter pares*, but you have to have the *pares*.

"As a group, Martyn Arbib and his cohorts at Perpetual have developed a collegiate centre of excellence. Paul Myners at Gartmore, now Nat West, is one to watch."

THERE'S NOTHING LIKE A GOOD NICHE . . .

. . . or possibly two niches. Bruno's was a big holding for Taube between 1973 and the late 1980s. Bruno's is an ethnic food supermarket chain based in Alabama. You have a subset of the overall market – ethnic food – doubled up with a subset of the geographic territory – Alabama. That gives you two barriers to larger competitors without reducing the market potential relative to the size of a small growing business. Growth within a defined niche is great. Bruno's business grew vigorously from a small base and turned £7,500 into over £1 million for Taube. PEP Boys Manny, Moe and Jack which developed a superior auto parts business is a holding of over 23 years. It has gone up more than thirty fold.

IF YOU AREN'T GOING TO BUY BIG POSITIONS, WHY BOTHER?

Leave on one side, for a moment, that Taube translates this into a licence to hunt wherever in the world he thinks fits. You find stocks in Taube's holdings which fit this category that are not exactly household names in their own market. The Italian telecom group discussed later on pages 333–4 got up to more than 10 per cent of several of his funds at one point.

It works both ways. Companies can become a large portion of his portfolio. Likewise, he is not afraid to own a large percentage of the free float in a particular stock in which he believes. He has held 8 per cent of the publicly available shares in Camellia plc. Kölnische Rückversicherung and CocaCola Amatil, which are covered later, are companies where Taube became a big shareholder.

Trying to sum up Taube's skills and stick this complex personality into small compartments with easily recognisable investment labels won't work. The nearest available would be Fundamental Analyst, but even that won't quite wash.

"Value is a catch phrase. What is the opposite of a value investor? Is there any such thing? I had a senior partner, once, who liked to say things like, 'I'm selectively bullish'. To which I said, 'Please let me know when you're indiscriminately bullish'. By looking at the opposite of a statement, you can often see the absurdity.

"I do like to be a contrarian, because I feel that the market is made up of people who act in a slightly hysterical way to both good and bad news. Price discounts both optimism and pessimism. So, when there's a lot of optimism in the price, I get exceedingly nervous and, as long as people are pessimistic, I am much more relaxed."

What you can see is that Taube revels in finding a situation where something has to give, because there is a *structural* flaw working against common sense and business logic which will lead someone to unlock the value he has identified. News International is a classic case in point. BAT was one early example. A late 1995 play came from Germany. Again, the element of international arbitrage is involved though, in this case, it is behavioural rather than financial.

> **Taube revels in finding a situation where something has to give, because there is a structural flaw working against common sense and business logic.**

"General Reinsurance, which is, I think, the most effective reinsurance company in the world, bought 75 per cent of Kölnische Rückversicherung (Cologne Reinsurance) from UAP/Colonia. They paid 1500 marks for 75 per cent, leaving 25 per cent in public hands.

"You could still buy these minority shares in the market after this happened for 800 marks because the Germans are used to the fact that the majority will rape the minority. So we bought about 20 per cent of the minority shares. Ultimately, General Re must integrate, because it is very difficult to run two insurance portfolios. They will want a common pool. There was a special holding company set up to give the French and Germans income on a seven year preference share. General Re sells at twice book value. If Kölnische goes to that value over seven years and grows at only 10 per cent, there will be an eight times return on it."

A second agenda which then stands out from this line of thought is that, contrary to widely held opinion on the subject, Taube can see virtue in being a minority shareholder in a business where there is a dominant majority shareholder. He is, of course, careful to qualify this concept. The characteristic of the majority shareholder is crucial. Their goals need to be understood to ensure that there is congruence between them and the growth in value for all shareholders. If these conditions combine, then the minority investor is, effectively, piggy-backing off the efforts of a motivated majority holder.

POLITICAL CORRECTNESS COMES TO FINANCIAL MARKETS

"Germans and French, when they control companies, do all sorts of funny things and don't always treat minorities with kid gloves. American and British companies are made to treat minorities properly and can't ride roughshod over the minority.

"As long as Cologne Reinsurance sells at a discount to General Re, then there seems to be no urgency in selling out when General Re is the natural buyer. In the meantime, I'm very happy to be a minority shareholder and let these people work for us.

"I don't do this in any aggressive way. I don't go into Rupert Murdoch at News Corp and say, 'Take me out'. I'm very happy not to be taken out. He's working for me. [The minority was bought out since this comment!]

"Ideally, I love to buy companies where there is a good majority shareholder, especially in different markets. If I could buy the minority shares of Phillips in India, if I could buy Unilever India or Glaxo India, I'd love it; for I would much rather be a minority shareholder of these people than have shares in Mr Tata's company or Mr Birla's company."

Underpinning all these ideas are the basic building blocks – the down and dirty detailed analyses of the numbers. Discussing financial analysis with Taube is rather like taking a temperature of a patient with a thermometer that contains no mercury. You know there is so much more going on that you can actually see. A sprinkling of insights conveys just how fast his mind works to make connections between different aspects of a business in arriving at an assessment of its value.

> *Whenever you buy a share, you don't just look at the share, you look at what you paid for a piece of the enterprise.*

"I pay a lot of attention to price times cash flow because, if a company at the end of a year has more money than it had before, or less debt, that's obviously useful. Arnold Weinstock once said to me 20 years ago that he looked at reports of a competitor which produced great earnings and, at the end of the year, they always had less cash than they had before; which made him laugh."

"Then you have to look at the enterprise value of the company itself. EBITDA is quite a good measure of enterprise value. Whenever you buy a share, you don't just look at the share, you look at what you paid for a piece of the enterprise.

"The reinvestment yield is hugely important. If you can get 20 per cent on your investment, that's a successful company. Then you look at the rate of growth they have achieved over the past few years. If the price earnings ratio is not much higher than the rate of growth, that's a nice yardstick."

You can't take Taube away from his favourite subject for long. Passing over financial ratios as 'the humdrum of business', Taube moves back into the aspect of investing which is a passion for him, and has proved so very profitable for his investors.

"The exciting thing is to look for something which is really different – where you are Columbus. To find these things, I do a great deal of reading, a lot of talking. One very clever man I talk to a lot is Bernard Selz in New York. In England, Anthony Bolton [Chapter 3] is a very capable man. We do not speak that often but we frequently overlap in stock ownership.

"John Hodson, my partner, has an encyclopaedic knowledge of the connections between people. He got interested 25 years ago in a company called Camellia Investments, in which we own 6–8 per cent. Then, by lateral thinking, we said if Camellia is so good, we should look at Williamsons (a tea company) and found you could buy 20–25 per cent of the company for about £4 million; and it's got 75,000 employees in India and a 25 per cent interest in an Indian tea company which contributes about 10 per cent and is about one tenth their size which is valued at more than half their market capitalisation. It's one of these goodies."

Selling is an issue for investment managers and one which somehow always seems fraught with more problems than buying. Taube is well aware of the problem, and makes sure he has thought through the ramifications of how to exit before entering into an investment. He also articulates a number of the sometimes contradictory calculations which have to be weighed before making a decision on whether to sell and, if so, how to execute a sale.

"If you have to sell £25 million worth of shares, the company has to be pretty big, or you have to be pretty patient – or you have to be very right. The other day, someone asked me how to sell a big position. I said, 'Like a porcupine makes love – very, very carefully!'

"The first thing is never to fall in love with a share just because it goes up. Ideally, a share never goes up as much as it should do and there's always a degree of undervaluation. Let me give you an example. One of our biggest positions is in News International, Rupert Murdoch's English subsidiary which owns *The News of the World, Sun, The Times* and *Sunday Times*, and has 40 per cent of BSkyB. He has an agreement between that company and its parent company, News Corporation, that the shares of News International are entitled to the same dividend and same rights as one and a half shares of News Corporation. 85 per cent is owned by him and about 15 per cent largely by four groups.

"Sooner or later, he will have to take out the minority because, if he uses the cash in this company to invest in other companies, he starts creating conflicts. Also, If I were him, I would want to take the cash out and use it elsewhere in the group. So, ultimately, I believe he will want to make a deal. Currently, that is about £6 versus a current market price of £3.10. As long as these shares remain at a near 50 per cent discount and as long as I like News Corporation, I'm happy. If they were valued at the same prices, I would be tempted to sell. And it's almost to our advantage that he doesn't do this, because News Corporation is growing and it will cost him more and more to do a deal later." [This has now happened. News Corp subsequently made an offer to exchange those shares for non-voting preferred ordinary in News Corporation at a value equal to £4.10p in June 1996.]

"The other example is Biochem Pharma, a Canadian company. They invented a drug which stops the AIDS virus mutating. Glaxo has a 13 per cent interest. By using a combination of Retrovir and this drug, 3TC, they have proved clinically that it can extend people's lives and can prevent people with HIV getting AIDS. The shares have gone up from $12/13 to $69 in the last six months, suddenly, after two years of doing nothing much. The valuation of the company is now Canadian $3.5 billion and an analyst who covers this company told us, 'If all goes well, they will make $200 million in the year 2000'. At seventeen times earnings four years from now, and the fact that the analyst was so bullish, suggests the ceiling isn't much higher. When it got up to $45, I decided to test the water and sold some shares. I worry when people start speculating.

"When something sells at a very substantial premium to the market, and to similar shares having similar growth rates, I would think of selling. Generally, you want to sell when everyone else gets euphoric. There should be an element of contrariness in what one does. Clearly, I have to be wary whatever I do. If it goes up further, I shouldn't have sold any and, if it goes down, I should have sold the lot; but you have to be careful and take the temperature first."

So seller's remorse is an occupational hazard for an investment manager, along with other prickly problems!

Seller's remorse is an occupational hazard for an investment manager.

As of 1996, Taube has reoriented his portfolio, positioning it to benefit from some fundamental macro-economic and political shifts which have introduced new elements to his variation on the theme of following values across borders. These are powerful forces, though finding the best way to play them is not always so obvious.

"Even today, with thousands of analysts, every now and again something is new; and you have to recognise when something is new and different and go for it.

"At the present time, one of our themes which we follow is that there are 1.3 billion people in the world who earn less than $1 a day. 57 per cent of the world's population earn less than $3 a day. These people are going to be earning more money and will spend it. Our reaction is to buy Nestlé, Unilever and Coca Cola, because they have the sort of products which people at this level of income buy when they move up.

One of our themes which we follow is that there are 1.3 billion people in the world who earn less than $1 a day. These people are going to be earning more money and will spend it.

"We have to think how to take advantage of themes. I'm scared about investing money in Russia, China or India, but I don't mind investing in Coca Cola, which sells syrup to these countries. The next step was discovering a company called Coca Cola Amatil, which is an Australian subsidiary (40 per cent owned). They were a preferred bottler in Australia and New Zealand, which have about 21 million in population. They make just under half their money selling and bottling soft drinks there. Because they are very capable, Coca Cola has let them buy concessions in Indonesia, which has about 195 million; Poland; the Czech Republic; Slovakia; Hungary; Switzerland; Austria; Romania;

the Ukraine and Byelorussia. They now have almost 400 million in the area they serve. They're growing like mushrooms.

"If people drink five bottles of Coca Cola in Indonesia and you've got 195 million Indonesians who can't drink alcohol, the likelihood is that this will become a very big business; which is how I like to play the developing world."

As an investment theme for the next decade, with his global view of the world, it should be no surprise that Taube focuses on emerging markets. Inevitably, the way Taube follows this theme is to tag along with world wide leaders in a specific sector and back their chosen company in the relevant country. It's a strategy which has served him well in the past, and one he expects to profit from in the future.

"The most important trend is the bringing up of Eastern Europe, and India, and China, closer to Western standards. In 1989 we started looking at Eastern Europe. We picked four situations in which we invested in 1992, two in Czechoslovakia and two in Poland. One was Philip Morris' subsidiary in Czechoslovakia called Tabak. We bought it at a very low multiple of cash flow. Then it went up four times or so, as everyone jumped in until it got so absurd we sold. Now it's back to where we started and we are buying again.

"Then there is Czokoladovny, controlled by Nestlé and Danone in the Czech Republic which also went up four times and has come back. We are studying that carefully, but the confectionery industry in the East started off at such a low level of hygiene and sophistication that they did not export as they could not meet the standards of Western countries. They will have to spend a great deal of money. In Poland we did exactly the same. We bought a company called Wedel, which was 60 per cent owned by Pepsi Cola. It's a chocolate and biscuit company. They went up eight times in nine months and we sold."

Taube is not so sanguine that these sorts of gains can be repeated in the same markets. So where is the next country to look at for 1996?

"I'm uneasy about China, because the West has got a love affair with China, but it's still a communist country. I don't like investing in countries which still have totalitarian regimes. I haven't put any money in Russia, because leopards don't change their spots that much and commercial law is not fully developed.

"Perhaps it's India. It is a feeling based largely on the fact that they have British law, the English language, a population of over one billion and a middle class that in numbers probably exceeds Europe's middle class."

In highlighting one industry Taube sees as having great potential for investors in the future, he returns to his roots and develops a new variation on an old theme – that of transatlantic valuation discrepancies.

"The new generation of cable in the UK is a combined licence for telephone and cable, which means that the better companies could have a great advantage over BT. These companies are valued at a fraction of the equivalent here compared to cable companies in America; and particularly because the American ones haven't had telephone until just now, so they are doubly attractive. The market here hasn't grasped this. They are about two years away from earnings and positive cash flow and appear to have financed themselves quite adequately, so they can be patient. This industry could be a serious winner.

"Nynex stands out and Bell Cable Media, to a certain extent. If you have cable, you can only make free calls to other people who have cable. So this should lead to concentration, which is a great attraction. Nynex, for instance, has Manchester and surroundings, which is a close contiguous area, and means that most people are likely to be on the same network and get these free calls. A free telephone service should be quite an attractive proposition, particularly to anyone with children in school. It also hangs together with the media revolution.

"Relative valuation means per subscriber and per population area. Ultimately, experience shows you get 40–50 per cent of your potential population. They are valued at $2,000 to $3,000 per subscriber in America and much less here."

Another sector, broadly defined, which has worked well for Taube and his investors is that of telecommunications. Hardly anyone who has watched the investment scene over the last decade can fail to be aware of the great gains that have been achieved in telecommunications stocks. Taube believes that more mileage can be extracted, though it is noticeable that he has found a more complex route that yields above average returns.

"They're fairly easy to analyse. We bought an enormous lot of the Italian telephone company, Telecom Italia, which has just spun out its mobile company. The fixed wire company is still only about 1.5–2 times cash flow. We got in at one times cash flow. We knew that the spending programme would come to an end in 1994, which meant that cash flow would then go into reducing debt. Thanks to Mr Berlusconi and the inability of the Government, we've been able to go on buying this fairly cheaply.

"We started off with warrants in STET, the holding company, which went from L2,000 to L60,000 and then consolidated them into convertible debentures of Telecom Italia.

"Our reason for holding such a large stake here was that we had sifted through most of the industry all around the world. We ignored the prejudice so many people have against Italy. I think Italy is nowhere near as bad a country as people make out. There are all these worries about mafia and politics which are problems, but not decisive."

ASSET ALLOCATION

Taube is a strong believer that equities are the way to build capital over the long term. His funds portfolios are concentrated almost exclusively on stocks and he has not much time for other asset classes. There have been occasions when he has bought bonds as a relatively short-term play relating to certain specific conditions in the markets.

"Supposing you have tremendous overheating in the stock market and the bond market goes weak. It's well worth paying attention. In 1987, the facts were screaming at you that the market was over-valued. The bond market had been falling for nearly nine months and the stock market continued to go up. In 1982/3 we shovelled money into American 30 year and zero coupon bonds, but based on an analysis of value rather than on any reading of the cycle."

Taube is not wedded to remaining fully invested at all times; rather the reverse. He has not been shy about stepping aside from stocks on occasion. He uses cash as ballast, but also will buy bonds when his macro-economic analysis suggests that fixed income securities will enjoy a period in the sun.

During the 1974 crash, Taube moved Bishopsgate Progressive to a 27.5 per cent cash position. By the end of 1975, he was down to 1 per cent as the market rebounded and Taube went on fast forward to put that cash to work. In 1990, Taube took the Special Situations Unit Trust up to 27 per cent cash, as he had foreseen a poor year ahead. The FT All Share was flat during the period, so he rode out that lacklustre year with less risk. In 1995, which surprised many by proving to be one of the best years to be fully invested, Taube was actually down to minus 1 per cent cash or 101 per cent invested.

Taube likes to have a cash cushion most of the time. It usually hovers around 10 per cent, which means he has achieved his level of performance with only a 90 per cent market risk in the portfolio. His careful use of cash as a temporary refuge from financial tempests, however, is more or less the full extent of Taube's trade-off between equities and other asset classes.

In similar vein, Taube professes himself to be a long-term investor who does not attempt to time the market and sit through the setbacks of a bear cycle.

"When the market goes higher, one has to get worried and be very careful which of our shares we want to live with in a bear market and accept we may lose some money. I'm not going to sell Williamson's Tea because there's a bear market in Japan. More market prone shares we probably should reduce.

"Everyone around always thinks, 'What's the market doing?' Of course, it doesn't really matter. You don't say Mr Rockefeller made a lot of money because the 1895 market went up. You acquire a slice of a business. Until that is valued at a silly price, one really shouldn't get too excited.

"The way we operate is to look at the valuation of companies, and think through their potential. We take a five year view and try to think how far this will go. If you think it can go up five times in five years and it doubles in six months, then that's only 2.5 times left and maybe I'm wrong. In those circumstances, you may take it off the table."

HALF AN EYE ON GOVERNMENT POLICY

While Taube shows his skill to best advantage when selecting individual securities, it would miss one whole dimension of the man if a description of his style did not include the area of macro-economic policy. Taube is always aware of the influence that Government can have on values, and this has worked to his advantage over a manager who is strictly a stock picker or only an asset allocator. Taube understands the interaction, as is demonstrated by an excerpt from the management report of Bishopsgate Progressive Unit Trust in November 1971.

In my report at this time last year I stated I was hopeful for a rise in equity share prices in 1971, on the basis that at that time they largely stood at levels discounting the problems of inflation and lack of growth in the economy. During 1971 the Government reduced corporate and personal taxation and increased both capital allowances for industry and the level of capital expenditure in the public sector of the economy. These measures, designed to stimulate the economy and hence to reduce the level of unemployment, take time to work through the economy.

Taube foresees that one unprecedented shift in the structure of society must have enormous consequences for financial markets, not so much over the next decade as over the next 25 years.

"The demographic situation in Europe is exercising my mind. *The Economist* and others have written really good articles showing the number of people of working age to the number of people in retirement or pre working age. Presently, the relationship is 4 or 5 to 1 and it looks like going down to 2.5 to 1 in Western Europe. Britain, Holland and, to some extent, the USA and Canada, have private pension schemes, but all the other countries are dependent on state pension schemes to such an extent that they probably will have to save twice the level of present GDP over the next 30 years and put them into private pension funds. The Germans will have to put at least £1,500 *billion* into these funds. The French and the Italians will have to develop organised pension funds.

"This means you will have institutional markets in those countries which are more like Anglo Saxon markets. A much larger proportion of the GDP will have to move to public markets either by privatisation or by companies going public. There's a sea change coming. To look after the old people, much more money will have to be saved; and the corollary of that statement is that rates of interest which, in the long run have been 3 per cent pa real will have to be rather higher than that for the foreseeable future."

It's always useful to hear the advice of not just one of Britain's, but of the world's, most successful managers on the qualities which make individuals stand out from their peers. Some are a tad tricky to spot from the outside. For those looking to find the person to trust with their future financial well being, perhaps, after looking at Taube's record, you might conclude the search is over.

"You have to be able to sleep well at night.

"You should never borrow so much or be so exposed in such a way that you can't have another shot.

"It's a mixture of steadfastness and just a dash of cowardice as well. To be totally stubborn is dangerous.

"Age helps. If you've lived through 1974 in England, it was quite unbelievable. People really thought the last trumpet had sounded. Seeing that, it paid you not to panic. There was hardly a share in the London market selling over £1 and you could buy Shell yielding 12 per cent. Things don't go on forever like that.

> *You should never borrow so much or be so exposed in such a way that you can't have another shot.*

"Industry is helpful. People imagine the likes of George Soros don't work hard. It's rather like going to Wimbledon and seeing a chap winning and not thinking you've got to be fit enough to be on a tennis court in the heat for four and a half hours, which means they have been working like a slave to get fit. The work ethic is so important, and yet the idea that gambling leads to success is ingrained. Using the words making money instead of earning it."

Taube eats his own cooking. One story doing the rounds – and not recounted to me by Taube himself – illustrates this point rather well. Some ten years ago, Taube had an operation requiring hospitalisation. Co-workers assumed they had heard the last of him for several days. Not so. While he was still in the recovery room, the first thing he did, after coming round from the anaesthetic, was to insist that the nurse brought him a telephone. Checking on his trading status that day had to be done before he got a boost of pain killers.

"Analytical skill are crucial. You have to be able to analyse things yourself. Knowing your own limitations is also crucial. You have to know when to call on other people."

Taube is essentially a modest man, so it is not generally well known that he uses his undoubted skills to benefit charitable endeavours. In particular, he looks after a foundation devoted to cancer research which, under his stewardship, started off with an endowment of £1 million 14 years ago and now is able to give away up to $1 million a year. While the capital continues to grow, Taube achieves a balance through judicious use of zero coupon bonds.

Taube also sits on the Estonian branch of the Soros Foundation, which gives away $3 million annually. He supports another charity which does work with children suffering from psychological disorders which he describes as "the best investment I know. If you can bring someone back into normal life and compare that to the cost to the state, if that person is not contributing, you can argue you are getting 100 times a year on what you are spending."

While that is an exceptional situation, Taube's shareholders have come to expect exceptional investment returns, and he has continued to find the sort of special situations which have continued to deliver these sorts of returns. Taube recalls one case where he put a client into Rembrandt Tobacco at one times cash flow in the early 1960s. Now named Richemont, part of the Rupert conglomerate, by 1996, a mere £1,000 invested then was worth more than £700,000!

The lesson could hardly be clearer though, as with everything else about investing, even hard and fast rules can bend.

"Everyone likes trading. It massages the ego if you make money quickly. My intention is to be a long-term investor, but I'm not hung up on these things. A long-term investment can become a short-term investment if it doubles tomorrow and a short-term one can become long-term if it goes down."

As for his investors, performance has been theirs for the taking. In only the second year of the fund's life, Progressive took off, beating the FT Actuaries All Share Index by a comfortable margin and the 36 per cent increase that year was nearly double the rise in the FT Industrial Ordinary Index. By the end of 1975, the Income Units were showing a six year gain *exclusive* of dividends, which was more than double that of either the FT All Share or the Dow Jones Industrial Average.

Such relative performance has become almost the norm for Taube, as he has retained an awesome consistency throughout his career. There is no better testimony than to end with the chart on facing page bound to bring a smile to every shareholder Taube has ever had. Chart 13.2 shows just how well Taube's philosophies and ideas about investing work in practice.

Chart 13.2 Relative Performance St James's Place Greater European Progressive versus FT Actuaries All Share (12.69 – 12.95)

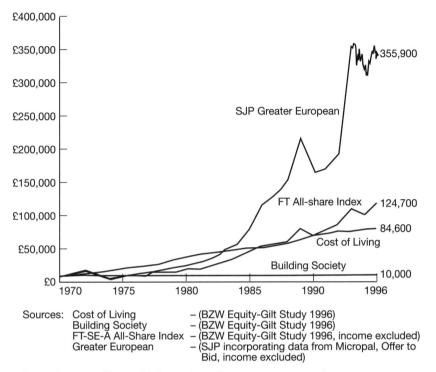

Sources: Cost of Living   – (BZW Equity-Gilt Study 1996)
          Building Society   – (BZW Equity-Gilt Study 1996)
          FT-SE-A All-Share Index – (BZW Equity-Gilt Study 1996, income excluded)
          Greater European   – (SJP incorporating data from Micropal, Offer to
                                    Bid, income excluded)

Data taken annually as at 31 December only.
Past performance is not necessarily a guide to the future.

339

Key to Successful Investing

It is all too easy to read through the profiles of these outstanding investors, put the book down, and carry on as before. Like so many New Year resolutions, the intention to improve in investing can wither among many more immediate, if less important, demands. That would be a waste. There's so much valuable advice on every page that the only real drawback is how to select a few pointers which can help most, so readers can skim the cream.

Many skills in investing are essentially timeless. Leading investors today pay tribute to Jesse Livermore and Benjamin Graham, neither of whom have been personally active during the last 20 years. Having had the privilege to talk at length with all our profiled investors and to study their techniques, it is now time for me to try to synthesise some common themes and sort out selected lessons which can be useful to every investor. They are my personal picks, and not necessarily the same ones our grand masters would chose. Please also be aware that the examples of specific investments cited are not meant as recommendations, but as illustrations of how an analytical approach can work. The aim is to enable readers to improve one or more aspects of their own investing performance. Since the territory covered has been extensive and the editor's pen has excised much material, I have divided these 'lessons' into three separate categories.

1. Secrets of Successful Investing

Here I have attempted to capture the key insights and investment strategies which have enabled our selected Grand Masters to do so much better than the market and rise to the summit of the investment profession. This cannot be a complete list. It is no litany of dos and don'ts. Investing does not work like that. We have extracted recurring themes, pointing to paths to be followed which, if the investor does not stray, should lead to, at least, a pot of silver, if not platinum.

No individual manager profiled in these pages will recognise his own idiosyncratic style in this section. Of necessity, what is presented is a blended composite of their separate and distinct skills; but there are a number of common traits, perhaps more than might be expected. The fact that certain themes do seem to recur should give added confidence about their efficacy. Using them can benefit professionals and individual investors alike.

2. Characteristics of a Successful Money Manager

Most people have neither the time, nor the inclination nor, if one is being realistic, the ability, to manage their own money. Investing is essential. Arguably, therefore, there is no more important decision than to whom one is going to entrust one's savings.

What is so tragic is that the average person, bombarded by slick marketing campaigns and barely disguised advertorials in the financial press, ends up going with a few so called 'household' names that get jammed into their head and act accordingly. The big finance houses get bigger; but big is not necessarily better. All too often, in the investment industry, the reverse is true. Big may mean mediocre performance with committee style management striving to be safely in the middle of the pack, or worse, inexperienced managers cutting their teeth on a small fund of nominal importance to the management company, but vital to the investor. Image all too often substitutes for real performance.

The temptation exists to throw up one's hands and dump the whole lot into a tracker fund. Resist the impulse. There is a better way.

Invest some effort into investigating the background of the manager(s) of top performing funds. When you buy into any investment scheme, it is vital not to forget that its performance will only be as good as the ability of the management. I have tried to extract from the background, experience and personality traits of these top managers, a few litmus tests anyone can use to decide whether to go with one investment vehicle versus another.

> *When you buy into any investment scheme, its performance will only be as good as the ability of the management.*

3. What Does it Take to be a Successful Investor or (for Someone Aspiring to Enter the Industry) a Good Investment Manager?

Always assuming the daunting prospect of immense amounts of drudgery does not put you off and you are actually determined to try, against the odds, to outperform the index, there are a few things which help even these odds. In the third section, you will find a few dos and don'ts to think about for those so minded. Please do not use these as a definitive checklist which will substitute as a suitability test or provide a personality screen. I make no claims to expertise in behavioural psychology and, to the extent that behaviour is an important element in the investing calculus, there is not any one definable profile that predicts success in investing; but I do believe there are identifiable traits which are more likely to be a plus than a minus, and I am convinced that certain preparatory steps are more helpful than others.

These are a blend of the psychological and the analytical, with a touch of homespun wisdom woven in at the end. Some are stand-alone but, for the most part, single dimensional approaches have limited validity. You have to combine concepts and tools. Multivariate methodologies is the name of the game.

1. SECRETS OF SUCCESSFUL INVESTING

(a) Think like a businessman, not an investor

The power of one has never been so sure as when applied to investing. The value of a security, both a Government stock and, more particularly, the common stock of a company, should not be some simple multiple of an accounting measure. The key is what is the whole enterprise worth, and then, backing out of that calculation, how much is one share worth?

That is a much more time consuming exercise than checking the yield column in *The Financial Times*; but it is an exercise that the best professionals discipline themselves to undertake before buying.

You won't find much mention of P/E ratios in *Investing with the Grand Masters*. What you will find is talk about 'underlying profitability', 'cash flow', 'sustainable profits', 'a businessman's point of view' and other similar lines of thought. How does that translate? The easiest short cut is to focus in on EBITDA – sometimes called the enterprise value – and develop a relevant multiple of that.

> **EBITDA is the calculation least susceptible to accounting inconsistencies or management manipulation.**

Earnings Before Interest, Taxes, Depreciation and Amortisation provides an approximation of the gross cash flow generated from the operations of a business. If this number is not positive, you have a problem. The Grand Masters in this book who focus on equities constantly return to some variation of this calculation like carrier pigeons coming home to roost. EBITDA is the calculation least susceptible to accounting inconsistencies or management manipulation.

As for the multiple, that's where the art comes in. Look at comparable companies within the same industry sector, within or across countries, and then make adjustments for factors like leverage or growth which impact on intrinsic value. The more highly geared company would deserve a lower rating; one with a comparable capital structure, but capable of achieving greater EBITDA growth, would warrant a premium to the sector average. Nothing out of the norm here. Common sense has a place in valuation.

Comparative analysis can often have even more meaning when you are dealing with a company which has multiple businesses and, for a classic conglomerate, is really the only reasonable way to derive an aggregated value.

That gets you to first base. There is one more element to the equation. Then assess who might buy this business, what they could make of it and, therefore, how much they might pay for it. This, of course, is the theoretical maximum and should not be used as a target price, merely as a guide to eventual upside; though there will be moments when prices can go way beyond this level and reality completely disappears.

The last step is simply to contrast the valuation with the current market price and see the level of discrepancy this approach throws up. One caveat. Even if you get all the analysis right, you can still be wrong if the majority of the market disagrees; but this latter point is generally one of timing. EBITDA valuations normally receive recognition sooner or later. Armitage and Licht, McLean, Moncreiffe and Taube all employ EBITDA as one very important route to assess fair value for a security. If this approach is not in your analytical tool kit yet, add it now.

(b) Comparative shopping makes for the best bargains

What we mean here is that you cannot look at investments in isolation. I am developing a theme touched upon briefly above. In particular, domestic markets in stocks and bonds are not as self-contained as they once were. Increasingly sophisticated fixed income investors compare the risk/reward profile of a Spanish peseta issuer with a company offering an instrument denominated in Mexican pesos, and seek to exploit inefficiencies on a global scale. Currency arbitrage allows, at a cost, more imaginative investment combinations. If a distributor of computer products has a 22 times P/E multiple in the US but rates only 11 times in Portugal, is that a realistic reflection of the relative potential in those markets, or could it be that the Portuguese are too conservative, or US investors too aggressive?

Another way to play this theme is to spot trends in one country which seem likely to occur in another. An understanding of why the introduction of a new technology, or a new retail concept, or even a new brand, worked so well in one environment, and how that should translate elsewhere, can give an investor an enormous edge. Nils Taube is one who has mastered this, and several examples are discussed on pages 318–20. You will find a similar philosophy at work in the way Howard Flight selects investments, and at a market level in how Peter Everington prioritises his country weightings, and Moncreiffe picks his imperfect pairs.

(c) Investors are not traders

There is a fundamental distinction between the two mind sets. While it may seem obvious that trading and investment are separate activities, all investors have to be traders at the margin, insomuch as they buy and sell securities.

The trick is not to be seduced into trading more often than is absolutely necessary. There are so many forces at work which stimulate trading. Start with your broker. If you are not trading, he is not earning a commission. Ditto for the market makers and, indeed, all the panoply of people providing support services to the investor. Next in line comes a

> *Most people who make a lot of money in the markets over the long term do not trade frequently.*

whole host of sound bite slogans, some of which are valid in certain circumstances, but all of which seem to suggest an imperative to trade often: 'Cut your losses early'; 'Take your profits'; 'Always be ready to replace one holding with something better'.

Most people who make a lot of money in the markets over the long term do not trade frequently. A 35 per cent turnover rate, which means the average holding period for an investment is about three years, would be close to an upper limit. Trading costs money. When you add in commission, stamp duty and a bid/ask spread which is always stacked against investors, someone who turns over their portfolio once a year could end up with annual costs of around 4 per cent. In illiquid securities, that number would be materially higher. That's a high handicap to claw back. Every trade you make is one more argument for a tracker fund.

Finally, there is an almost in-built imperative to action. One of the most difficult things for any investor is to have the patience to hold on. There will be times to cut losses, or even to sell a static stock, because no-one likes 'dead' money, but think hard before making that decision. Activity may make you feel better in the short run. There's a certain satisfaction in being able to say you've done something; but there's no guarantee that you will be financially better off in the long run. 'Think before you trade' should be stamped on every stock certificate, or etched into every computer keyboard.

A consistent theme across nearly all these great money managers is that they hold stocks for longer periods, on average, than less good managers. Four and five years is common. There are some survivors in their portfolios with 20 plus years' longevity. Many that are in for only a short time are not sold, but bought out due to a takeover. Look at the portfolios of the likes of Bolton, Hart and Moule and you'll find old friends that have been there a long, long while. Even in the currency market, and it is hard to find any environment where the pace is more frenetic, cycles take years to work through.

Trading in many asset classes is a zero sum game with costs attached. There is a thrill to trading akin to playing Donkey Kong. Instant gratification is there for the asking. But who is the donkey? Most people invest because they have long-term goals like school fees, buying a house, or retirement. If your investment goals are long term, you should manage your portfolio for the long term.

Let us counter with a few other adages: 'Let your winners run'; 'Average down on cheap stocks'; 'Hesitate to swap a security you know well for one you don't know so well'. Colin McLean puts this case better than any other. I must stress again: every investor has to trade. Do dump dogs and always strive to find new opportunities, but most people who take time to examine their own history agree they could do better by trading less.

(d) Don't be bashful – make big bets
The best investors do not hesitate to take large positions in companies. This is true across the board. You can rarely, with the one possible caveat being liquidity, have too much of a good thing.

Let's review a few examples: Leonard Licht is the Grand Master in this department. Some of his bigger positions are found on page 188. Colin McLean ends up with large holdings in most of his funds. Anthony Bolton runs a rather concentrated portfolio, as does Richard Hughes. Most of our leading money managers exhibit an unusually high degree of concentration in their stock portfolios. It's about backing your own judgement, and it's also about focus. No-one can be master of the whole market. Grand Masters are the best on their own particular patch. It makes sense to pick your spots and make sure you spend time where it will do the most good – on a few good stocks.

There are exceptions to this latter point, and the counter argument does deserve consideration. Risk diversification has been all the rage; but modern theorists now feel 12 holdings are sufficient to diversify away 90 per cent plus of systematic stock market risk. Armitage and Moncreiffe employ carefully considered strategies to overcome this problem and are able to balance that with uncorrelated portfolios, while still managing big bets. Calculations in bond markets are more complex.

> **Buffett puts a lot of eggs in a small number of baskets.**

Overall, it is easier to make money if you have a concentrated portfolio. For most people, eight or nine stocks should provide sufficient diversification to reduce the systemic risk of holding individual securities. After that, the benefit of further risk reduction may be more than offset by the danger of losing touch. It is difficult even for professionals to follow all developments in their portfolios. For an individual with a few hours a week to spare, it is well nigh impossible. Do not spread yourself too thin.

In passing I think I should note that this theme mirrors the words of wisdom from the great Warren Buffett "Diversification is a protection against ignorance." Buffett puts a lot of eggs in a small number of baskets.

(e) Personal characteristics of management don't merely matter: they are critical

This does not seem like exactly the sort of statement one would expect when discussing the quality of management. Surely it should read, 'Must be experienced in the industry,' or 'have excellent academic qualifications and a good CV,' or 'can communicate goals and motivate employees'. All these attributes can be a plus, of course. What is fascinating is that the emphasis of our top investment managers, to a large degree, lay elsewhere: on honesty, integrity, and on personal commitment.

Colin McLean was the most clear and most cogent in expounding on this theme, but others hold similar views. Management and shareholder interests need to be aligned, in particular, in the way in which management are compensated. The structure should be skewed to equity returns. Investors need to take note of how much executive directors are taking out versus putting in or, at least, retaining, in both absolute and relative terms. There can be no upper limit on an individual building equity capital alongside the outside shareholders but, if someone highly paid only has a small stake in the creation of corporate wealth, that can be a bad sign. Congruence of objectives is the key.

Excessive lifestyles are usually a give-away of a management more likely to reward themselves than shareholders. The old chestnuts about private jets and three inch carpets in luxury head offices have more than a grain of truth. Get Licht on the subject. He shares McLean's sentiments to the tee. Hughes takes a different view of the same problem. He looks out for this behaviour to signal potential opportunities, but only after the mess has brought the company to a restructuring and has cost its shareholders much of their original investment. Sadly, it's hard to spot the worst abuses such as private condos and wild parties that disappear into T&E budgets; but flamboyance is usually visible somewhere. Extravagant behaviour in a personal life often carries over into the office. Oversized egos usually lead to deflated stock prices. Everington makes the point that this is a global consideration. Many managements see companies as their own personal fiefdoms. Investors should stay away both from their equity and any debt instruments.

Oversized egos usually lead to deflated stock prices.

Above all, answer the question: 'do you put your shareholders first?' Armitage avoids "management which is promiscuous with shareholders' equity". This is one key litmus test. It is an extension of the issue, 'what is more important: empire building or creating value in the equity?' These two objectives are not mutually exclusive, but they can clash, and frequently do. An over aggressive acquisition policy is a bad sign – especially if financed with a flurry of paper. When shareholders are constantly asked to stump up more cash, it's hard to get a good return on investment. Armitage is also concerned that big increases in sales more often lead to larger management salaries than higher share prices.

In a different vein, Flight finds the same sort of criticism to make about Government policy. Monetary conditions which are too loose can devalue the currency and destroy value in the bond markets. Fixed income values react like equities: when there is too much around, you cannot give the stuff away. Yields levitate. Everington hammers home the virtuous liquidity cycle which can categorise good and bad countries in the same way that investors can rank companies.

Moncreiffe puts a different slant on this whole issue. He is concerned about cosy relationships on the board which can be harmful to investor wealth when management of closed-end funds carry on collecting fees even if they are trading at a deep discount, while the directors look the other way.

Investors need to be aware of these concerns and be on the lookout for management featherbedding. The corollary holds true, as well. Seek out managers who have material amounts of their own capital at risk, and who have a much larger financial stake in the success of enhancing the equity value than in any current compensation package. Then you have found a properly motivated person.

The Prince of Wales has proved how powerful this philosophy can be, applied at all levels. What matters in a large business is life and death down in the small company sector. There is no substitute for using personal values as a screen in a start-up investment when, in the early days, the entrepreneur is the business. He lays extraordinary emphasis on this in making investment decisions at The Prince's Trust.

(f) There is no room for romance

"A love affair is not on in the stock market" (Michael Moule). Nothing is easier than becoming enamoured of an investment. Once upon a time, someone bought North Korean bonds at par, and Polly Peck stock was worth a lot of money. Glamorous concepts can be an investment lure. Even sound old favourites which have performed so well can turn sour. How many large companies from the 1970s are still around?

You take a very sick dog down to the veterinarian to put it to sleep. A dying investment is a liability which deserves much less consideration. Investors must monitor developments closely and, if something starts to go off the tracks, if the driving forces change, or if the rationale which led to the initial purchase decision alters, it is time to trim. Richard Hughes' investment style is a classic case in point. Once a recovery security has recovered, it should be sold, however well it has done, and almost in spite of having prospects for continued, if less dramatic, growth in the future.

(g) There's value in them there shells

The UK market is somewhat unique in this respect, but bombed out companies can be beautiful. What you are looking for is a small company which has shrunk to the point where it has lost visibility and is neglected by the market, but can come back. Leonard Licht made killings along this line, and Richard Hughes has scored some stunning successes with such a tactic.

The second route is to seek a shell where new blood comes in to change the business and its rating. If Ian Gowrie-Smith, Luke Johnson, Bob Morton or Nigel Wray suddenly appear on the share register, something is likely to happen soon, and savvy investors can expect a stirring ride. Even Grand Masters with large portfolios like Anthony Bolton and Nils Taube cannot resist the money making potential in a good shell. Colin McLean and Peregrine Moncreiffe extend the strategy to investment trust shells which can be rejuvenated with just as much benefit to shareholders as any ordinary operating company.

Shells are commonplace in the US, but their reputation, on the whole, is a lot less savoury. So far, other markets do not seem to have hit on how to exploit this niche. Trawl the small cap sector of Scandinavia or the *deuxième marché*. Shells sound good in any language if they come clean and with an entrepreneur attached.

Rumour which may or may not be reliable has it that endless psychological studies were carried out before determining that telephone numbers should have seven digits. It seems that seven is the maximum numerical sequence a human brain can easily store and access. Let's make this easy and stop before exceeding the limit. Let me repeat an earlier caveat. This list is not exhaustive, nor is it a summary of all the useful investment ideas contained in *Investing with the Grand Masters*. I have extracted seven themes which crop up with regularity, which have worked well in the past and which, employed wisely, should prove rewarding in the future. The next section involves a more qualitative diagnosis and calls for a little soul searching.

2. CHARACTERISTICS OF A SUCCESSFUL MONEY MANAGER

(i) Start making money early

The lesson from the lives of these top investment professionals is simple and easy to apply for any parent. If little Johnnie or little Jane show an interest in a hobby that can make money, give them every encouragement. Teenagers who want to start a business, however small, may be the next super investor.

Stamps are a particularly good grounding. Leonard Licht cut his initial investment teeth in that field. Gardening, car washing, all can yield excellent returns on capital. Almost any collectible engenders a sense of value early on. Coins are the most obvious example, along with cards. Michael Moule was big at bartering those. Howard Flight made money out of harvesting water cress. Peter Everington conducted a wholesale business while at school. Others had even more interesting examples but we agreed not to print them!

Success in these sorts of ventures can provide the stimulus to look seriously at the investment field, as well as giving confidence to the budding entrepreneur. This indicator is one thing the Prince of Wales is looking for when he talks about people with the right personality. There is no substitute for practical training, even on a small scale. Enjoying the profits or learning how painful losses can be while the risks involved remain limited is of great help later on, when the sums of money can be scary and decisions may have wide reaching ramifications.

Yours truly tried his hand at just about everything. I found that vegetable stalls had very attractive characteristics, particularly if you got the produce for nothing and sold it to your neighbours (no distribution or sales and marketing costs). Coins and stamps both were a source of income and capital gain while I was at school. Collecting and trading the collection called for an understanding of the price mechanism and an eye for spotting other people's errors – or, in pure investment terms, identifying inefficiencies in market valuation.

One other observation relates to pocket money. A shortage of cash can be a good incentive to go out and make some. Unless an allowance is earmarked for some kind of productive purchase (buying a chemistry set?) or is slated for saving, a generous parent can, unintentionally, deprive a child of motivation. A pocketful of loose change can be too much of a good thing.

(ii) Start managing money late

Most of our managers were never allowed near other people's money until they had been around the City for considerable periods of time. When they were initially let loose on the clients, they already had a good understanding of the mechanics of the market and a sense of value which had evolved from years of observation and indirect involvement. Michael Hart was at Foreign & Colonial for 16 years before moving into the investment side of the business. He served a long apprenticeship. Michael Moule spent 14 years in various subsidiary roles before being given real responsibility to make investment decisions; but that length of time was not unusual pre the mid 1980s. Leonard Licht spent nearly 6 years at Warburgs before getting his hands on his first client portfolio; and then he was given the crumbs from other brokers' tables.

Perhaps the insight here, if one can call it that, is that the investment business is akin to any other. Experience counts, and someone who understands what they are doing before they start has a leg up on someone who is expected to learn on the job. The fact that formal training did not exist in the 1960s and 1970s in the way that is institutionalised in 1996 does not take away from the value of the experience available at that time. Learning by osmosis requires rather more astute antennae and an ability to sift sound advice from that other, less helpful variety. So, in one way, people who swam to the top in such an environment were better suited to succeed in the investment business.

(iii) MBAs need not apply

Don't worry if you don't get a first from Oxbridge – or even go to Oxbridge, for that matter. Only two of these top money managers went down that route. There is absolutely no correlation between academic achievement and success in the investment business. Most of the leading players in Britain could be considered deficient in the degree department.

This is not to say that there is nothing on offer in schools or universities today that can be of practical value to investment managers of the future, but it is an area of education which is noteworthy, mostly by its absence. That said, no-one has made a case that any formal investment education, such as an MBA, makes a big difference. No-one has yet come up with a convincing case that fluency in foreign languages or classics makes for better investment performance, either.

The message to take away is that education in general, or any specific sort of education, cannot, on its own, determine whether a manager will do well. Entrusting money to a manager from New College, Oxford, may feel better than investing with someone who worked through night school to receive a qualification as Company Secretary, but may actually leave you worse off financially, particularly if that Company Secretary was Michael Hart. Equally, if the Ladies Investment Club of Beardstown can beat the averages, who's to say a group of retired investors in Bath cannot pool their experience and expertise and go one better, even if they cannot muster a single BA between them. Someone starting out with drive, ambition, commitment and a willingness to learn can more than compensate for any perceived academic disadvantages. What more powerful evidence could you want than the success stories at The Prince's Trust?

In case you feel a need for further confirmation, let's look at a sample of the academic backgrounds of our superstar investors. What do we have here? Those that do have degrees are an eclectic lot, and only just out-number those without. Post Graduate education is conspicuous by its absence. Howard Flight is the only one of our Grand Masters to call the MBA his own.

- John Armitage   History
- Peter Everington   Aeronautical engineer
- Leonard Licht   One A Level. Went straight to the City at 16
- Michael Moule   Seven O Levels. Went straight to the City at 17.

Not exactly a list brimming with obvious academic indicators of investment talent! Some interest in economics is the only clue. On the other side of the coin, I am not aware of any firms where you will find this set of credentials used as screening criteria for selecting the intake for their trainee positions.

(iv) Don't start as you mean to go on

It doesn't seem to matter where you begin, as long as the first job is in the investment industry, broadly defined. This appears to hold true for both the position within a firm and the pedigree of the firm itself.

- Anthony Bolton began life as a graduate trainee for Keyner Ullman, a once proud name long lost in the mists of the 1970s.
- Michael Moule's first stop was as a runner at GIT, a firm only real fanatics in the field of investment history trivia would be familiar with today.
- Leonard Licht started at Warburgs, but as a clerk filing telegraph cards.

- Michael Hart's first real job was in the Company Secretary's office, and on the lowest rung of the ladder in that profession.
- Richard Hughes began his career as a trainee accountant at Derbyshire County Council – nowhere near the City, nor even involved in any peripheral activity, though his first, full position was in the pension management department.

The changing structure of the financial services industry, with increasing requirements of specialisation, may mean that people wanting a career in investment management will need to follow a more restricted path in the future. It is, however, my contention that the top names in the field 20 years from now are toiling in some obscure position and probably have not yet migrated into the managing of money. The age of the gifted amateur has certainly given way to the era of the analyst. There is still room for original thought; indeed, perhaps, the need has never been so great. Top investment records never rose out of conventional wisdom.

(v) Continuity is a virtue

Nearly all of these top names have been closely associated with only one fund or institution for most of their careers. You can argue that our sample is somewhat biased; and that is true, to the extent that one of the criteria required to appear in this book was a ten year plus track record at the pinnacle of the profession. That aside, it is not just time served in the industry which is the point at issue: it is stability.

- Michael Hart has managed FCIT for 26 years
- Nils Taube ran St James's Place Progressive for 26 years
- Leonard Licht was looking after clients at Mercury for 24 years
- Michael Moule has been around Bankers for 20 years
- John Armitage has only 14 years' history, but 12 of those were at Morgan Grenfell, focusing on Europe
- Richard Hughes has been at the Recovery Fund almost from the day he started at M&G

A high percentage of the best money managers do not move around. They stay in one place and build up a client base, consistently applying their investment philosophy in a work environment which is supportive of their efforts. Recognising the value of stability and low turnover among top performers is important for individual investors looking to leave their money in secure hands without having to worry about whether what you see today is not what you will get tomorrow.

I would like to end this section by paraphrasing a precis of personal skills direct from the mouth of one of the Grand Masters, in this case Peter Everington.

"Bright, numerate, with a logical understanding of how things work. Decisiveness and the ability to extract and distil key issues from a wide range of reading material. Of these, decisiveness is the most important. The difference between a good manager and a

> *It is the inclusion of indecision into the process that is the downfall of most managers.*

bad manager does not come down to the balance of good versus bad decisions. Rather, it is the inclusion of indecision into the process that is the downfall of most managers."

3. WHAT DOES IT TAKE TO BE A SUCCESSFUL INVESTOR?

Most of this chapter has been devoted to what is the more substantive analysis of the most pertinent common threads that emerged from looking at some of the brightest minds in the investment business of the 1990s. I should like to bring the curtain down on a rather lighter note with a collage of helpful hints for actual, or would be, investors.

(i) Do not be discouraged if you make a bad investment

If this sounds silly, it is not, because making a mistake is only natural. Most people get depressed when they lose money, be it ever so small a sum, and to a much greater extent than any kind of corresponding uplift that might brighten the day when they make a profit. This imbalance holds true even when the profit is much greater than the loss. Psychology seems to extract some sort of intrinsic pain/gain ratio – and, in the investment world, the ratio appears heavily stacked in favour of the pain. A thousand pounds to the good more or less offsets £250 down the drain.

On a rational basis, such a swing in mentality makes no sense; but empirical observation shows that this sort of a skewed reaction is the norm. Experience also shows that most people lose money in the market on most investments most of the time but, when they do make money, the profit on the ones that work out ends up being a multiple of the total losses on the two or three that failed to perform. Two simple explanations solve the puzzle. You can never lose more than 100 per cent (unless you short unhedged), but there is no end, in theory, to the profit potential; and most people cut their losses well before a total write off.

It should be of great encouragement to note that most of our experts expect to lose money on at least 40 per cent of their investments. I am not saying that Robert the Bruce is a good investment model but, in the interests of getting away from homespun wisdom of any variety, let me stress how important it is to be prepared to lose money and learn from a mistake. Just because Uncle Joe's sure thing tip on Biotank performed with the same sort of result as his last past the post nap on the 3.25 at Cheltenham does not mean that a thoughtful application of the tried and tested investment precepts elaborated in this book will not do better. They will. Used as intended, they should reward the patient investor with superior returns.

I am not sure that I go all the way with Michael Moule, who believes it is "probably best if you lose money on your first investment", but he has a point. Investment is a serious business. You can enjoy investing and should have fun, but the consequences of taking it lightly can be very detrimental to your bank balance.

> **Most people will lose money frequently. As long as you control your losses, your wins should more than compensate.**

A small loss first time out of the box has the virtue of underlining this point at minimal cost, and should cause all but inveterate gamblers to treat their investment activities with more respect. Most of the best investors do seem to lose money on their first investment. But they learn from this experience. Tag along with Moule, Hughes and Bolton and if you feel a little let down after a loss, console yourself with the thought that you are in very good company.

In case the point has not got across, let me reiterate. Most people will lose money frequently. As long as you control your losses, your wins should more than compensate. As long as you can step back and do not allow yourself to be sucked into the psychological trap of feeling awful each and every time one goes sour, but focus on the overall progress of your portfolio over the medium term, you will feel better over time and be better placed to take advantage of foolish decisions by others who have grown discouraged by markets – usually at just the wrong moment.

(ii) Listen, listen, listen

Lots of us feel we are good at asking questions. Some people make a career out of this activity. A good politician knows how to ask questions better than people in any profession. Does this make him or her a good investor – or good at anything, for that matter?

"If there's one feature of my investment life, it's that I'm a good listener" (Michael Moule).

The neglected flip side and poor relation in the equation is listening. If information is the lifeblood of the investment industry, then a good listener has a built-in advantage over a bad one. Listening well is difficult, and almost impossible if you are talking, which suggests a regimen of short, focused questions that demand long, involved answers. That extra item gleaned from a conversation in which someone else is contributing well over half can be the tool that gives an astute investor an edge. John Armitage structures his interactions with investee companies around this precept. The Prince of Wales is one of the world's great listeners.

(iii) Know how to filter

Lawyers have a head start, here. They spend so much time searching through millions of worthless words to find the key phrase on which a legal opinion rides, and which can sway the case to the plaintiff or defendant.

Investors today are faced with a mega data overload. The need for focus has never been greater. Skill in synthesis and the ability to discard the extraneous while homing in on key facts are at a premium. The proliferation of material on the Internet is only the latest in a long line of developments; but there is no correlation between the amount of data available and good investment decisions.

Most stuff that comes our way is not helpful. One thing I noticed about all our star investors was that they had a very high degree of focus. They covered a lot of ground, absorbing vast amounts of data, but discarding most very quickly as not relevant to their needs. Leonard

Licht has a talent for picking the *one* point that matters out of an entire presentation. Colin McLean exhibits the same skill.

Even if global in outlook, most portfolios tended to be remarkably concentrated and focused on a few anchor investments. If money managers can do this with hundreds of millions, it should not prove too tough a challenge for someone with £50,000 to invest.

(iv) Buy Shell Transport and Trading

This point is not entirely tongue in cheek though please be clear I am not recommending this specific stock. Anyone smart enough to have ploughed through every page of *Investing with the Grand Masters* may have noted the appearance of this specific security several times. For those seeking a short cut, check the index. If there is one single company which has been prominent in the portfolios of several of these top notch investors over the last 20 years, Shell T and T fits the bill. Hart has had it in FCIT from day one, and the Company still remains his largest position after 24 years. Moule has held it for over 18 years. In 1983, it was his largest position. Bolton owned Shell T and T for a while, as did Taube.

The real lesson here is almost as simple. If you want to go for individual investments rather than entrust your portfolio to the top professionals, buy the same things that the best managers hold. Tap the collective wisdom of this group, and it's hard to imagine that you could go wrong.

> **If you want to go for individual investments buy the same things that the best managers hold.**

Look around the world. The story repeats itself. The portfolios of the Grand Master travel well. You will find the same stalwarts crop up time and time again. It is no coincidence that both Everington and Moncreiffe were early buyers of San Miguel, the leading beer company in the Philippines, and both banked very large profits on that holding.

You can extend the proposition to include top industrialists and even certain corporate financiers who are more deeply involved in their deals. Follow the leader and you could come in second which, given the length of the investment continuum, translates into exceptional returns. (See also *The Financial Times Global Guide to Investing*, page 304, by this author.)

The interchange of good ideas is the lifeblood of the investment industry. The best ideas reside in the portfolios of the most successful

investment managers. Many of them run public funds, so this information is readily available. You can call up and ask for the annual report
and see just what the large holdings are at Bankers or FCIT or St James's
Place Special Situations. If you start to spot names which recur across
these portfolios, it is highly probable you have found an investment
which will outperform the market.

(v) Enjoy yourself

I have said this several times, and want to end on a positive note. If you
cannot have fun with your portfolio then, at best, you are missing out
on half the satisfaction available to anyone directly involved in their
own investments. You may also surprise yourself by how well you do.
My mother, who is well past the pension age and has never had any
involvement in the City, looks after a small selection of shares she mon-
itors herself. Since 1992, she has beaten the performance of her professional investment manager, who will remain nameless to spare his
blushes, each and every year. She enjoys reading about the companies
in which she is a shareholder and following their prices in the Saturday
Financial Times. Not that she has matched the returns achieved by the
people we have profiled in *Investing with the Grand Masters*, but she has
done well with the 15 per cent of her retirement nest egg which she personally directs, and she has fun playing with that small portion of her
portfolio.

You can also tell, talking to John Armitage, or Peter Everington, or
Peregrine Moncrieffe, or the Prince of Wales, or any of our investment
Grand Masters, that they really enjoy their work. Are they so good
because they are doing what they enjoy, or are they enjoying themselves
because they are so good? I shall leave that one to Mystic Meg. My
observation is merely that you will be a better investor if you approach
the activity with the right mindset and only put capital at risk which
you can afford to lose. Take away that pressure, start out with a subsidiary goal to get pleasure out of your investing and you probably will
achieve that, as well as superior returns.

Tips for the Top

(Up and coming Money Managers for the Next Century)

To reach the pinnacle of the investment profession requires a combination of persistence, consistency and endurance, as well as a touch of genius. Few make it, but once there, looking back is rather easier. For investors as well, it is easier to identify those managers who have already demonstrated their pedigree by racking up superior returns over many years. There is no shortage of historical information and picking winners and losers from the past is a simple numerical exercise.

It is a tad trickier to predict who will emerge as the most talented investment professionals of the next generation. Yet, if we want to do well in the future with our investments that information is of great interest. The problem in trying to pick the winners of tomorrow is that the money manager who was number one last year is more likely to prove to be a shooting star than a safe pair of hands. It takes time to build a track record. Younger managers who may show up at the top of the ten year performance tables in 2006 are likely to leave faint footprints today. So how can the average investor track down these people?

What better way than to ask those who have already proved themselves to be the cream of the crop? We took a poll asking our chosen Grand Masters to name Brits below the age of 37, as of January 1996, who they felt had the potential to fill their shoes down the road. We also interviewed a number of fund managers whose job it is to know these things and blended in their recommendations.

We have listed the results in alphabetical order to avoid any indication that one person is preferred over another. What we can say about all of them is that by inclusion on this list they have achieved the highest accolade a money manage can ever receive – recognition by the best and most knowledgable practitioners in their own profession. These are people who deserve watching as some of them are bound to be the Boltons and Taubes of tomorrow.

Name	Firm	Area of Expertise
Mike Balfour	Edinburgh Fund Managers	Far East
Rod Birkett	Fleming/S&P	Japan
Andrew Crossley	Invesco	Smaller companies
Mark Evans	Montpelier Asset Management	Emerging market debt
William Garnett	Henderson	Japan, esp. smaller companies

Name	Firm	Area of Expertise
Patrick Harrington	M&G	High income
Scot Meech	Threadneedle Asset Management	Income
Bradley Mitchell	Commercial Union	Smaller companies
Stuart Mitchell	Morgan Grenfell	European equities
Chris Poil	Mercury Asset Management	UK equities
John Richards	Mercury Asset Management	UK equities
Steve Russell	Sun Life of Canada	UK smaller companies
David Shapiro	Universities Superannuation Service	Smaller companies
John Stopford	Guinness Flight	Global bonds
Martin Taylor	Barings Asset Management	Emerging European equities
Neil Woodford	Perpetual	High income

The two managers mentioned more than once were Patrick Harrington and Neil Woodford. Proving that this selection is not coloured by the composition of the panel the only organisation with more than one name to make this list is not featured or currently associated in any way with the people voting – Mercury Asset Management. In the interests of additional disclosure I want to add that only one name on this list was nominated by someone at the same firm.

The other interesting feature to note is the preponderance of smaller company specialists in the list. Stock picking is at a premium at the low end of the market and the difference between a good and bad manager in the smaller company sector is more pronounced. Since smaller company stocks tend to outperform the broader market over time it is encouraging to see such good representation in a sector which should be of great interest to individual investors.

Ditto for Asia. Younger UK managers have turned in some strong performances in this region which is such an important financial market and likely to be even more critical in the future. Other representation in the emerging market category is also a plus given the positive long term trends for investors in those markets.

It is useful to see some balance with the appearance on the list of several income orientated managers. This should be of particular relevance to older readers more concerned to maximise current income.

When we come to updating *Investing with the Grand Masters* in the year 2006, it will be interesting to see which of these individuals have emerged as senior statespersons of their profession. I cannot predict the actual individuals, but am confident some names from the above list will have achieved industry-wide recognition ten years on from today.

B

Recommended Reading for the Serious Investor

Dedicated investment professionals immersed in their work have few hours in the year to devote to books. Life is a litany of annual reports and analysts' ruminations to say nothing of the constant daily battle to keep up with the *The Financial Times, Investors Chronicle* and other essential reading. When they do make the effort above and beyond the required minimum, it has to be something special to justify that most precious and transient of commodities – their time.

If that is true for the average fund manager, it is even more so for the superstars who appear in these pages. A referral on a work considered worth reading from them is high praise indeed. They are also most alive to the changes and developments that affect the investment industry and the best possible source of ideas about investment literature which they felt had helped their performance. We asked what books they would recommend to the individual investor.

The one winning the most plaudits is that stock market bible, *The Intelligent Investor*, by Ben Graham. Interestingly that is the one book which Warren Buffett has gone on record as recommending. He emphasises Chapters 8 and 20. *The Intelligent Investor* is generally regarded as the definitive text on value investing. It is held up as inspirational by such investing gurus as Peter Cundill and the firm of Tweedy, Browne. It is fundamentalist in approach, and perhaps a bit overly purist for most of today's stock pickers, but following the approach outlined in this book continues to spawn success stories even fifty years after it first appeared in print: which goes to show that the best investment advice can be timeless. With today's mega multiples the cautionary note sounded by Graham is a dose of fresh air.

Several were kind enough to mention *The Financial Times Global Guide to Investing* in positive terms. With nearly 750 pages and contributors from over 140 leading investment practitioners *The Financial Times Global Guide to Investing* is the most comprehensive book available today. Topics covered range from an overview of all main asset classes and geographic markets to explanations of analytical tools and pointers on how to use global trends to find profitable investment themes. Contributors include Sir Ron Brierley, Dr Marc Faber, Mario Gabelli, Nicholas Knight, Neil Mackinnon, Michael Price, Stephen Roach, Terry Smith, Sir John Templeton and John Train. It is a must for every serious investor.

The other books recommended are listed below with a brief comment on their main merits. Since you have already purchased *Investing with the Grand Masters*, it seems safe to give credit where credit is due, even to other investment books. One interesting note is the emphasis on economic history and market behaviour and the absence of analytical offerings, other than the works by Graham and by Terry Smith. There is also a general recognition that the best, and perhaps the only way for individuals to get usable insights into improving their investment performance is through books written by or which profile the most successful professional investors. Some may see this reasoning as circular but the views of our Grand Masters validate the premise for writing this book. Their selection is as follows:

Accounting for Growth Terry Smith
Known as 'The Book They Tried To Ban', no other work on accounting has generated so much controversy. Smith's work is a damning indictment of how accounting conventions allow companies to manage reported earnings while retaining unqualified audit opinions. If that seems academic the impact is very real. Smith explains how proper analysis and understanding of published accounts can enable investors to steer clear of potential time bombs where they could lose a lot of money. Smith is now regarded as the top analyst in this field in London and his insights are invaluable to any concerned investor who should check every portfolio holding against Smith's accounting red flags.

Extraordinary Popular Delusions and the Madness of Crowds Charles Mackay
Another work which proves the point that there's no fool like an old fool. This perennial best seller explains how market valuations can depart radically from underlying value, which is when the great investors can make the most money. Its focus is psychology rather than analysis. Henry Ford would not agree but this is essential reading for anyone who wants to avoid repeating the mistakes of the past in investment markets.

Liars Poker Michael Lewis
Not exactly Salomon's shining hour but a lot of laughs for everyone else on the Street. Lewis's semi fictional(?) account of life as trader has a serious side as it lays bare some of the more callous chicanery whereby clients are parted all too readily from their funds while intermediaries focus on counting up commissions. Every investor needs to strike the word 'churn' from their vocabulary. Once you appreciate the trading mentality there is no excuse for taking their bait. Enjoyable and educational.

One up on Wall Street Peter Lynch

When someone as savvy and successful as Peter Lynch, the former manager of The Magellan Fund, writes a book it makes sense to read it. Lynch manages to cross over the professional barrier and explain his investment approach in terms every investor can understand. He gives practical advice on how to implement his ideas. If there is any flaw in this book it is perhaps an oversimplification. If investing was this easy we would all be able to do as well as Peter Lynch.

The Alchemy of Finance George Soros

Soros is a charismatic individual who is part politician, part philosopher and part philanthropist. This makes for a complex man, and *The Alchemy of Finance* is a somewhat complex book with investment strategies interwoven with analysis of global trends, which move markets. Of course, Soros is well known as the man who can control currencies; at least if anyone can Soros can. A fascinating read but without a cast iron stomach, an unusual level of intuition and large funds under management it is hard to see how much practical help can be gleaned from this book.

The Great Crash J.K. Galbraith

The Great Crash of 1929 is embedded in the collective consciousness of the financial market and its memory, accurate or otherwise, is still capable of moving markets today. The story of what happened makes a fascinating read, and the characters who populate the book provide an object lesson in manipulation. Perhaps this is essential reading for all emerging market investors. Hopefully those of us who are confined to the more mature markets will not experience its like again; though some have suggested Japan came close to a carbon copy catastrophe in the late 1980s.

The Money Masters John Train

John Train is a true renaissance man and one of the most important figures in the investment profession. He is no mean money manager himself but is best known for his portraits of other great figures in the profession, many of whom are his personal friends. He also regularly contributes to the *Financial Times*. *The Money Masters* profiles some of the great investors of the 1980s, including Soros, Lynch, Steinhardt, Rogers and Neff. Still going strong after fifteen years the stories of these successful practitioners contain a ton of practical advice; and Train is an excellent writer. *The New Money Masters,* his follow up work, is another good reprise along the same theme.

The Rise and Fall of the Great Powers Paul Kennedy

It is useful not to lose sight of the big picture. Kennedy illustrates long wave socio/political and economic cycles as he traces the rise (and fall) of nations. There is a certain inevitability about the transience of being at the top. At a time when too many people measure markets in minutes, this long view provides a useful balance and suggests important investment insights about the need for global diversification.

The Wealth of Nations Adam Smith

Another oldie but goodie. The power of a few simple ideas is often lost in the clutter of data and the proliferation of technology that drives financial markets in the 1990s. Smith is now revealed as the father of free trade and the leading prophet of comparative advantage. Port from Portugal for cloth from England is easy to remember and it always seemed to me that the UK got the better of the bargain. With a glass in hand some of the language is easier to swallow. Going back to basics is necessary if markets are not to get detached from the true reasons for creation of wealth. Words of wisdom from a genuine libertarian have as much relevance today as they did in 1776, possibly even more.

Ultimate Risk Adam Raphael

If you are not aware of the problems at Lloyds you have not been awake during this decade. Raphael is a 'Name' on three of the most affected syndicates and provides a revealing insight on risk run riot. There is many a cautionary tale in his exposé of what went on. Perhaps only those not affected can enjoy this book, but this story contains almost too many useful reminders that there is no such thing as a free lunch or a free golf invitation.

Index